HARLEY-DAVIDSON

HARLEY-DAVIDSON

Roy Bacon, Denis Chorlton, Richard Fleury, Ian Kerr

THUNDER BAY
P·R·E·S·S

bibliography

Magazines

The Motor Cycle: December 1913, July 1915, October 1915, November 1915, June 1917, November 1940, September 1941.

Motor Cycling: November 1914, January 1915, October 1917, December 1917, December 1918, November 1938, April 1942, October 1942.

La Revue Motocyclyte August 1923.

All American Heroes Jan/Feb 1994.

The Classic Motorcycle February 1984.

Books

Genat, Robert and Robin, *Harley-Davidson Police Motorcycles*, Motorbooks International,1995.

Rafferty, Tod, *The Complete Harley-Davidson Encyclopedia*, Bramley Books, 1997.

Sucher, Harry V., *Harley-Davidson, The Milwaukee Marvel*, (3rd Revised Edition) Haynes, 1985.

Wright, David K., *The Harley-Davidson Motor Company: An Official Eighty-Year History*, Motorbooks International, 1987.

Burns, Max and Messenger, Ken, *The Winged Wheel Patch*, Vanwell Publishing, 1993.

Motorcyclist, *Questions and Answers by Uncle Frank* (Army Service Edition) Western Journal 1943.

Saladini, Albert and Szymezak, Pascal, *Harley-Davidson, A Way of Life*, Aurum Press, 1997.

Palmer, Bruce, *How to Restore your Military Harley-Davidson 1932-1952*, MBI Publishing Company 1998.

Page 2: The Harley lifestyle. Garry Stuart

Right: Road Glide. Ian Kerr

Published in the United States by
Thunder Bay Press
An imprint of the Advantage Publishers Group
5880 Oberlin Drive
San Diego, CA 92121-4794
www.advantagebooksonline.com

Produced by PRC Publishing Ltd

64 Brewery Road
London N7 9NT

ISBN 1 57145 231 1

Library of Congress Cataloging-in-Publication Data available upon request.

4 5 01 02 03

Printed and bound in Taiwan

contents

Introduction

Richard Fleury

To the bandana-wearing "Hognoscenti," a Harley-Davidson motorcycle is much more than the sum of its steel, chrome, rubber, plastic and leather parts. Ask converts why these machines are special and you'll hear a variety of misty-eyed eulogies evoking hazy concepts like "soul," "feel," "character," "legend" and "heritage."

To the committed Harley enthusiast, the world is divided cleanly into believers and those poor, unenlightened souls who will never understand. Talk to the latter group and you'll hear other, less charitable words. Words like "slow," "crude," "dinosaur" and "anachronism."

Yet few vehicles have ever inspired such devotion and ferociously partisan brand loyalty as the "Hog." It's one thing to wear a company's trademark on a T-shirt; it's quite another having it tattooed across your back for the rest of your life. But go to massive annual Harley parties like Sturgis or Daytona and that's exactly what you'll see, along with Harley fans ceremonially pummeling Hondas and Suzukis into scrap metal with sledgehammers in front of gleeful, cheering crowds.

People ride Harley-Davidsons for very specific reasons; reasons which have nothing whatsoever to do with handling, outright performance, sporting supremacy or engineering one-upmanship.

To some they represent a timelessly charismatic antidote to the clinical excellence and technological rat-race of cutting-edge sportsbike design. Others are attracted to the look; the in-your-face chrome'n'leather glitz. And then there's the noise. Harleys sound like no other motorcycle, especially with the almost-compulsory loud aftermarket exhaust. Growling through open pipes, their signature tune — that famously unmistakable "potato-potato" rhythm — is a ground-shaking bass rumble that Hell's Angels author Hunter S. Thompson once described as a "burst of dirty thunder."

But more than anything, for today's Harley riders a down-payment on a new Hog is a passport to the past, a way of buying into a rose-tinted, chrome-plated dream of America's glory years. Or rather one particularly golden chapter in America's past; the era which embraced the heroism of World War Two and the limitless optimism of the 1950s.

Fans know it, Harley-Davidson descendant and design guru Willie G. Davidson knows it and the Milwaukee marketing men's jobs depend on it. As the machines rolling off the Harley-Davidson production line become more technologically sophisticated, the styling draws more and more heavily on the good ole days.

Today's Harleys are curious, stylized hybrids of old and new. The factory spends millions developing new hi-tech ways of making their machines ride like modern motorcycles while looking like automotive antiques.

With the help of some clever techno-trickery, modern Harley riders can have their retro cake and eat it. Fake hardtails — the "Softail" bikes — and redesigned Springer front forks mimic the look of the primitive suspension of yesteryear without compromising ride quality or triggering a haemorrhoid-ointment sales boom.

After decades of fighting for its survival against the onslaught of mass imports from Japanese manufacturers, Harley-Davidson has finally learned how to play to its strengths. By capitalizing on its heritage and American-ness, Milwaukee has staked its claim to a large and lucrative and loyal niche market. A rapidly-growing niche market it is too.

The past, after all, is permanent and in Harley-Davidson's

All the photographs in the Introduction are by Simon Clay.

case, it is the one unique asset the company's Japanese rivals could never copy or improve upon.

Their bikes may be faster, cheaper and more reliable but when it comes to heritage, no motorcycle company in the world can overshadow Harley-Davidson's illustrious history. It's the oldest remaining marque in the world and if its current growth is any indication, its longevity is unlikely to be challenged for some years to come.

The likes of Honda and Yamaha have studiously aped the Harley look with varying degrees of success. But however well-engineered these Japanese "factory customs" are, to a significant chunk of the U.S. two-wheeled community, they will always be dismissed as just so much "Jap Crap."

American bikers love Harleys with a passion verging on obsession. It's fuelled by pride in the fact that it's the world's oldest marque and partly by a patriotism borne of Harley's postition as the last remaining major American motorcycle maker. That patriotism has helped the company last for almost a century and saved the company's hide in the 1980s, when Ronald Reagan — one of the most shameless flag-wavers to occupy the White House in recent times — was persuaded to impose protectionist import taxes to save this beleaguered national treasure from overwhelming competition from Japan.

But their appeal isn't confined to the Land of the Free. Yankophile Harley owners around the world love the bikes precisely because they are as exotically American as Hollywood, the

Wild West, Las Vegas and the Superbowl.

Some critics sneer that Milwaukee has been building the same bike for most of this century. That may be true, but that's exactly why Harleys remain so desirable today. The marketing men call it pedigree. By rumbling on fundamentally unchanged for so long, the 45-degree V-twin powered iron horse has become an iron icon, a powerful symbol of 20th century America.

The first Harley-Davidsons were designed as a motorized alternative to the horse in the wide-open rural expanses of the American Mid-West. They were hefty, agricultural-strength machines built to withstand batterings from farm tracks and dusty backroads without breaking down and stranding riders in the middle of nowhere. Simple and durable, they were built to last and if something broke, there was a good chance it could be fixed by the local blacksmith.

Out in the Big Country, any means of transport had to be tough and dependable. Harleys were more rugged than machines produced by the hundreds of other tiny manufacturers which made up America's emerging motorcycle industry. Consequently Harley-Davidson survived and thrived while its early rivals fell by the wayside. It was a lesson Milwaukee never forgot.

Ever since, simplicity and durability have been Harley bywords. Cutting edge technology? No thanks. If it ain't broke, Milwaukee don't fix it. And with a few exceptions, Harley-Davidson has always set

great store in building bikes that don't break . . .

Like the heavyweight V-twins it has made since 1903, the company itself has never been comfortable with sudden changes in direction. Throughout its history, Harley-Davidson's leading lights have been forced reluctantly into change like they were forced into racing by the sporting successes of rival manufacturers like Indian and Excelsior. And like the bikes, the Milwaukee management isn't always quick off the mark, but once rolling forward it has the momentum of a steam locomotive.

In tune with the finest principles of the U.S. constitution, Harley-Davidson can justifiably claim its products have a classless, democratic appeal. Cops or congressmen, hairdressers or Hell's Angels; Harleys are genuinely bikes for everyman.

That said, Milwaukee has a long tradition of high-profile celebrity customers. Rock'n'rollers ranging from the sublime (Elvis Presley owned a stable of Harleys including 1956 KH) to the ridiculous (Billy Idol broke his leg when he ran a red light aboard his customized Hog) have ridden Harley-Davidson machinery.

Actors and movie stars have always been eager to land a role in the Milwaukee Hall of Fame too.

The first recorded Harley-Davidson celebrity publicity stunt involved a flamboyant vaudeville artiste with the unlikely name of Trixie Fraganza, who was asked to pose in the saddle by a Seattle dealer.

Movie stars from Clark Gable to George Clooney, Sylvester Stallone and Mickey Rourke have been photographed aboard Milwaukee metal, as well as Whoopie Goldberg, Marlene Dietrich and Liz Taylor. Even today, Hollywood has its own Harley owners' club, called the Three Point Motorcycle Club.

But to the company's horror, the Harley-Davidson name has been linked to as much infamy as fame. It began in 1947 when thousands of beery, Harley-riding, ex-services city boys terrorized locals in the sleepy California town of Hollister. The incident was splashed all over papers and immortalized in film a few years later in *The Wild One* starring Marlon Brando. America's latest bad boy icon, the outlaw biker had arrived.

This wasn't the kind of publicity those conservative men of Milwaukee wanted and they were quick to sweep its underground following under the carpet. There must have been more tense moments in the Harley-Davidson publicity department in the mid-

1960s when Harley-gunning outlaw bikers again gripped the public imagination in the fearsome shape of the Hell's Angels. And once again, in 1969, with the huge success of the movie *Easy Rider* starring Peter Fonda and Denis Hopper as a couple of cocaine-dealing, drug-munching hippy bikers cruising across America on — you guessed it — a pair of Harleys. Fonda blasted across the screen aboard an ex-police panhead with ludicrously raked-out forks and Old Glory paintjob, while Dennis Hopper rode an extensively-chopped Duo-Glide.

Just as it took a long time for Harley-Davidson to realize the full marketing potential of its American Retro image, the company only dared acknowledge the less respectable side of its heritage long after the dust had settled in the streets of Hollister.

It started to happen in 1971 with the launch of the radical new FX Super Glide, Harley's first ever "factory custom," a successful attempt to jazz up the company's staid image by producing its own readymade answer to the "choppers" being built in backstreet workshops all over America. The Super Glide was the inspired invention of Willie G. Davidson, the grandson of one of the company's founders and he fol-

lowed it up in 1977 with the FXS Low Rider custom-styled cruiser.

Part of Willie G. Davidson's genius was to embrace the whole of Harley-Davidson's history, official and unofficial, famous and infamous, mix it all together and recycle it with a slick modern marketing spin. Under Willie G.'s guidance, Harley turned once unwelcome counter-cultural associations into a whiff of danger calculated to make the bikes all the more desirable. Especially to the older, more affluent motorcyclists who were beginning to buy

into the Harley legend. Before long, middle-aged riders whose occasional fiddled business expenses were the nearest thing to a felony they were ever likely to commit, would be slipping on their leather waistcoats, firing up their Hog and playing Dennis Hopper for the weekend.

And just as he incorporated subtle outlaw references in his designs, Willie G. began to turn styling throwbacks and engineering anachronisms into selling points. Sensing that Harley's best bet for the future lay in nostalgia, he

took the company in the retro direction which has proved so profitable since.

Today, the Harley image is more sharply defined than that of any other motorcycle. And the Harley Davidson corporate identity — it's name and famous logo — are guarded fiercely by the company's lawyers. With good reason; Milwaukee's merchandizing wing is worth millions of dollars a year, and the Harley Davidson name appears on everything from branded clothing, cigarette lighters and belt buckles to aftershave and

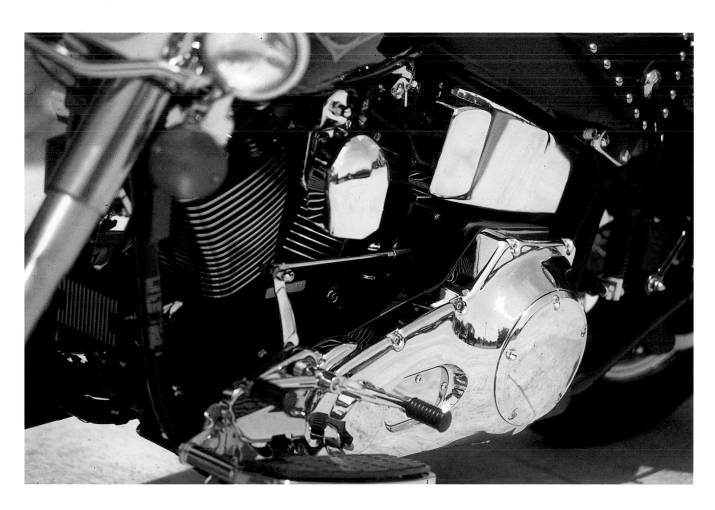

kiddies' pencil cases. But despite its huge current success, Harley-Davidson is still missing valuable marketing opportunities and has some strong new homegrown competition to deal with. American manufacturers such as Titan and the California Motorcycle Company — although smaller than Harley-Davidson — are moving into the heavyweight V-twin cruiser market with their own high-quality Hog clones.

Recently CMC has even stolen Harley's thunder from right under Willie G.'s nose by producing its own Peter Fonda-endorsed replicas of the *Easy Rider* bikes and signing up stunt legend Evel Knievel (who performed most of his most famous jumps on Harley machinery) to design a special limited edition cruiser. As if that wasn't enough, CMC has also relaunched the Indian marque; once Harley-Davidson's greatest rival.

At this rate, the next chapter of the Harley-Davidson story could well prove as interesting as its past . . .

Harley History

Richard Fleury

Even legends have to begin somewhere — and the origins of the Harley-Davidson Motor Company are as humble as any.

The Harley-Davidson saga began in a simple wooden shed in America's mid-West at the turn of the century. Like many mechanically-minded young men at the time, 21-year-old William S. "Bill" Harley and his friend Arthur Davidson, aged 20, became interested in a new form of transport emerging in Europe.

The early motorcycles were little more than a compact engine hitched to a bone-shaker bicycle frame. So, figuring it couldn't be that difficult, the two friends attempted to build their own version.

They weren't alone; backyard hobbyists were trying the same thing all over the U.S. and in the next few years hundreds of new motorcycle manufacturers would spring up across the country.

But only one company would still be building bikes nearly 100 years later; Harley-Davidson.

Both the men worked at the Barth Manufacturing Company in Milwaukee; William as a draftsman and Arthur as a pattern maker. By happy accident a colleague, Emil Kruger, had priceless insider knowledge of the new internal combustion engine developed by pioneering Frenchmen Albert

DeDion and Georges Bouton. The German draughtsman had worked on the DeDion petrol engine — which powered an early motorised tricicyle — back in Europe. And when he emigrated to America, his precious drawings came with him.

Drawing on Kruger's expertise, Bill and Arthur started work on their first motorcycle. Basically a 10cu in (167cc) single-cylinder, four-stroke engine bolted into a bicycle frame, it had direct belt drive to the rear wheel, and according to Harley-Davidson lore, a carburettor which began life as an old tomato tin! It worked . . . but only just. Power, at around 2bhp, was on the feeble side, riders had to pedal the machine uphill and the tubular bicycle frame was too flimsy for the job.

Nevertheless this wobbly prototype paved the way for greater things to come and, in 1903, the pair became the Harley-Davidson Motor Company.

Important lessons learned, they went straight back to the drawing board and the Harley-Davidson "factory" — a tiny, wooden shed in the Davidson boys' back yard thrown together by their dad — became a hive of activity.

The second prototype and two production bikes were underway by the end of the year. It wasn't

quite what you'd call mass production — but it was a start. The next engine was bigger, at 24cu in (405cc), and with 3bhp on tap, slightly more powerful. And to avoid the chassis flexing which afflicted its predecessor, Bill Harley built a sturdier loop frame.

The bikes were finished and sold in 1904. A decade later the company would cite the longevity of one of these original production bikes, which clocked up 100,000 miles without any major repairs, to advertise the durability of Harley-Davidson machinery. Not bad for a machine knocked up by amateurs in a garden shed equipped with little more than a second-hand lathe.

Durability was important; more so then than now. America is a vast, mainly rural country, and early motorcycles had to be tough to withstand the battering they took from potholed roads and rutted farm tracks

The following year, the company expanded its cramped premises and recruited its first employee — Arthur Davidson's big brother Walter. Walter was a railway machinist by trade, and he was soon joined by an assistant. Very much a family business,

Right: Engine of a 1905 Single.
Garry Stuart

Right and throughout chapter: Sportster detail. National Motor Museum via Roy Bacon

Arthur even enlisted the artistic talent of his Aunt, Janet Davidson, to finish the paintwork on each machine.

Meanwhile, realising he needed a sound grounding in engineering, William Harley enrolled at the University of Wisconsin to start a degree.

The fledgling firm had a little to learn about naming its products too. The most exciting name they could come up with for their first production bike was the evocative "Silent Gray Fellow." Sets the pulse racing, doesn't it?

Yet there were good reasons for this comically dull name. In 1906, Harley-Davidson customers were offered a different paint option for the first time — Renault Gray — and the machine's well-constructed silencers were indeed quieter than rival manufacturers'. But beyond advertising the practical aspects of its motorcycles, the new firm was anxious to forge a reputation for reliability and to project a respectable corporate image.

Production leapt to 50 machines in 1906 and a generous loan from the Davidson's rich uncle, James McLay, allowed the promising little company to move to a new 2,400sq ft site which would later become Harley-Davidson's famous Juneau Avenue factory.

Another classic early Harley-Davidson anecdote dates from this time. It seems that no sooner had the brothers built the building's shell, they were told part of it encroached on land owned by the railroad company. Rather than risk a legal battle with the powerful railroad bosses, a gang of ten men physically hoisted it up and moved

it back a foot. By 1907, the enterprise was gaining momentum and soon became Harley-Davidson Inc. The oldest Davidson brother, toolmaker William, joined the ranks as works manager and the quartet were working like Trojans, producing 150 machines by the year's end — three times the previous year's output.

While engineering student Bill Harley devoted his spare time to designing a new V-twin engine, Walter and William Davidson traveled to Chicago to learn the latest welding techniques. Sales supremo Arthur started setting up a dealership network and oversaw the company's first national advertising campaign. Under Arthur's thorough stewardship as sales manager and company secretary, Harley-Davidson was turning into an altogether more serious venture.

Phenomenally committed and hard-working — as witnessed by the subsequent mushrooming of their business — Harley-Davidson's founding fathers were a close-knit and by all accounts virtuous lot. Stoical, sensible men, the Scots-immigrant Davidson brothers were also known for financial prudence.

Their cautious, naturally conservative approach would remain a characteristic trait throughout the Harley-Davidson

story. Come what may, technological advances would be considered and deliberate — a process of careful refinement. Evolution, not revolution. It was, and still is, the Milwaukee way.

The philosophy served them well for nearly half a century, producing durable machinery

Below Left: First Harley, of 1903, restored by factory. Garry Stuart

Below: Model J of 1925. Garry Stuart

which carried the Harley-Davidson name through economic calamities, two World Wars and stiff competition from rival U.S. motorcycle giants. Later on, however, it was almost responsible for the firm's downfall. When swift change rocked the motorcycle market in the latter half of the century, Milwaukee was slow to react.

Nevertheless, the idea of development by gradual improvement remains part of the Harley-Davidson legacy today. If it ain't broke, Milwaukee don't fix it . . . at least not in a hurry.

Driven by the original Harley-Davidson dream team's blend of talents and personalities, sales trebled again to 450 in 1908, thanks to Walter Davidson's prestigious competition triumph in the Federation of American Motorcyclists endurance run. Walter finished with a perfect 1,000 points, a great achievement since he rode the whole 175 miles without a support vehicle — or even any spares!

In 1909, the improved 5-35 model went on sale for the first time. This was also the year Bill Harley took the step which would define the future of Harley-Davidson. He built the first Milwaukee V-twin, the Model D.

Vee-engined bikes were already helping rival U.S. manufacturers such as Indian,

Excelsior, and Merkel, carve out racing reputations and customers were pressing Harley-Davidson to follow suit.

Just a handful of these bikes, which used two 5-35 cylinders angled at 45°, were produced and the factory didn't make any the following year. Although a motorcycling milestone, the new model — sold exclusively to privateer racers — was flawed. Not only was it expensive at $325, but the engine's atmospheric inlet valves were not ideally suited to a V-twin, and reliability suffered as a result.

Despite this hiccup, the company continued to make strong progress. In a series of early sales coups, Walter Davidson sold motorcycles to the Bell Telephone Company, police forces and several public utilities. Once again, production trebled and by now, the workforce was 150-strong.

The V-twin made a comeback in 1911 in a much-improved form, when the 49.50cu in 810cc pocket-valve engine design made its debut. It was still expensive, at $300, but the new model was faster, stronger and more user-friendly. Although sales records for this crucial year were destroyed in a flood, Harley historians estimate production to have been between 5,000 and 6,000 machines.

By 1912, the twin was outselling the single and this year's

new models showcased improvements and technological innovations including a lower-slung frame, the first effective motorcycle clutch, optional chain drive and saddle suspension in the form of the "ful-floteing seat."

The prospect of an official, factory-backed racing effort also took a step closer to reality when a privately-fielded example of the new X8E V-twin left the opposition for dead in the San José road race.

A time of frantic expansion for Harley-Davidson, the years 1912–1920 would develop into a golden age for motorcycling. More ordinary Americans aspired to motorised mobility — and motorcycles were significantly cheaper than cars.

The market was growing and Milwaukee was enjoying a healthy slice of the cake. The factory worked hard to keep up with demand and 12,966 machines were built in 1913

In its first decade, the firm had watched more than 100 rival U.S. manufacturers spring up only to fall by the wayside. But now, as two-wheeled transport grew in popularity, Harley-Davidson began to reap the benefits of its cautious approach.

It wasn't the only company profiting from the two-wheeled boom. For most of the period

Below: The finish and the silent running led to the "Silent Gray Fellow" tag. A 1907 Single. Garry Stuart

Harley-Davidson's success, though impressive, was overshadowed by Indian and Excelsior-Henderson.

In 1914 production moved to a new factory facility on the existing Juneau Avenue site. Output held steady at around 13,000 bikes a year, with an initial 350 machines destined for the new European market. The U.S. Mail alone was running 5,000 Harley-Davidsons and the company was selling to police departments all over America.

Milwaukee embarked on an urgent recruitment drive to cope with the rise in sales. By 1915 more than 1,500 employees were working at Juneau Avenue.

More than 15,000 bikes were built in 1916 — the year bicycle-style pedals finally disappeared to be replaced by a kick-starter, and Harley-Davidson launched its own company magazine, *The Enthusiast.*

By the end of World War One, Harley-Davidson's main rival, Indian, ran into trouble after giving almost its entire output of 20,000 machines over to the war effort, while whittling profit margins down to a dangerously low level. A patriotic gesture it may have been, but it allowed Harley-Davidson (which cannily only produced 7,000 bikes for military service) to seize control of the home market when hostilities ended.

By 1919, Harley-Davidson was the world's biggest motorcycle manufacturer. Production had soared to 23,000 motorcycles and 16,000 sidecars — and with its export drive in full swing, the company was going truly global. Milwaukee-made bikes were selling well in 67 countries around the

world via Arthur Davidson's network of 2,000 dealers. But as the Roaring Twenties drew to a close, motorcycling's first golden era also came to an abrupt halt.

Harley's sales halved between 1920 and 1921 as the post-war economy suddenly boiled over and sank into unexpected decline. In a bold cash-conserving move, the company immediately axed its highly successful motor sport department when the all-conquering Wrecking Crew factory team was at the very height of its fame.

The biggest blow to the U.S. motorcycle market came from the desperate tactics adopted by car manufacturers. The dumping of Ford and General Motors cars at below cost price, for instance, bit a huge chunk out of the motorcycle market.

Suddenly motorcycles were no longer selling for a third of the price of the cheapest automobile. With the Model T Ford rapidly becoming the affordable transport for the American family, motorcycling was relegated to the province of enthusiasts or the poor.

Right: Hog cognoscenti admire the "Silent Gray Fellow." Garry Stuart

Below: The front cover and frontispiece of the 1911 brochure with the famous Milwaukee address. via Roy Bacon

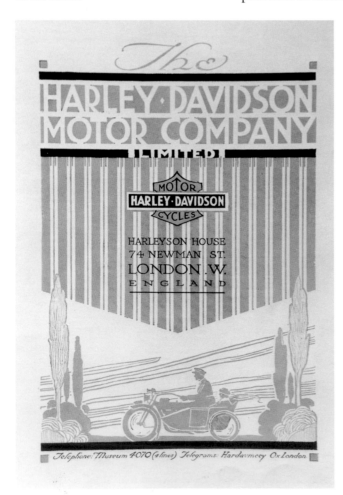

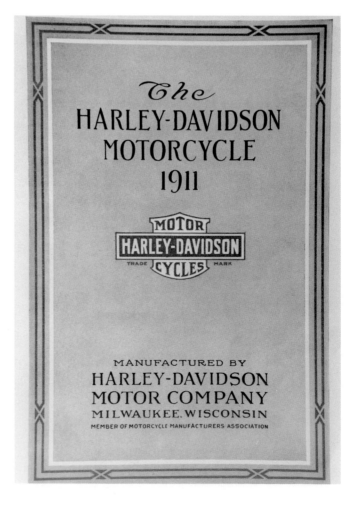

Eager to maintain industry confidence in the Harley-Davidson name, the company did what so many firms do when the chips are down — it summoned hundreds of dealers to an urgent sales conflab. Gathered at Harley-Davidson's Milwaukee headquarters, motorcycle dealers from all over the U.S. listened patiently as worried bosses talked up Harley-Davidsons future and painted a rosy picture of the firm's financial health.

With the domestic market shrinking, Harley-Davidson's burgeoning international sales network became a vital asset. In the next few years, more than half of Harley-Davidson's production was geared to export sales. In Britain, Fred Warr became the leading Harley-Davidson dealer.

Hungry for more overseas markets, Arthur Davidson dispatched his top salesman, Alfred Rich Child, around the world to drum up sales in countries as far-flung as Africa and Japan. Child's expedition was a success and he even set up a deal allowing a Japanese company, Sankyo, to make Harley-Davidsons under licence. Several years and a great deal of bureaucratic wrangling later, the Japanese Harley — a copy of the VL side-valver — was finally built as the "Rikuo." The name translates roughly as "King of the Road."

The operation was rapidly reorganized in response to the threatening economic climate. Although most of it efforts were geared towards survival rather than expansion, Milwaukee compensated for falling domestic sales by moving into the aftermarket by producing a range of official branded accessories — from extra lights and instruments, to engine oil, and riding coats. Fleet sales also helped the company weather the storm. By 1924, 1,400 police departments were riding Harley-Davidson mounts.

The First

Despite the motorcycling slump and the wheeler-dealing that followed, Harley-Davidson still found the time and money to keep developing its products.

Milwaukee toyed with ideas for a four-cylinder bike to compete with the successful, super-smooth, four-pot motors made by Indian and Henderson. An experimental engine was built in 1924 but received the thumbs down. The company decided to stick with the V-twin layout, choosing to upgrade and refine the tried and tested design instead.

A cheaper and less-risky path to follow, it led to the much-needed update of the J model, which had evolved directly from the V-twin bikes of 1911. The big bore twins got their makeover in 1925. The 61cu in and 74cu in JD model pocket-valve V-twins became the first Harley models to boast streamlining and the teardrop gas tank. Determined to stay on top of the still-sluggish market, Harley-Davidson kept prices at or below those of the previous year.

At the same time, company executives decided to drop the Model W Sport twin. This light-weight, horizontally-opposed side valve twin, launched in 1919, was basically a rip-off of the British-built Douglas motorcycle. But despite good sales in the U.K., it had never captured the imagination of American buyers. Instead, domestic customers had opened their hearts, minds and wallets to Indian's V-twin counterpart — the Sport Scout.

To fill the gap at the bottom of its range left by the departure of the Model W, the factory once again turned its attention to singles, producing a budget side-valve roadster and an overhead-valve racer — the "Peashooter."

In 1928, Milwaukee introduced the race-derived, twin-cam models the JH and JDH. These fast, pocket-valve V-twin road bikes were the first machines to come equipped with Harley-Davidson's latest pioneering innovation, the front brake. American riders were slow to appreciate the benefits of the new front anchor but it worked wonders for the safety of Harley's heavy bikes.

By the time the J series was finally killed off to make way for the VL V-twins in 1929, more than 70,000 examples had been produced. More than any other Harley-Davidson machine, the J model pocket-valve twins had established the marque's credentials in every motorcycling arena. As board racers, utility vehicles, hillclimbers and day-to-day transport, they had secured

23

Harley-Davidson's reputation, defined its strengths and laid the groundwork for the breakthrough bikes to come. Other engine configurations had been tried with varying degrees of success but none had worked as well as the heavyweight Vs. The Wall Street Crash and the Great Depression which followed, subjected U.S. manufacturing to a brutal form of natural selection. It was the greatest test yet for Harley's cautious, "evolutionary" ideology.

In October 1929, the stock market collapse sent the American economy into a disastrous tailspin. The postwar mini-slump of the early 1920s seemed like a minor blip in comparison. Anticipating the hard times ahead, Milwaukee cut its 1930 range from 13 to six models.

By 1933, the Depression had laid waste to great swathes of American manufacturing. With 25 percent of the U.S. labor force out of work, few people could afford a motorcycle and manufacturers were hit hard. Industry-wide, production plummeted from 32,000 to just 6,000 machines.

As the economic contagion spread across the Atlantic, export sales crumbled as European countries hiked up import tariffs to protect their own manufacturing industries.

Milwaukee was on its knees, as production dried up to just 3,703 machines but the company was still alive. Miraculously, even at this perilously low point, the company still managed to turn a modest profit. Other motorcycle producers didn't fare as well. Hundreds of rival manufacturers had already bitten the dust, including major players such as Henderson-Henderson, which went under in 1931

In fact, the Depression's death toll was so high that only Harley-Davidson and Indian survived. But while Indian was helped through the worst crises by multi-millionaire benefactor E. Paul DuPont, Harley-Davidson had only its own resources and business acumen to fall back on. Some workers were laid off, but the Milwaukee management was determined to keep as many employees on the payroll as possible, if only to retain their skills ready for the eventual economic recovery.

So instead of announcing drastic job cuts, they cut wages and shortened the working week.

Desperate to keep the cash flowing and factory running, the company branched out into the utility market in 1932 with the production of the Servi-Car, an odd-looking trike supplied to police, garages and delivery services.

Not the most aesthetically-pleasing Harley ever created, it was nevertheless well-designed and solidly-engineered. Incredibly, demand was such that the Servi-car remained in production until the 1970s, getting a Hydra-Glide front end along the way in 1958.

• Harley-Davidson •

In these increasingly dire financial circumstances, any new idea or sales gimmick which might help Harley-Davidson keep its head above water was worthy of consideration. In an attempt to make its motorcycles look more appealing, Milwaukee jazzed up its machines' paintwork in 1933 with an uncharacteristically extravagant new range of colors and Art Deco graphics. It wasn't what customers had come to expect from the company once responsible for the "Silent Gray Fellow" but they seemed to like it. So much so that Harley-Davidsons have sported vivid color schemes ever since.

But it was the motorcycles, and one well-loved model, in particular which enabled Harley-Davidson to ride through the hardships of 1929–36. In 1929 Harley-Davidson's 74cu in big twins were complemented by two less expensive new bikes.

The 30.5cu in 500cc Model C single (known as the "Thirty-fifty") proved short-lived, but it was the other newcomer, the new small Model D twin, which would sustain Harley during the impending economic catastrophe. It was soon joined by the bigger 74cu in (1,200cc) VL side-valver but the VL was too heavy, only slightly quicker and less reliable than the J series machines it replaced.

The "baby" side-valve (or "flathead") Model D 45cu in (750cc) V-twin, on the other hand, was a rugged and reliable workhorse. More than any other machine, it was responsible for the marque's survival as the Depression tightened its stranglehold on the U.S. motorcycle business. And with only minor alterations over the years, the "45" went on to become Harley-Davidson's longest-serving model, remaining a staple of the range until it was eventually succeeded by the K Model in 1952.

By 1930, three versions of the original Model D were available: the low-compression D, the high-compression DL and the DLD, also known as the "Special Sport Solo." Renamed the Model R in 1934, the machine was improved and renamed yet again in 1936 as the Model W.

This crude, harshly-sprung and ponderous machine just went on and on. Fast it wasn't, but for sheer unburstable durability the 45 was second to none. Cheap to make, simple to maintain, tough, dependable, and functional, it was exactly the kind of motorcycle the country needed to keep it chugging along through the adversities of the Depression years.

By 1935, the economic pall was starting to clear and by the

following year, Milwaukee had recovered sufficiently to launch two new models. One was the latest incarnation of the 45cu in side-valver, the Model W. The Model UL V-twin, which boasted a monstrous 80cu in (1,340cc) motor was another addition to the range.

But the year 1936 was notable for the debut of one very special new model; the Model E — better known as the mighty "Knucklehead." So called because the contours of its lumpy rocker box were said to resemble a clenched fist. The Knucklehead was a radically reworked version of the 61cu in (1,000cc) V-twin and the precursor to today's Harleys.

The Knuckle was developed by the factory race department under the direction of Harley-Davidson's legendary racer Joe Petrali. It showed too. The engine kept the same bore and stroke as the J model twin but gave double the power and a whopping 90mph top speed, thanks to an innovative new overhead valve system.

The new machine — designated Model E — featured a recirculating oil system, beefed-up frame, forks, clutch, and four-speed gearbox, built to handle the extra horses. Somehow even the styling seemed to ooze brute horsepower.

Determined to make sure the world sat up and took notice

of his creation, Petrali immediately took a race-tuned Knuckle-powered streamliner to a record-breaking 136.83mph at Daytona Beach, beating the previous record held by Indian.

There was no denying it; Harley's handsome new flagship was an engineering tour-de-force and a living, breathing testament of Milwaukee's newfound, post-Depression optimism.

Many believe that without the Knucklehead, Harley-Davidson may not have lasted until the end of the decade. Bolstered by sales of this stunning new bike, 1937 sales climbed to 11,000. Sadly, works manager and Vice-President William A. Davidson also died the same year.

Surviving the Depression by the skin of its teeth thanks to innovative marketing and financial prudence, Milwaukee emerged looking stronger than ever. Once again, it had produced the right motorcycle for the times. And the lessons learned about styling and finish during the lean years proved just as useful once business picked up again.

With the spectre of war hanging over Europe, Harley began developing a military model in 1937. Two years later (just months before Germany invaded Poland) a pair of military-spec Model W bikes, designated WLA, were delivered to the U.S. Army for testing. The 45's finest hour was about to begin. The same robust virtues which had earned the side-valve 45 such affection during the grim years of the Depression would soon make it a battle-zone hero.

The 74cu in (1,200cc) Knucklehead, built to take on rival Indian's famous big twins, appeared in 1941. Its 95mph-plus top speed, power, and sturdy build quality, made it attractive to police departments — traditionally an important market for Milwaukee machinery. But just as the Knuckle, the first all-American superbike, seemed poised for global success, the Japanese bombed Pearl Harbor, and the factory immediately threw itself behind the war effort.

Even before Uncle Sam officially stepped in to join the war, Milwaukee was busy building 5,000 military bikes for the British government. Triumph's factory had been hit during the bombing of Coventry and the American replacements were a godsend for the both British Army and the R.A.F.

By that time Harley-Davidson's fortunes were once again in the ascendant — and World War Two, just like the First, proved good for business.

At the end of 1941 production had bounced back to more than 18,000 as the first wave of military-spec machines were prepared for duty. Soon almost all of Milwaukee's output was for military use. The factory suspended production of racing models and the WLDR was dropped from the range.

One of Harley-Davidson's less well-publicized wartime duties, was that their engineers were charged with the task of stripping and examining captured enemy motorcycles. And Major John Harley, (later a company executive) was responsible for training army riders at Fort Knox.

Production was cranked up from 11,000 in 1940 to more than 20,000 in 1943. And Milwaukee mourned as one of its original founders, 65-year-old Walter Davidson died in 1942, followed by Bill Harley in September 1943 at the age of 66.

By 1945, Milwaukee had produced 88,000 military machines, mostly WL 45s. Canceled government orders towards the end of the war created a mountain of surplus machines which helped to expand the company's market share in the immediate post-war years.

As the conflict drew to a close, Knucklehead production

Below: For World War Two the firm built the 45cu in model in this WLA form for the U.S. forces and as the WLC for the Canadians. Garry Stuart

Harley-Davidson

increased apace. Fewer than 1,000 machines were built in 1945, but the number grew to 4,000 bikes in 1946, and more than 7,000 in 1947. The bigger 74cu in variant proved far more popular with customers than its 61cu in sibling.

Milwaukee was still feeling the pinch of wartime shortages in 1946, limiting paint options to red and grey for the first half of the year. But the spring fork shock absorber — an attempt to improve rider comfort — appeared for the first time this year.

Looking ahead to a period of post-war prosperity, the factory was busily developing and testing innovations such as the telescopic forks which would later see the light of day on the Hydra-Glide model of 1949; and with the help of tuner Tom Sifton, its racing department was experimenting with foot-operated gearshifts, rear suspension and stronger brakes. All improvements which would eventually filter through to road-going machinery.

Despite Milwaukee's deep commitment to gradual, cautious development, its crystal-ball gazers were predicting a change in the motorcycle market which could not be ignored. The designs of the future would have to be more user-friendly, more accessible to less mechanically-minded owners and more reliable. Hand-gear

shifts, oil-leaks, and a punishing ride would not sell motorcycles in this fast-approaching new era. It had served the company well, but the Knucklehead's days were numbered.

In 1947, Harley-Davidson opened a new 269,000sq ft factory facility on Capitol Drive, Wauwatosa — a suburb of Milwaukee — in anticipation of increased peacetime demand. War-weary motorcyclists returning from duty were looking forward to getting back in the saddle and hitting the open road.

But returning to their hobby wasn't going to be cheap. Post-war inflation was rising and so was the cost of motorcycling. After a six-year freeze, the price of the top-of-the-range 74cu in ohv machines — the last of the Knuckleheads — leapt from $465 to $605. More

than half of Milwaukee's total production was given over to the Knucklehead in 1947, with almost 12,000 examples built.

As part of Germany's post-war reparations, manufacturing rights to the country's DKW (Dampf Kraft Wagen) motorcycles had been surrendered. Divided between Milwaukee and British bike maker BSA, they gave Harley-Davidson the opportunity to build its own lightweight two-stroke bikes, without incurring development costs.

Although the antithesis of Milwaukee's trademark big V-twin four-strokes, these bantamweight budget bikes — designated the S Model — provided the company with an instant entry-level machine in 1948. Simple, economical and cheap to buy, it was hoped the 125cc Model S would bring new blood into the world of motorcycling. Coincidentally it was the first Harley-Davidson badged roadster to feature the new foot gearshift which would soon find its way on to mainstream machines as European manufacturers begun shipping bikes across the Atlantic in ever-increasing quantities.

The S-model's neat little teardrop gas tank often found its way on to race bikes as a weight-saving measure, eventually becoming one of the key styling cues of the Sportster. The learner-friendly 3bhp single, later christened the Hummer, didn't go down well with dealers, however who remained preoccupied with selling "proper" Harleys. But nevertheless it was an ideal starter bike for a generation of young novice riders who often graduated on to more powerful machines.

As far as Milwaukee was concerned, the war had produced other spin-off benefits too. Technological advances driven by military conflict had accelerated progress in the engineering world. And when peace came, civilian manufacturers were ready to reap the rewards of the military's steep learning curve.

In Harley-Davidson's case, the lessons learned would help produce machines tailored towards a new breed of rider who was more interested in riding than spannerwork.

In 1948, Milwaukee announced the Knucklehead's replacement, the "Panhead." The new model was powered by a development of the Knuckle's big twin engine. Externally, the Knuckle's distinctive, nobbly rocker covers were replaced by cylindrical alloy items shaped like upside-down cooking pans; hence the new unofficial moniker.

Offered in both 74cu in and 61cu in forms, the new powerplant featured hydraulic tappets or valve-lifters requiring less frequent adjustment, aluminum heads and a much more oil-tight lubrication system.

The sum of the improvements made the Panhead an easier motor-cycle to live with than its predecessors, showing that Milwaukee was serious about making motorcycling available to a wider public. To promote the new model, a national advertising campaign was launched and dealers re-introduced finance schemes to tempt potential customers.

Its first year sales figures showed Harley was on the right track. More than 13,000 Pans rolled off the line in 1948, a year in which overall production had grown to 29,612 motorcycles.

The following year, Milwaukee took the unprecedented step of giving a new model an official name. They must have had high hopes for the new Hydra-Glide Panhead.

The company's optimism was understandable. The machine bore Harley-Davidson's version of the hydraulic suspension fitted to the latest European motorcycles; The Hydra-Glide fork. The new system gave a smoother, more comfortable ride than the old leading-link springer front end which had graced Harleys for the past 40 years. There was still no suspension for the rear end though — Harley riders would have to wait a little longer before the spine-battering rigid frame was replaced with a more forgiving rear set up.

The more modern, enclosed styling of the new telescopic forks also helped bring the bike's appearance up to date. The Hydra-Glide's seamless forms, sweeping curves and rounded edges typified the automotive styling trends of the late 1940s and early 1950s. With its fat tyres, thick seat, and large, elegant mudguards or "fenders," it was a fine-looking heavyweight cruiser with all the classic Harley charms.

When, 40 years later, Milwaukee decided to mine its own back-catalog by building a range of retro-styled models, it was the Hydra-Glide which designers turned to for inspiration.

But even the celebrated first-ever Glide couldn't stop sales slipping slightly to 24,000 in 1949. Production numbers were levelling out by 1950; the year the last of the original company founders, 69-year-old Arthur Davidson died in a car accident.

The 1950s should have been a golden decade for Harley-Davidson. The war over and a new age of

Below: The early Hummer two-stroke, derived from a prewar DKW, became the 165cc Super 10 in time.
Garry Stuart

peace and prosperity beckoning, the American people were developing a new-found confidence. Anything seemed possible and as industry picked up, living standards improved and the future began to look brighter than ever in the Land of the Free.

Boom time had arrived. By the mid-1950s, a staggering 40 percent of the world's entire industrial output would be produced and consumed in the U.S.A.

In keeping with the exhuberant mood of the times, proud Harley owners with cash to spend were individualizing their machines with custom paintjobs and bolt-on extras. Picking up on the trend, Milwaukee decided to capitalize on this by offering its own options and add-ons such as two-tone paint, windscreens, and chromed "cheese-grater" fenders. The Harley-Davidson line of factory-issue accessories and clothing was extended and leather saddlebags became popular with touring riders. The term "full-dresser" was first coined in 1951, to describe a machine decked out with a full complement of luggage and touring paraphernalia.

In the circumstances, Harley-Davidson should have been raking in record profits and expanding as fast as gas in a combustion chamber. Instead, Milwaukee was worried. Why?

Because the British were coming! When Triumph set up a U.S. dealer network in 1951, Harley had good reason to fret. A young and dynamic company, Triumph offered a greater choice of models and the bikes were both technically superior and cheaper into the bargain.

Plainly terrified by the prospect of a British invasion, Milwaukee leaned heavily on dealers who might be tempted to stock the dreaded imported machines. But these restrictive trading

practices (later ruled unfair by a U.S. Government commission) weren't enough to stop faster, lighter bikes from across the Pond luring buyers away by the thousand.

A European-style foot-shift was offered as an option for the first time on the Hydra-Glide Panhead in 1952. The same year, overshadowed in the sales figures by its big brother, the 61cu in Panhead was discontinued.

In a bid to compete with the influx of sporty European machinery,

Harley also unveiled the new 45cu in (750cc) K model in 1952.

This replacement for the now tired old 45 side-valve design featured a foot-shift and a hand clutch. It was also the first Harley ever to sport hydraulic suspension at both ends

On paper it looked promising. The styling was sporty, the design modern, the handling good, but, alas, performance remained stodgy. Milwaukee coordinated a dealer push to promote the new bike as

its share in the middleweight market came under attack from the increasing number of dealers selling European bikes.

At the same time, Harley-Davidson demanded Government protection. It lobbied for a 40 percent import tax, together with import quotas to restrict the number of machines shipped over from Britain. The appeal fell on deaf ears. After weeks of tortuous legal hearings, America's Tariff Commission threw out Harley's complaints and condemned the company's restrictive practices.

As Milwaukee celebrated half a century of non-stop production in 1953, its great rival Indian went out of business. Once just one of hundreds of American motorcycle manufacturers jostling for a piece of an overcrowded market, now Harley-Davidson stood alone. And with the stream of imported British bikes threatening to turn into a flood, the sole surviving American motorcycle company was feeling the pressure.

After a shaky start, race-tuned K Model bikes were beginning to find their form on the track in 1953 with a welcome Daytona win. But on the street, the sluggish road going K was being blown into the weeds by the latest imported overhead-valve rivals from AJS, Matchless, Triumph, and BSA. Production

Left: Side-valve engine of the competition KR model in road racing form. Garry Stuart

Below: The KR set up for off-road events rather than for flat track where rear suspension and front brake were not fitted. Garry Stuart

slid down to 14,050 machines. Realising it was losing ground, Harley-Davidson began development work on the replacement middle-weight performance bike which would emerge a few years later as the Sportster.

In the meantime, 1954 saw the introduction of a hopped-up version of the K Model. The short-lived KH was bored out to 54cu in (883cc) boosting power to 38bhp and providing a stop-gap sports model while Milwaukee prepared its answer to the growing Brit threat. Harley's accessory sideline

was still selling well, and in 1954, the range was extended with new products including fishtail exhaust tips and Speed King leather saddlebags (The daft but aptly-named Fringe King was the fringed version).

Hot-rodding became a popular pastime in the America of the mid-1950s. Young gasheads with money to burn — literally — were no longer content with stylish looks. They wanted horsepower and plenty of it. Bike or car, if it wasn't a street racer it wasn't worth having. Alarm bells rang as sales dipped below 10,000 in

1955. It was time to give the old Hog some more muscle, reasoned Milwaukee, and the 74cu in FLH got 60bhp and a top speed of 105mph. With all four original founders gone, a new generation was now running the show at Milwaukee. William J. Harley was treasurer and chief engineer, John Harley was product engineer, Walter C. Davidson was company secretary and William H. Davidson was vice-president. By the mid-1950s, these guardians of the family business were ready to lock horns with the best of British.

In 1956, after a short production run of around 4,000 bikes, the KH bowed out to make way for Harley-Davidson's great new hope: the XL Sportster. The U.S. motorcycle scene was pleasantly surprised, rather than bowled over, when the Sportster made its debut appearance in 1957. Even so, this low, lean, modern machine must have struck a chord with the hot-rod generation, because Harley-Davidson production was climbing back up to 13,000 units by the end of the year.

With iron cylinder heads, large gas tank and big rear mudguard, the Sportster wasn't quite as single-minded as some had hoped. More of a sports tourer than an a no-frills, backstreet scratcher, it represented only a slight performance gain on the KH. But the performance potential from the new overhead-valve motor was there even so. Feedback from Sportster buyers made it abdundantly clear that performance was what they craved.

Milwaukee listened and the Harley range was split down the middle from that moment onwards — Sportster or Glide — performance or touring.

The throttle-happy contingent didn't have long to wait. The purposeful XLCH

Below: In 1958 the Panhead gained rear suspension to become the Duo-Glide. Garry Stuart

Sportster (The CH supposedly stood for "Competition Hot") arrived in 1958 — it was a winner from the word go. An aggressively-styled, lightened version of the XL, it remains one of the most beautiful Harley-Davidson designs ever built. It boasted alloy wheels, magneto ignition, a compact, "peanut" fuel tank swiped from the 125cc Hummer two-stroke and a powerful 54cu in (883cc) engine with domed alloy pistons. It looked the business and, more to the point, could hold its own against most of its imported rivals.

An immediate hit, 2,000 of these minimalist masterpieces were sold in the first year of production.

Also new for 1958 was the FLH Duo Glide luxury tourer; it was basically a Hydra-Glide with hydraulic suspension at both ends. For the first time, Harley's big twin got swinging-arm rear suspension and a hydraulic rear brake. By now the foot-shift model was selling three times as well as the traditional hand-shifter.

Production was still hovering around the 12,000 mark in 1959, as the U.S. motorcycle market grew increasingly overpopulated. Norton, Triumph and BSA continued their expansion into the Harley heartland, while Japanese motorcycles gained a toehold as a brace of lightweight Hondas appeared on the scene.

The early 1960s saw Milwaukee's planners make some uncharacteristically experimental forays into uncharted territory.

The weirdest of these has to be the Topper. Unleashed on an unsuspecting public in 1960, the 165cc Topper was Milwaukee's wildly optimistic stab at the scooter

• Harley-Davidson •

Below: Yes, Harley-Davidson did produce a scooter for a short time; built for 1960–65, it used the 165cc two-stroke engine. Garry Stuart

market already cornered so profitably by Italian marques Vespa and Lambretta.

A hideously unattractive, boxy affair, it boasted some eccentric features including an outboard motor-style starting cord and a parking brake. Against the odds, production lasted a full five years before the Topper was put out of its misery in 1965 after a run of just 3,000 machines.

As the lightweight motor-cycle market started to grow, Harley-Davidson took the unexpected step of buying a half-interest in the Italian company Aeronautica Macchi in 1960 for the very reasonable sum of $250,000.

There was method to the madness, however. Aermacchi (as Harley's Italian manufacturing arm became known) specialized in small singles; two-strokes in particular.

Harley knew its own Hummer lightweight two-strokes would soon be past their sell-by date, if they weren't already, but it wasn't prepared to throw away its slice of the small bike market. By hooking up with the Italian manufacturer, it could bypass the cost of tooling up for the production of new models. One year after the acquisition, the 250 Sprint single was introduced to the American public.

An ugly duckling of a motorcycle, the Italian-built Sprint was initially unpopular despite a strong, four-stroke engine which had been tried and tested in European road racing. U.S. racers eventually took the machine to their hearts and the factory built a brace of bikes, including some successful sporting variants which sold well during the 1960s. Between

43

• Harley History •

1961 and 1974, around 40,000 250cc and 350cc Sprints found American owners.

Nevertheless, Milwaukee's Italian hook-up came too late to stop Honda staking its claim to America's lightweight motorcycle market.

By the mid-1960s, Japanese manufacturers dominated the sector and had the middleweight market firmly in its sights. But with Aermacchi's help, Milwaukee had at least established a presence in this increasingly profitable arena despite the Japanese onslaught.

Meanwhile the humble Hummer two-stroke remained in production and by 1963, had mutated into a series of 175cc bikes called the Ranger, Pacer, and the bizarrely-named Scat.

William G. Davidson, grandson of founder William A. Davidson, joined the company as styling director in 1962. Sadly he arrived too late to veto the launch of the ugly and ill-advised Topper, but the legendary "Willie G." has held the job ever since, personally shaping the Milwaukee look for almost four decades.

In 1963, with plastic and glassfiber becoming more versatile materials, Harley-Davidson bought a glassfiber boat factory in Tomahawk, Wisconsin. The company later used the facility to make sidecars, motorcycle bodywork and even a Harley golf cart.

The mid-1960s saw the unstoppable Honda posting unprecedented sales figures. The sudden boom caught Harley-Davidson napping. By 1965, the Japanese were busy transforming the whole complexion of the U.S. motorcycle market. American buyers

Below: An Electra-Glide with Panhead engine and thus from 1965, the only year that combination was offered.
Garry Stuart

couldn't get enough of the exciting new lightweight and middleweight machines appearing in dealerships around the country.

By contrast, Harley-Davidson wheeled out the Electra-Glide, an update of the Duo Glide featuring a push-button electric start. In genealogical terms, the Electra-Glide represented an important stage in Harley-Davidson's evolution. A gargantuan, laid-back tourer, the '65 version was also the last of the Panhead models to leave the Milwaukee production line. Ironically, more Panheads were built in 1965 than during any preceding year; almost 7,000 as it turned out.

In 1965 Milwaukee bosses made the historic decision to list Harley-Davidson on the stock market and thereby surrendering control of America's last great motorcycle company.

More than 1.3 million shares were sold over the next four years. Initially, shareholders were pleased with Milwaukee's performance. But before long, awkward questions were being asked as Japanese manufacturers continued to seize an ever-larger slice of the domestic bike market. Their aggressive push into the U.S. motorcycle scene seemed relentless. Honda, for instance, would soon advance from the middleweight

• *Harley-Davidson* •

market into the heavyweight sector with the introduction of the revolutionary, high-performance CB750 four.

By 1966 Harley production had hit 36,320 — a peacetime record — thanks to Aermacchi's considerable contribution.

The long-serving Panhead was superseded by the 74cu in "Shovelhead" engine, first seen on that year's Electra-Glide models. Again, the new motor was a development of the previous big V-twin. While the bottom end of the motorbike remained largely

unaltered, it was mated to a new top end featuring aluminum rocker boxes said to resemble the shape of a coal shovel.

Soon afterwards, Milwaukee was confronted with a hostile takeover bid from an international conglomerate led by the Waukesha Engine Company. It bought up Harley-Davidson stock at an aggressive pace, leaving Harley-Davidson with few doubts about its long-term intentions.

Seriously rattled by these predatory maneuvrings and desperately requiring an injection

of capital to help his company grab a generous share of the exploding U.S. motorcycle market, William H. Davidson entered talks with sporting goods manufacturer American Machine and Foundry in 1968.

AMF's chairman Rodney Gott had been a Harley fan since the 1930s and negotiations led quickly to a merger between Harley-Davidson and AMF — at least that was the official line. In reality the deal was widely viewed as a takeover masquerading as a merger. Either way, Milwaukee

Below: Aermacchi single from Italy, a
fine motorcycle but not fully suited for
American roads. Garry Stuart

publicly backed AMF, urging shareholders to support the buy-out.

By December 1968, it was a done deal. AMF's coffers were $21 million lighter and Harley-Davidson was in new hands. But the relationship was rocky from the outset. As boardroom battles between the long-established family firm and its new corporate owners grew more heated, some of Milwaukee's top executives walked out in the first few years.

Unsurprisingly, the ill-will soon spread to the strongly unionized workforce and many

Harley aficionados believe this deterioration in employer-employee relations had a profound effect on the build quality of bikes produced under the AMF regime.

Although frequently cast as the villains of the piece, AMF invested huge sums of cash in machinery and plant. Sales grew dramatically during this period but the profits were slim and the marque's reputation suffered as quality-control slackened.

By the end of the 1960s, almost half of Harley-Davidson's production was coming from

Aermacchi's factory in Varese. By 1969, 4,575 Italian-built 350 Sprints had been imported, a significant figure when you consider that only the Electra-Glide and XLCH Sportster models had managed to shift more than 5,000 units in the same year.

The arrival of Honda's 123mph 750 Four in 1969 sent a chill wind whistling around Milwaukee. Proof positive that Mr Honda was deadly serious about building big bikes, it signalled nothing less than the start of the Japanese domination of the world's

motorcycle industry. In the coming decade, a tidal wave of Eastern imports would create a new U.S. market bigger than anything Milwaukee had ever imagined.

By the time the Sportster-derived XR750 race bike made its first appearance in 1970, production was at 29,000. As the 1970s progressed, the U.S. Government tightened regulations on safety, emissions, and noise. For Harley-Davidson, that meant bigger and better brakes, exhausts, and air cleaners. Officialdom also insisted on standardized operating controls for all motorcycles sold in the U.S market, which meant Sportster models had to be converted from a right to left foot shift. All of which added to production costs and cut into AMF's profits.

Output increased to 37,000 in 1971, a year which also saw Milwaukee's styling maestro Willie G. Davidson make a splash with a dazzling new design — the FX Super Glide factory chopper.

Destined to attain modern classic status, the FX was the first of many inspired ideas dreamed up by the innovative Willie G. The first-ever "factory custom," the FX big-bore sports cruiser was an imaginative attempt to cash in on the flourishing custom and chopper scene. But for Harley-Davidson, it was a risky departure. A long-established family business founded

on conservative values, from the very beginning Harley-Davidson had done everything in its power to distance itself from motorcycling's more "anti-social" elements. And yet here it was, selling a machine deliberately styled to resemble the bastardized creations ridden by the worst kind of longhair outlaw bikers. By Milwaukee standards, this was revolutionary stuff.

Willie G didn't get it exactly right at the first attempt though. Marred by a clumsily-designed boat-tail rear fender, the 1971 model wasn't an instant winner. But demand increased when the offending article was removed the following year — until the FX was soon outselling Sportsters.

In 1972, with output heading for 70,000, the Harley-Davidson assembly line was transferred from it's spiritual home in Milwaukee to AMF's premises in York, Pennsylvania; an empty former arms factory hurriedly adapted for motorcycle production. Harleys are still assembled there today, although their hearts — those soulful big Vee engines — are still forged in Milwaukee.

Misgivings about the increasingly dubious build quality of Harley machines were widespread by the early 1970s but AMF's marketing know-how somehow kept sales afloat.

By 1973 the York plant was producing a healthy 71,000 bikes a year. An impressive figure. At least it sounds impressive until you consider that, by that time, the total U.S. motorcycle market had ballooned to a mind-boggling 1.3 million machines a year. Harley-Davidson had never dreamed such a market existed. But Japanese manufacturers had somehow predicted, created, and successfully exploited, it within an extremely narrow timespan.

To make matters worse, Japanese motorcycles were cheaper, better engineered, and more sophisticated, than U.S. iron and they quickly made Milwaukee's big twins look like overpriced antiques. At the same time, the Japanese invasion was also beginning to squeeze out the British-built machines once seen such as a grave threat to Harley's future.

Worsening industrial relations were also becoming a problem for AMF, with production disrupted by a three-month strike at the York plant in 1974.

In 1975, with production figures exceeding 75,000, AMF appointed a new boss for Harley: Vaughn L. Beals Jr. Improving quality quickly became priority number one for troubleshooter Beals.

Harley's reputation for durability had taken seven decades

to build and just few years to bring down. Many of the AMF-era big twins had been afflicted by oil leaks and electrical faults and customers were losing patience. Lucrative fleet contracts had been lost and Harley models were receiving an increasingly rough ride from the motorcycle press, both at home and abroad.

Harley's Milwaukee management brought as much pressure as they could muster to bear on Beals; something had to be done, they urged. The evidence was compelling and, sure enough, AMF agreed a significant hike in quality was urgently needed.

Even more disturbingly, Harley-Davidson was steadily losing its grip on the U.S. heavyweight motorcyle market. At the beginning of the 1970s Milwaukee's domination of the sector was almost unchallenged. By 1980 Harley could claim less than half of America's big bike sales.

As if to ram the point home, in 1975 Honda launched the Gold Wing, a four-cylinder, 1,000cc tourer aimed squarely at the heavy-weight tourer market which had been Milwaukee's undisputed domain for more than half a century.

Willie G's next burst of creativity led to 1977s FXS Low Rider, a new version of the factory custom featuring shortened suspension and a cut-down seat

height, and the XLCR Café Racer. Primarily a design exercise, this sinisterly stylish street racer looked fast but sold slowly. With a production run of just two years, it was a short-lived model Although it failed to catch on at the time, it's a sought-after collector's item today.

In 1978 — the company's 75th birthday — it was a panic-stricken delegation of Harley and AMF top brass which, once again, went running to Washington alleging that Japanese manufacturers were dumping bikes on to the American market at a loss. Trade officials conceded some dumping had taken place but insisted the company's profits had not been affected. Harley's current ills, they concluded, were of its own making. Harley-Davidson had failed to adapt to a rapidly-changing market — that's all.

The Aermacchi factory was sold off the same year. Communication and supply lines between Italy and Milwaukee had deteriorated over the years and more pertinently, the small-capacity bikes were now outclassed by cheaper machines from Japan.

AMF's enthusiasm for the motorcycle business had cooled by the end of the 1970s. The predicted massive profits had never arrived, leaving Harley-Davidson's parent company frustrated by its

own inability to transform Milwaukee's dated manufacturing methods into profitable mass production on a truly international scale. Its ambitious — some say misguided — plan to play the Japanese at their own game had ended in disappointment. AMF wanted out. The scene was set for a pivotal moment in the company's boardroom history: 1981s bold management buy-out.

A dozen Harley big cheeses, led by chairman Vaughn Beals, raised more than $80 million from investors, including finance giant Citibank, and took control of the firm after lengthy negotiations with AMF.

"AMF has failed to make the company a going concern," said the simple statement announcing that the troubled marriage was to be dissolved.

Production had more than trebled during the AMF decade but nevertheless, the uneasy partnership had finally reached its natural conclusion. Consequently, in June 1981 the Harley-Davidson Motor Company opened up shop.

The new owners publicized their acquisition with a mass Hog ride from Milwaukee to York, Pennsylvania. Harley-Davidson, the "People's Motorcycle," was back in the hands of true motorcycle enthusiasts, they declared.

Below: Super Glide FXE Liberty from 1976, built to celebrate the U.S. Bicentennial. Garry Stuart

Enthusiastic and committed they may have been, but they were only too aware of the hard work and numerous pitfalls which lay ahead. Production had fallen from 50,000 in 1979, to under 42,000 in 1981, but more dangerously, profitability was questionable and Harley-Davidson's credibility was at an all-time low in the aftermath of the AMF era.

With impeccable timing, Honda transferred production of its big selling Harley-rival tourer, the Gold Wing to Ohio in 1981. The gauntlet was well and truly thrown down.

The newly-independent Harley-Davidson lost $25 million in 1982. Output had dropped again to around 30,000 bikes and by the following year Harleys accounted for less than a quarter of America's annual big bike sales.

The race was on to reverse the company's declining fortunes before time and money ran out. Beals and his team called in America's top industrial consultants, toured rival Japanese factories, overhauled working practices and reconsidered marketing strategies.

In 1983 Milwaukee again begged Washington to impose protectionist taxes on Japanese imports. This time it worked. President Ronald Reagan gave Harley-Davidson what it had been asking for since the early 1950s.

• Harley-Davidson •

Below: The 1979 XLCR Sportster Café
Racer built 1977–78. National Motor
Museum via Roy Bacon

Tariffs of up to 45 percent were imposed on big bike imports for the next five years, long enough to allow the privately-owned Harley-Davidson company to improve its products and rebuild its tarnished reputation.

Repairing the damage done to its public image during the AMF years was a crucial first step. So in 1984, the company sank $3 million into a publicity campaign aimed at winning back the hearts and minds of American motorcyclists. Coast-to-coast advertising was backed up with a promotion giving free test rides to tens of thousands of potential Harley-Davidson converts.

Another PR triumph was the setting up of the Harley Owners' Group, an official enthusiasts' organisation launched by Milwaukee to foster customer loyalty. The first club of its kind, HOG was a massive hit from the outset and has remained hugely popular ever since with getting on for half a million members around the world.

But the factory knew clever public relations would only do so much to recapture the confidence of the enthusiast market. The product would have to live up to the hype. Efforts to bring Harley hardware up to date had been underway for the last couple of years. But the moment of truth

arrived in 1984 with the unveiling of the V2 Evolution engine. The new mill — the long-anticipated Shovelhead replacement — came in both 80cu in (1,340cc) and 55cu in (883cc) guises. Less leak-prone, lighter, torquier, cleaner, smoother, and more powerful, than the outgoing Shovel, the new "Evo" motor made its debut in the new 1984 Softail. The Softail also gained the distinction of being the first in a long line of models to boast retro styling.

Ironically, the Harley look took off in this overtly nostalgic direction at just the same time as the factory produced some of the most sophisticated and modern

engineering to bear the Harley-Davidson name in many decades. The Softail, in particular, showcased an ingenious new feature. Its monoshock suspension was cleverly concealed behind the engine to mimic the rigid-framed, hardtail look of yesteryear. Refined, modern, and reliable, but still every cubic inch an authentic Harley-Davidson big V-twin, the Evo engine was the ideal antidote to Milwaukee's lingering image problems. It was soon powering a multitude of striking new models beginning with the Heritage Softail in 1985.

Heritage soon became the byword at Milwaukee. The flourishing retro theme was part of some shrewd image-management emphasizing Harley-Davidson's strongest asset — its "American-ness." Harley, after all was unique; the only major U.S. motorcycle manufacturer, with the best part of a century's worth of history behind it. Before long, the company was shamelessly playing on the romanticism of 1940s and 1950s America. It revived long-dead styling touches such as tombstone tail lights and fishtail exhausts, name-checked its illustrious founders in sale brochures and generally harked back to past glories at every available opportunity.

Below Left: Electra Glide 1200 from 1978 with Shovelhead engine and alternator electrics. via Roy Bacon

Below: Aermacchi road racing RR-250 built in Italy with a twin-cylinder, two-stroke engine. National Motor Museum via Roy Bacon

Over the next decade, the Harley-Davidson image would undergo a comprehensive makeover. Milwaukee's marketing men reinvented these (in many ways anachronistic) American heavyweight machines, turning them into desirable modern icons.

Slowly but surely, Harley-Davidson was putting its house in order. But some doubters still refused to believe the company had a future. Unfortunately Milwaukee's own bankers were among them. Expecting the worst, Citicorp decided to sell its interest four years before import tariffs were due to be lifted. Milwaukee's credit was immediately cut, plunging the company into financial turmoil.

Chairman Beals spent much of 1985 struggling to generate interest among potential investors. The soul-destroying search for Milwaukee's savior dragged on for six months without a glimmer of success. Then, just as bankruptcy seemed inevitable, the company was thrown a last-minute lifeline by the Heller Financial Corporation. A deal was agreed in December securing Harley-Davidson's future and providing nearly $50 million worth of working capital. Back from the brink again . . .

Beyond the life-or-death boardroom drama, 1985 had its upside. While Harley's marketing spin doctors were busily promoting

company's uniquely American identity, the sales department landed a valuable government contract to supply shell cases to the U.S. military.

Back on a rather more solid financial footing, a buoyant Harley-Davidson enjoyed a good year in 1986. Harley overtook Honda's Gold Wing in the U.S. sales charts, improved its share of the big bike market to 33 percent, and posted profits of $4.3 million

In yet another smart move from Willie G, a back-to-basics 883cc Evo-engined Sportster was offered as an entry-level Harley at the bargain price of $3,995. The low cost, coupled with a tempting buy-back option, helped shift 10,000 Sportsters in its first year.

The same year, Willie G, Vaughn Beals and the rest of the Harley-Davidson management hierarchy embarked on another high-profile ride; a marathon cruise from LA to New York. The run was timed to coincide with the refurbishment of the Statue of Liberty. A canny piece of media management, the event was contrived to reinforce the link between Harley, Liberty and the Good Ol' US of A in the public imagination.

Meanwhile, respected Harley-Davidson engineer and former roadracer Erik Buell left to develop a handbuilt Harley-based sports bike, setting up his own facility at

Mukwonago, Wisconsin. The resulting RR-1000 machine was campaigned in the Battle of the Twins series, blazing the trail for a range of road-orientated Buell sports bikes. Harley-Davidson later bought into Buell and the company now operates as Harley's sports bike arm.

An extraordinary thing happened in 1987. In bullish mood, with 47 percent of the big bike market to its name, Harley-Davidson asked the government to remove import tariffs a year early. Milwaukee announced it was ready to take on the Japanese without government protection. Fighting talk — and a sure measure of the company's newfound confidence.

For the second time in its history, the company was publicly owned, as a stock market floatation raised $30 million.

In 1988, retro-styling reached a new extreme with the introduction of the Softail Springer, featuring a modern revival of the girder forks as used on Harley-Davidson machinery 60 years before. Meanwhile, sales accounted for 54 percent of the heavyweight market. Harley-Davidson was on a roll.

A massive capital investment program in the early 1990s saw the company grab an even bigger 61 percent share of the big bike market with production at 65,000 units.

By 1991 all models boasted five-speed transmission and by 1992 belt drive was also standard across the range. Striking new additions including 1992s Heritage Softail Nostalgia FLSTN and 1995s super-retro FLHR Road King developed the nostalgia motif, while the hi-tech Buells, such as the 1994 S2 Thunderbolt and the 1996 S1 Lightning, kept the sports bike flag flying.

In 1995, fuel injection also appeared for the first time on a Harley, on the FLHTC-1 Electra-Glide. Production topped 105,000 the same year, passing the magical 100,000 for the first time. A new paintshop at Harley-Davidson's York, Pennsylvania assembly plant helped speed up output and the one million square feet assembly plant now produces between 540 and 560 bikes in a day. (The current record is a whopping 600 machines in a single 24-hour period).

A $90 million factory was opened in Kansas City, Missourri, in 1998, where today's Sportster models are turned out at an average rate of one every 55 minutes.

Below: The Fat Boy was coded as the FLSTF and built from 1990 with the solid disc wheels. via Roy Bacon

Output increased to just under 160,000 in 1998. Harley's 80cu in big twin engines and the new (from 1999) 88cu in are still built at Milwaukee, although today the Juneau Avenue building is the company's conference center and service school.

By the time it celebrates its centenary in 2003, Harley-Davidson aims to be turning out 200,000 motorcycles a year. President Ronald Reagan once famously described the Harley saga as "An American Success Story." Looking at the numbers, it's hard to disagree.

But perhaps the greatest measure of that success comes from its old adversary, the Japanese motorcycle industry. They say imitation is the sincerest form of flattery and the recent advent of the Japanese-built big V-twin Harley clone must have raised a wry smile or two in Milwaukee.

Machines like Yamaha's Royal Star cruiser look the part and sell for less, but something's missing. Call it soul, feel, character, pedigree — whatever, the fact is it doesn't matter how many copies you make, there's only ever one original!

Right: WL45 flathead. Garry Stuart

Harley Types

Roy Bacon

A Single Start

Harley-Davidson is best known for its V-twin engines, but has used other forms, beginning with a single. From the start Harley differed from most of its contemporaries who based their machines on a heavy-duty bicycle with an engine hung in place. William Harley and Arthur Davidson aimed for something more solid and better able to cope with the road conditions of the time, so their machines were heavier, sturdier, and more reliable.

To propel the machine, and give it the ability to deal with hills, they chose to use capacity rather than tuning. The result was a relaxed machine with an easy travel style, limited stress on the engine parts, and little wear over long periods. It might have used more gas than others, but this was of little account for many years by when the style was long established for the firm. It was one that later worked equally well for Henry Ford and his model T.

The first Harley-Davidson engine was built in 1903 and had a modest 10cu in capacity but was quickly replaced by one of 25cu in. Construction was simple with a vertically-split crankcase in which the crankshaft ran in bushes with a

split, bushed, big-end bearing. The one-piece, cast-iron cylinder and head was inclined forward a little, and fitted with a side exhaust valve and overhead automatic inlet valve — the latter operation known as aiv. The layout was referred to as inlet-over-exhaust (or ioe) abroad, and as pocket-valve in the United States, but became as well known as the F-head.

A crankshaft gear drove the half-speed camshaft that also carried the points cam for the basic battery ignition. Lubrication was by a total-loss system, with the flow into the crankcase controlled by a

needle valve and the oil encouraged up onto the cylinder bore by crankcase baffles and piston suction.

The engine was installed in a robust loop frame and drove the rear wheel by a flat belt; and there was a choice of three engine pulley sizes to enable the owners to gear the machine to their needs. A slave pulley on an arm controlled by a lever set the tension, allowed for the various pulleys, dealt with belt stretch and acted as a crude clutch. There were pedals, the rear hub had a coaster brake, but there was no front brake then or for many a

Early Singles

Model . . . . **Single**
Years. 1903–05
No. cylinders. 1
Valves. . . . . aiv, ioe
Bore/stroke inch. . . . . . . 3 x 3½
Capacity cu in 24.74
Capacity cc 405
Ignition . . . . coil
No of gears 1
Drive system . . . . direct belt
Suspension . . . . rigid
Wheel type . . . . wire
Rear brake. . . . . coaster
Wheelbase inch 51

Model . . . . **Single**
Years. 1906–08
No. cylinders. 1
Valves. . . . . aiv, ioe
Bore/stroke inch . . . . . . 3⅛ x 3½
Capacity cu in 26.8
Capacity cc 440
Ignition . . . . coil
No of gears 1
Drive system . . . . direct belt
Front suspension . . . . . . rigid, 1907
. . . . leadinglink
Rear suspension. . . . . . . rigid
Wheel type . . . . wire
Rear brake. . . . . coaster
Wheelbase inch 51

Model . . . . **Single**
Years. 1909–12
No. cylinders. 1
Valves. . . . . aiv, ioe
Bore/stroke inch . . . . . . 3⁵⁄₁₆ x 3½
Capacity cu in 30.16
Capacity cc 494
Ignition . . . . coil, magneto
. . . . option
No of gears 1
Drive system . . . . direct belt
Front suspension . . . . . . leading link
Rear suspension. . . . . . . rigid
Wheel type . . . . wire
Rear brake. . . . . coaster

Left: Engine of the early singles, this restored one from 1913–14. via Roy Bacon

Above and Right: 1911 engine with timing cover off to show gear drive to magneto. via Roy Bacon

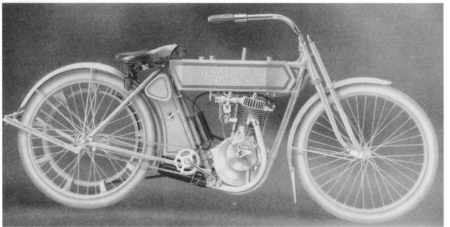

year, as it was not thought desirable with most American roads unpaved. It was a good, solid foundation built on a concept that was just right for the U.S.A. with its vast distances and cheap gas.

Production expanded and changes came along with an effective muffler and a move from the early black finish in 1906 introducing the "Silent Gray Fellow" name.

For 1907 there were leading-link front forks in a form the firm would use for over four decades, and in 1909 the engine grew to 30cu in with magneto ignition an option — this fitting behind the cylinder where it was driven from the camshaft by a gear train within a case.

There were piano-wire controls concealed within the handlebars, matching tanks for gas and oil, and the option of a V-belt in place of the flat type. That year saw the first V-twin but it was not a success.

Left: 50th Anniversary celebration restored 35cu in 1912 "Silent Gray Fellow." Garry Stuart

Below: 1913 twin. Garry Stuart

Right: 1915 989cc twin. Roy Bacon

Below Right: Lonnie Isam of Houston's Competition bikes: restored single of 1905 on floor; unrestored 1907 on workbench. Garry Stuart

The First Twin

It was 1911 before the V-twin made its true debut in a form that would stay with the firm from then on. The V-angle was set at 45° — just as now — and this allowed the engine to tuck neatly into the loop frame with little change. It was this angle, and the single carburetor, that gave the exhaust note the characteristic beat it retained down the years to become part of the Harley legend.

Construction of the V-twin engine was much as for the single, but it differed in having a mechanically opened inlet valve from the start. This was easily done by replacing the automatic assembly with one that included a rocker and its support. A pushrod, with external return spring, and a few timing chest changes completed the revision with little alteration to the F-head cylinder casting.

The 1911 twins were of 49cu in and retained the rear-mounted magneto and belt drive. The singles kept to aiv while the frame design was altered to provide a straight downtube in place of the older curved type. The frame was changed again for 1912 to slope the top tube and lower the saddle that was then suspended on a spring concealed in the seat tube.

All this gave much improved comfort, while performance was enhanced thanks to the addition of a 61cu in engine size and roller big ends. On the transmission side a clutch went into the rear hub and one model was offered with chain drive. Production rose to over 9,500 units.

Most models had chain drive for 1913, when the singles adopted a mechanical inlet valve with its cam mounted on one of the magneto-drive gears. At the same time it was enlarged to 35cu in to become the 5–35 series. A forecar kit was an option, this replacing the front forks with twin wheels that had a trade box suspended between them. There were two speeds in the rear hub for 1914 when all engines had roller-bearing big ends and most models had a drum rear brake. A sidecar was listed and proved popular.

The final step in the process from primitive to complete basic motorcycle came in 1915 when the engines gained an oil pump and the machines a three-speed countershaft gearbox with all-chain drive via a dry clutch. There was also a magneto-generator listed as

Below Right: A 1915 advertisement. Copies were sold to provide food parcels for prisoners of war during World War One. via Roy Bacon

Bottom Right: A 1914 twin as seen in the 1991 brochure. via Roy Bacon

an alternative to acetylene lighting. In this way all the component parts were in place and for over a decade it was a case of steady development and refinement for the V-twins.

Rounded tanks came in 1916 and an olive paint finish for the next year. The singles were dropped after 1918 and during this period the factory went racing with eight-valve twins and to the war in Europe. By then the American market had shrunk, thanks to Henry Ford, and in time the home industry was reduced to a few firms, dwindled to two, and then there was just Harley-Davidson.

The firm concentrated on V-twins with the occasional single, but in 1919 introduced the Sports Twin that differed in many radical ways. For a start it had a 35cu in flat-twin engine that was built in unit with a three-speed gearbox. The engine had side valves, all opened by a single camshaft, and to suit this the inlets were installed at an angle. Each cylinder and head was cast in one piece, as was the combined inlet and exhaust manifold set on the right side of the engine. An external flywheel went on the left end of the crankshaft and the magneto sat on top of the crankcase. Three helical gears took the drive up to the gearbox located in the top of the crankcase, while final drive was by a fully-enclosed chain.

This interesting engine unit was a stressed member in the tubular frame that had front suspension by trailing links that connected to a single, central spring just in front of the headstock. The front fender was well valanced and fully sprung but the frame was rigid at the rear. All told, it was an enterprising design but expensive to build, down on power in comparison with its Indian Scout rival, and lacked the expected V-twin exhaust note. By 1924 it was no longer listed.

Below: The first twin was this Model 7D of 1911, with magneto ignition.
via Roy Bacon

Bottom: The 7–9hp V-twin engine with 45° angle between cylinders used by Harley from then to now.
via Roy Bacon

1911–1920

Model	Single
Code	5–35
Years	1913–18
No. cylinders	1
Valves	ioe
Bore/stroke inch	3⁵⁄₁₆ x 4
Capacity cu in	34.47
Capacity cc	565
Ignition	magneto
No of gears	1, 1914-2, 1915-3
Drive system	chain
Front suspension	leading link
Rear suspension	rigid
Wheel type	wire
Rear brake	drum

Model	Twin
Years	1911–12
No. cylinders	V-twin
Valves	ioe
Bore/stroke inch	3 x 3½
Capacity cu in	49.48
Capacity cc	811
Ignition	magneto
Drive system	belt
No of gears	1
Drive system	belt
Front suspension	leading link
Rear suspension	rigid
Wheel type	wire
Wheel size inch	22
Rear brake	drum
Wheelbase inch	59.5

Model	Twin
Years	1912–20
No. cylinders	V-twin
Valves	ioe
Bore/stroke inch	3⁵⁄₁₆ x 3½
Capacity cu in	60.32
Capacity cc	989
Ignition	magneto
No of gears	1, 1913-2, 1915-3
Drive system	chain
Front suspension	leading link
Rear suspension	rigid
Wheel type	wire
Wheel size inch	22
Rear brake	drum
Wheelbase inch	59.5

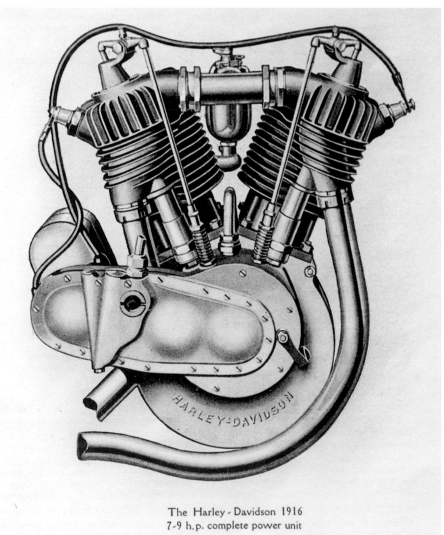

The Harley-Davidson 1916
7-9 h.p. complete power unit

Below: The 1916 Model 16C single of 4hp with magneto ignition and three-speed gearbox. via Roy Bacon

Bottom: The 1916 sidecar A fitted on the left for the UK market and usually powered by the V-twin engine. via Roy Bacon

A Larger Twin

A new and larger V-twin appeared in 1921 as the Seventy-four — a name that would continue in use to 1980. The existing twin continued as the Sixty-one, both designations referring to the engine capacity in cubic inches. The larger had both an increased bore and the longer four-inch stroke of the 5–35 single but retained the ioe F-head layout.

Two versions were offered, the F model with magneto ignition and the J model with a generator. Both kept the existing features of chain drive, three-speed gearbox, robust rigid frame, leading-link front forks, and a single rear brake. A full electrical system was fitted and the increased power kept the Harley well up with the competition without sacrificing reliability.

This made the big twin a fine machine for the U.S.A. of the 1920s as the highway system expanded and riders made longer journeys. For more local work the firm offered the 37cu in CD single, essentially the Seventy-four minus the rear cylinder, but it had few buyers so was dropped after two seasons.

The twins ran on through the decade with minor changes for all years and major ones now and then. The early olive finish gave way to Brewster green for 1922, but reverted to olive green in 1924. A major change was a new frame for 1925 that lowered the seat height by three inches and enabled a more modern tank style to be adopted which much improved the line.

Singles returned to the Harley-Davidson range for 1926 as a means of offering lightweight models. All were known as Twenty-ones, from their capacity, but both side-valve and overhead-valve versions were listed, each in two forms. For one, magneto ignition and no lights were specified, for the other it was battery ignition and lighting.

All were quite conventional in their construction with a vertical cylinder and detachable head, that of the side-valve engine designed by Ricardo. The timing gears and cams went on the right so the side valves were vertical, as were the pushrods up to the rockers and inclined overhead ones. The electrics went behind the cylinder with gear drive and the models continued the Harley practice of making the tanks as two halves that joined in the center to appear as one, with the left carrying oil separately from the fuel, the right one fuel only. Transmission was by chain but the three-speed gearbox was of the cross-over type so the final drive went on the right, the primary and clutch on the left under a cover. A simple, rigid frame, had leading-link front forks, and the usual sprung saddle, but a sprung front fender. Also built for some years was a competition version of the ohv model known as the Peashooter.

The ohv road singles were dropped after 1929 while the side-valve model was stretched to become the Thirty-fifty for 1930, this being rejoined by the side-valve Twenty-one in 1932 with both models continuing to 1934. After then it was twins only for a long time.

Little was altered for 1927 although the ohv singles benefited by the fitment of new Ricardo-designed cylinder heads. For 1928 the V-twin engines adopted the Two Cam system in the timing chest, an arrangement used in the competition motors from 1919 and one that now gave better valve control to the road engines. With more power and speed, and many more paved miles of highway, the marque finally fitted a front brake, albeit none too powerful. A cylindrical toolbox was fitted to the front fork below the horn and headlight, while 1929 brought twin headlights of a more streamlined form.

Then it was the end of the decade, the start of the Depression years and time for Harley to replace the old F-head twin. It had served them well since 1911 but a valve in the cylinder head was still regarded with some suspicion. It was noisy, let oil mist out, and could cause serious damage if it broke and fell into the engine.

Until all this was overcome, there was great attraction in the simple side-valve so that was the route the firm decided to take. Not such a bad choice as a large side-valve twin would offer enough performance from its wide power band with less noise, good reliability, and easy servicing.

• *Harley-Davidson* •

Below Left: Side-valve single of 1930 and of 21cu in capacity, 350cc in the UK. via Roy Bacon

Below: Later Model J from 1928, hence front brake, of 74cu in or 1,200cc. via Roy Bacon

Bottom: The 1923 Model J of 61cu in or 1,000cc. via Roy Bacon

1921–1929

Model 37
Code . . . . CD
Years. 1921–22
No. cylinders. 1
Valves. . . . . ioe
Bore/stroke inch . . . . . . 3.424 x 4
Capacity cu in 36.83
Capacity cc 604
Ignition . . . . magneto or coil
No of gears 3
Drive system . . . . chain
Front suspension . . . . . . leading link
Rear suspension. . . . . . . rigid
Wheel type . . . . wire
Rear brake. . . . . drum

Model 21
Code . . . . A & B
Years. 1926-29,
. . . . 1932-34
No. cylinders. 1
Valves. . . . . sv
Bore/stroke inch . . . . . . 2⅞ x 3¼
Capacity cu in 21.10
Capacity cc 346
Ignition . . . . magneto or
. . . . coil
No of gears 3
Drive system . . . . chain
Front suspension . . . . . . leading link
Rear suspension. . . . . . . rigid
Wheel type . . . . wire
Wheel size inch 20
Front brake. 1928-drum
Rear brake. . . . . drum
Wheelbase inch 56.5
Seat height inch. 28.5

Model 21
Code . . . . AA & BA
Years. 1926–29
No. cylinders. 1
Valves. . . . . ohv
Bore/stroke inch . . . . . . 2⅞ x 3¼
Capacity cu in 21.10
Capacity cc 346
Ignition . . . . magneto or coil
No of gears 3
Drive system . . . . chain
Front suspension . . . . . . leading link
Rear suspension. . . . . . . rigid
Wheel type . . . . wire
Wheel size inch 20
Front brake. 1928-drum
Rear brake. . . . . drum
Wheelbase inch 56.5
Seat height inch. 28.5

Model . . . . Twin
Code 61
Years. 1921-29
No. cylinders. . . . . V-twin
Valves. . . . . ioe
Bore/stroke inch . . . . . . 3⁵⁄₁₆ x 3½
Capacity cu in 60.32
Capacity cc 989
Ignition . . . . magneto
No of gears 3
Drive system . . . . chain
Front suspension . . . . . . leading link
Rear suspension. . . . . . . rigid
Wheel type . . . . wire
Front brake 1928-drum
Rear brake. . . . . drum

Model . . . . Twin
Code . . . . 74F or 74J
Years. 1921–29
No. cylinders. . . . . V twin
Valves. . . . . ioe
Bore/stroke inch . . . . . . 3.424 x 4
Capacity cu in 73.66
Capacity cc 1207
Ignition . . . . F-magneto,
. . . . J-coil
No of gears 3
Drive system . . . . chain
Front suspension . . . . . . leading link
Rear suspension. . . . . . . rigid
Wheel type . . . . wire
Front brake. 1928-drum
Rear brake. . . . . drum

Model . . . . 35 Sport
Code . . . . WA
Years. 1919–23
No. cylinders. . . . . flat twin
Construction . . . . unit
Valves. . . . . sv
Bore/stroke inch . . . . . . 2¾ x 3
Capacity cu in 35.64
Capacity cc 584
Ignition . . . . magneto
Primary drive. . . . . gear
Final drive. . . . . chain
No of gears 3
Front suspension . . . . . . trailing link
Rear suspension. . . . . . . rigid
Wheel type . . . . wire
Wheel size inch 20
Rear brake. . . . . drum
Wheelbase inch 57
Seat height inch. 29

Left: The side-valve single for 1926.
Garry Stuart

Below Left: 61cu in Model J of the
1920s. Garry Stuart

Right: Flat-twin Model WA sold as the
35 Sport. Ian Kerr

Below Right: The 350cc overhead-valve
single of 1928. via Roy Bacon

Bottom Right: A 1926 side-valve single
in good condition. Garry Stuart

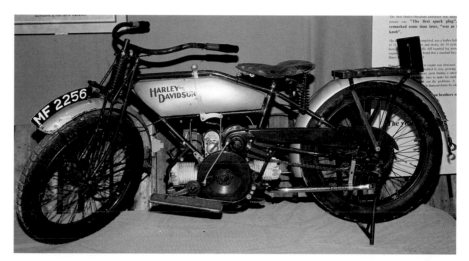

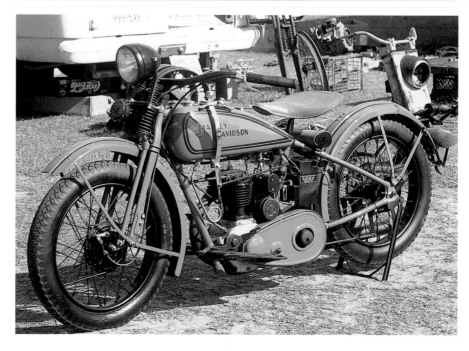

Right: Brochure front cover for 1931. (Back cover at Left.) via Roy Bacon

Side-Valve Twins

The new range of side-valve twins was first seen in 1929 and listed as the model Forty-five. Essentially simple, with its 45cu in, 45° engine, it followed the well established Harley-Davidson practice of sturdy construction, well able to cope with its duties.

It would prove to be reliable and easy to service. Coil ignition and total-loss lubrication continued to be used while the generator was installed on the left, adjacent to the front cylinder, and driven from the timing chest by a cross-shaft and bevel gears.

The gearbox had three speeds and cross-over drive (as on the singles) so the clutch continued on the left but the final drive went on the right. The frame and leading-link front forks were also based on the singles and the fixtures and fittings much as those on the older F and J twins. Several versions were offered aside from the stock Model D, one with raised compression ratio, one in sports form and one for sidecar work.

Below: 1938 Model UL side-valve V-twin. Garry Stuart

Right: Servi-Car in action. Garry Stuart

Side-Valve Twins

The Forty-five came along at the right time for it was firmly in production by the time of the Wall Street crash and its price and specification suited the decade to come. Not that the firm ignored the market for the larger machine, for in 1930 they introduced a new Seventy-four as the Model V with a side-valve engine. There were four variants that kept the existing engine dimensions, three speeds, leading-link forks, and coil or magneto ignition, but it was a new design, on the lines of the 45.

Problems beset the new Seventy-four when the first

shipment went out late in 1929 and the firm had to work hard to deal with these. Rectification kits went out to dealers while production was halted for a while — the outcome was a considerable drop in demand. In time they improved as riders found that the model was essentially better than the older type, but by then the Depression was tightening and sales fell to a low in 1933, that year being little better than 1910.

All firms struggled with reduced production, lay-offs, and lower wages. Police sales were one outlet both Harley-Davidson and Indian fought over with models fitted out with equipment to suit the special needs of the customer. Other needs were looked after by the sidecar, a long-standing addition to the motorcycle that continues to be listed to today.

There was also its commercial variant — the Parcelcar — that was popular with tradesmen for town and local use for many years. It was cheaper to run than a truck and easier to park in traffic, while well able to carry the tools of the trade and some advertising material on the sides.

In 1932 Harley-Davidson added the Servi-Car that was based on the Forty-five and destined to remain in production until 1974. It was laid out as a tricycle with two rear wheels; its frame was

designed for the job, not adapted from the motorcycle type. The transmission include a differential in the rear axle and above it sat a box container. A tow bar was attached to the front fork. The idea behind the Servi-Car was for it to be ridden to a car, hooked to it, and the car then driven to the garage for its service with the tricycle in tow. It survived for the many years it did by being taken up by traffic police who found it handy for their work. They can still be seen in some cities today.

Back in the 1930s the firm generated more revenue by extending their option list to include more machine accessories, plus Harley-Davidson clothing, and items for rider and passenger. This would continue into modern times and become a major part of the company business with all manner of products carrying the firm's logo.

Another deal, that would have a profound effect in time, was for their machines to be built under licence in Japan. This led to the sale of tools, dies and engineering knowledge which led to the creation of the "Rikuo" and the spread of technical information in that far-off land.

Machine evolution continued with the Forty-five becoming the Model R in 1932, the year the smaller side-valve single returned

to the line. Most of the work was on the details, but for the police the firm turned to producing radio receivers. They tried making industrial engines, but industry was buying few of those, and such devices as a tractor which the operator walked behind, and an outfit for painting lines on roads.

It was a desperate time with little real change on the technical front and it was late 1935 before another model appeared. This was the Eighty model V, essentially the Seventy-four with a longer stroke, and with it came the option of four speeds in the gearbox for both models. However, just round the corner was the forerunner of the modern Harley-Davidson.

Left: The 1936 VLH. Garry Stuart

Below: Big twin flathead of 1935–41 with 80cu in engine. Garry Stuart

Side-Valve Twins

Model	30–50
Code	C
Years	1930–34
No. cylinders	1
Valves	sv
Bore/stroke inch	3⅜ x 4
Capacity cu in	30.07
Capacity cc	493
Ignition	magneto or coil
No of gears	3
Drive system	chain
Front suspension	leading link
Rear suspension	rigid
Wheel type	wire
Front brake	drum
Rear brake	drum
Wheelbase inch	57.5
Seat height inch	26.5

Model	45
Code	D, R, W
Years	1929–51
No. cylinders	V-twin
Valves	sv
Bore/stroke inch	2¾ x 3¹³⁄₁₆
Capacity ce i	45.29
Capacity cc	742
Ignition	coil
No of gears	3
Drive system	chain
Front suspension	leading link
Rear suspension	rigid
Wheel type	wire
Wheel size inch	18
Brakes	drum
Wheelbase inch	57.5
Seat height inch	26.5

Model	74
Code	V
Years	1930–36
No. cylinders	V-twin
Valves	sv
Bore/stroke inch	3.424 x 4
Capacity ci	73.66
Capacity cc	1207
Ignition	magneto or coil
No of gears	3, 1936–4 option
Drive system	chain
Front suspension	leading link
Rear suspension	rigid
Wheel type	wire
Wheel size inch	19
Brakes	drum
Wheelbase inch	60
Seat height inch	28

Model	80
Code	V
Years	1935–36
No. cylinders	V-twin
Valves	sv
Bore/stroke inch	3.424 x 4½
Capacity ci	78.84
Capacity cc	1292
Ignition	coil
No of gears	3, 1936–4 option
Drive system	chain
Front suspension	leading link
Rear suspension	rigid
Wheel type	wire
Wheel size inch	19
Brakes	drum
Wheelbase inch	60
Seat height inch	28

Side-Valve Twins

Left: Big twin flathead in later years. Garry Stuart

Below Left: The 80cu in big flathead twin. Garry Stuart

Bottom Left: A 1936 VLH. Garry Stuart

Right: 1933 VL. Garry Stuart

Below Right: Bobbed VL. Garry Stuart

Below: Model 45 from late 1930s. Garry Stuart

Side-Valve
Twins

Left: Big twin flathead. Garry Stuart

Right: Engine of a late-1930s Model 45. Garry Stuart

Below Right: Servi-Car. Garry Stuart

Overleaf: The 1937 Package Truck. Garry Stuart

Below: Late 1930s Model 45 with dynamo alongside front cylinder. Garry Stuart

Servi-Car

• *Harley-Davidson* •

Below, Left and Right: The Servi-Car survived much longer than could have been anticipated thanks to its adoption by police services. The Japanese built Servi-Cars under licence. All Garry Stuart

Left, Below Left and Bottom Left: 1930s' VLs. All Garry Stuart

Right: 1936 80cu in Model V. Garry Stuart

Below Right: 1934 VL. Garry Stuart

The Knucklehead

During five of the most difficult years in the company history, work continued on a new overhead-valve twin. Finally launched for 1936 as the Model E series and listed as the 61 OHV, it was effectively a new machine, for there was little from the past other than the firm's tradition of building strong machines — it was the start of a new era.

The engine kept to the dimensions of the past so retained the usual 61cu in capacity, but had just one camshaft to operate all four valves. This meant that each pair of pushrod tubes had to splay out to run up to the respective rocker box which supported each rocker on a shaft held by a large domed nut on the right-side end. From their appearance came the model nickname of "Knucklehead."

The rest of the engine was conventional with the cylinders at 45°, built-up crankshaft, and gear drive forward to the generator and points housing. Different was the use of dry-sump lubrication with the oil carried in a tank under the saddle. A dry clutch drove a four-speed gearbox and kept to the usual foot operation as did the left-hand lever for the gears. The rigid frame and leading-link forks were

new developments of the old, as were the wheels, brakes, sprung saddle, and other details.

The use of twin gas tanks continued and these had a top panel carrying, mounted on it, the speedometer, instruments and switches. The overall styling was superb with machinery filling all the spaces to look just right, substantial but not heavy, reliable but not dull. With the new model came the start of the fitment of accessories in groups at the factory. Two packages were offered and this practice would continue and expand. There were some early snags with the machine, soon dealt with, but despite these the new model sold better than the firm had expected.

The new frame, forks, tanks, and wheels, went onto the Seventy-four and Eighty for 1937 when these became the Model U series. All the side-valve twins changed to dry-sump lubrication that year, the smallest becoming the W series — this set the main part of the firm's range in place for a good many years, although there would be other models.

There were some detail changes and for 1938 these included full valve enclosure for the 61 OHV. While Europe went to war the firm looked at supplying the Forty-five to a military

Below: A 1937 Knucklehead. Garry Stuart

specification and built a flat-twin
model, the XA, based on the
layout of the shaft-drive BMW. For
1941 the road range added the
74 OHV by stretching the bore
and stroke of the 61E, but not
copying the dimensions of the
74U engine. It was known as the
Model F, but few were built before
civilian production was replaced by
wartime needs early in 1942.

*Below: Postwar Knucklehead for 1947
after restoration.* Garry Stuart

• *Harley-Davidson* •

The Knucklehead

Model	74	**Model**	61OHV
Code	U	Code	E & EL
Years	1937–48	Years	1936–48
No. cylinders	V-twin	No. cylinders	V-twin
Valves	sv	Valves	ohv
Bore/stroke inch	3⁵⁄₁₆ x 4⁵⁄₃₂	Bore/stroke inch	3⁵⁄₁₆ x 3½
Capacity cu in	73.79	Capacity cu in	60.32
Capacity cc	1209	Capacity cc	989
Ignition	coil	Ignition	coil
No of gears	4	No of gears	4
Drive system	chain	Drive system	chain
Front suspension	leading link	Front suspension	leading link
Rear suspension	rigid	Rear suspension	rigid
Wheel type	wire	Wheel type	wire
Wheel size inch	18	Wheel size inch	18
Brakes	drum	Brakes	drum
Wheelbase inch	59.5	Wheelbase inch	59.5
Seat height inch	26	Seat height inch	26
Model	80	**Model**	74OHV
Code	U	Code	F & FL
Years	1937–41	Years	1941–48
No. cylinders	V-twin	No. cylinders	V-twin
Valves	sv	Valves	ohv
Bore/stroke inch	3⁵⁄₁₆ x 4⁵⁄₃₂	Bore/stroke inch	3⁵⁄₁₆ x 3³¹⁄₃₂
Capacity cu in	79.46	Capacity cu in	73.66
Capacity cc	1,302	Capacity cc	1,207
Ignition	coil	Ignition	coil
No of gears	4	No of gears	4
Drive system	chain	Drive system	chain
Front suspension	leading link	Front suspension	leading link
Rear suspension	rigid	Rear suspension	rigid
Wheel type	wire	Wheel type	wire
Wheel size inch	18	Wheel size inch	18
Brakes	drum	Brakes	drum
Wheelbase inch	59.5	Wheelbase inch	59.5
Seat height inch	26	Seat height inch	26

Left: The Knucklehead engine.
Garry Stuart

Below Right: The 1947 Knucklehead.
Garry Stuart

Left: Dutch AA solo, a WLA restored and in suitable colors. Garry Stuart

Below Left: A WLA 45, restored to civilian colors. Garry Stuart

Right: 1945 WLA 45 finished in red rather than khaki. Garry Stuart

Below: WLA 45 upper engine and tank top. Garry Stuart

Three beautifully maintained WL 45s in civilian guise. All Garry Stuart

102

Postwar

After the war Harley-Davidson was well placed to pick up where the company had left off. The Forty-five had never really ceased production and was soon joined by the Seventy-four Model U and the two overhead-valve models, the 61 and 74. Only the Eighty was left off the list.

The first new postwar model was a totally new type for the firm and aimed at a completely different market sector to their usual customer. First seen late in 1947, it used a 7.5cu in, 123cc, two-stroke engine built in unit with a three-speed, footchange gearbox. This went into a rigid frame with pressed-steel girder forks, drum brakes, a saddle and basic equipment. In fact, it was not new at all but a copy of a 1935 German DKW taken as part of the war reparation and also built by BSA in Britain as the Bantam, in Russia as the Voskhod, and later by Yamaha as the Red Dragonfly, while continuing at DKW whose works were in East Germany after partition.

The model remained in production until 1959 with a change to the telescopic front forks in 1951, when it was called the Tele-glide. In 1953 the engine was stretched out to 164cc but two years later the 125 returned and both versions were known as a Hummer. Intended for local use, other small two-strokes would replace them in the 1960s, but while all sold quite well, they were never perceived as true Harley-Davidson models — they sat uneasy alongside the big V-twins in showrooms.

In 1948 the overhead-valve engines had a new top end with light-alloy cylinder heads, hydraulic valve lifters, and fully-enclosed

Below: Hydra-Glide with Panhead engine. Garry Stuart

Bottom: Detail of Hydra-Glide. Garry Stuart

valve gear. This introduced a single rocker box cover held by a ring of small bolts to each cylinder head and the form, much as a baking pan, soon led to the model being known as the Panhead. That year was also the last year for the venerable side-valve Seventy-four Model U.

For the next year the suspension was improved by a change to telescopic front forks for the two overhead-valve models which became known as Hydra-Glides. With the forks came smaller wheels, fatter tyres under well-valanced fenders, and a styling

Postwar

Model...........................45
Code ....K
Years 1952–53
No. cylinders ....V-twin
Valves.............................sv
Bore/stroke inch.............2¾ x 31¾₆
Capacity cu in 45.29
Capacity cc 742
Ignition...........................coil
No of gears 4
Drive system...................chain
Front suspension ....teles
Rear suspension................s/a
Wheel type ....wire
Wheel size inch 19
Brakes ....drum

Model...........................55
Code ....KH
Years 1954–56
No. cylinders ....V-twin
Valves.............................sv
Bore/stroke inch.............2¾ x 4⁹₆
Capacity cu in 54.20
Capacity cc 888
Ignition...........................coil
No of gears 4
Drive system...................chain
Front suspension ....teles
Rear suspension................s/a
Wheel type ....wire
Wheel size inch 19/18
Brakes ....drum

Code 61EL
Years 1949–52
No. cylinders ....V-twin
Valves.............................ohv
Bore/stroke inch.............3⁵₆ x 3½
Capacity cu in 60.32
Capacity cc 989
Ignition...........................coil
No of gears 4
Drive system...................chain
Front suspension ....teles
Rear suspension................rigid
Wheel type ....wire
Wheel size inch 16
Brakes ....drum
Wheelbase inch................60.5
Seat height inch...............31

Code 74FL
Years 1949–65
No. cylinders ....V-twin
Valves.............................ohv
Bore/stroke inch.............3⁷₆ x 33½₂
Capacity cu in 73.66
Capacity cc 1,207
Ignition...........................coil
No of gears 4
Drive system...................chain
Front suspension ....teles
Rear suspension................rigid, 1958-s/a
Wheel type ....wire
Wheel size inch 16
Brakes ....drum
Wheelbase inch................60.5
Seat height inch...............31

Model...........................Hummer
Code ....S
Years 1947–59
No. cylinders 1
Valves.............................t/s
Bore/stroke mm ....52 x 58
Capacity cu in 7.52
Capacity cc 123
Ignition...........................flywheel
......................................magneto
No of gears 3
Drive system...................chain
Front suspension ....girders,
......................................1951-teles
Rear suspension................rigid
Wheel type ....wire
Wheel size inch 19/19
Brakes ....drum
Wheelbase inch................50

Model...........................Hummer
Code ....ST
Years 1953–59
No. cylinders 1
Valves.............................t/s
Bore/stroke mm ....60 x 58
Capacity cu in 10.0
Capacity cc 164
Ignition...........................flywheel
......................................magneto
No of gears 3
Drive system...................chain
Front suspension ....teles
Rear suspension................rigid
Wheel type ....wire
Wheel size inch 1⁹₉
Brakes ....drum
Wheelbase inch................50°

trend towards the de luxe tourer that the Glide series would keep to modern times.

For 1952 the big overhead-valve twins went over to a foot gearchange and hand clutch which brought them into line with the flood of imports coming into the United States from Europe. But the old system remained available for the traditional Harley rider. At the year end the Model E was dropped, for the F was only a few dollars more and performed better.

More important, although none too apparent at first, was the addition of the Model K which replaced the elderly Forty-five. While it remained a 45°, side-valve, V-twin of the same 45cu in capacity, it was a totally new concept for the firm as it had unit construction of the engine and four-speed gearbox. Inside the engine was much on the lines of the past with four camshafts, gear driven in a row, the generator at the front, and the points housing on top of the timing cover. The cylinder heads were in light alloy and the valve gear fully enclosed.

Primary drive was by chain on the left to a dry, hand operated clutch, while the gearbox had footchange and was of the cross-over type, so the final drive went on the right. Lubrication was dry sump for the engine and separate for the transmission. The engine unit was housed in a tubular frame with telescopic front suspension and pivoted-fork rear, while the wheels were 19in diameter, with wire spokes, and drum brakes.

Unfortunately for the firm, the K had a number of minor trouble spots and, more important, failed to deliver on the road. The performance was around 80mph tops and the acceleration less than exciting when matched against the British imports. In 1954 an engine stretch to 54cu in did little to help matters, but for all that the KH, as it had become known, led to one of the firm's best loved and long running series of models, the Sportster.

Far Left: A 1945 WL45. Garry Stuart

Left: WL45, postwar. Garry Stuart

Left and Right: A 1947 WL in civilian finish. Garry Stuart

Below: The unit construction KHK of 1955. Garry Stuart

• *Harley-Davidson* •

Below: Customized K model.
Garry Stuart

Bottom: 1952 Model K. Garry Stuart

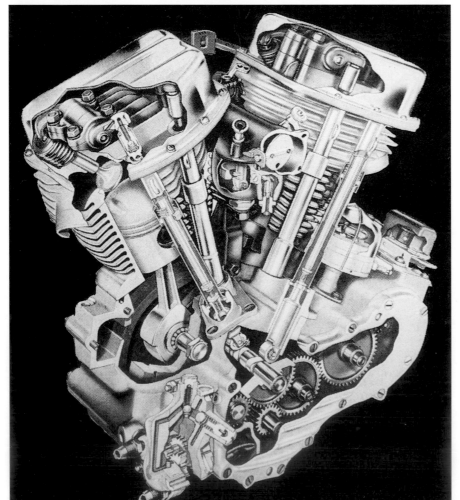

The Panhead engine was the postwar Harley-Davidson answer to the problems of overheating encountered with the old iron Knucklehead. Announced in Fall 1947, the Panhead made its entry onto the market in 1948.

Above Left and Above: Panhead-engined Electra Glide. Both Garry Stuart

Left: The Panhead engine. via Roy Bacon

Above Right: The first Panhead of 1948. Garry Stuart

Right: Hydra-Glide. Garry Stuart

Sportster

The Sportster arrived for 1957 as the XL model and in essence was the KH with overhead valves. However, in the process the bore was increased and stroke reduced to leave the capacity at 54cu in. This meant new heads, barrels, flywheels, and cam gear, but the transmission and cycle parts stayed virtually as they were. It had always been Harley-Davidson practice to make haste slowly and change one area at a time — something the firm would continue to do down the years.

As a smaller machine than the Hydra-Glide, the Sportster came with a single seat in its basic form, but with a host of options for dealers to profit by and owners to customise their machines with. It was the start of the modern Harley style which would lead to the factory creating new models by a mix-and-match process using the base machine and the option list. Then each owner could go on to add their individual ideas with further options. Much of this was well in the future but the Sportster was at the start, along with the Glide. The process would lead to a massive expansion in the range of models with many sequences of code letters to help identify them.

Both the Glide and Sportster were affected for 1958 when the 74FL (as the big twin had become) added rear suspension to be renamed the Duo-Glide. The basic Sportster XL was joined by the XLH and XLCH, the first for the highway and the second much quicker thanks to a tuned engine. This came about from the model being successfully run in competition, and it sold well in all forms — never two the same — but most either set up for road or sports use, the latter usually with magneto ignition.

This line took the firm to the end of the 1950s and well into the next decade, for it was in 1965 that the big twin gained electric starting, 12-volt electrics, and the name of Electra-Glide. The next year brought a change to the top end of the engine with each rocker box separate and bolted to the cylinder head. Their shape ordained the new type name of Shovelhead and this took the Electra-Glide up to 1969.

Meanwhile, the Sportster was given 12-volt electrics for 1965 to keep it in line with the Glide and gained electric start for 1968.

Right: A 1972 XLH. Garry Stuart

Sportster

Code	XL
Years	1957–59
No. cylinders	V-twin
Valves	ohv
Bore/stroke inch	3 x 3¹³⁄₁₆
Capacity cu in	53.90
Capacity cc	883
Ignition	magneto or
	coil
No of gears	4
Drive system	chain
Front suspension	teles
Rear suspension	s/a
Wheel type	wire
Wheel size inch	1⅝₈
Brakes	drum
Wheelbase inch	57
Seat height inch	30.5

Code	XLH & XLCH
Years	1958–71
No. cylinders	V-twin
Valves	ohv
Bore/stroke inch	3 x 3¹³⁄₁₆
Capacity cu in	53.90
Capacity cc	883
Ignition	magneto or
	coil
No of gears	4
Drive system	chain
Front suspension	teles
Rear suspension	s/a
Wheel type	wire
Wheel size inch	1⅝₈
Brakes	drum
Wheelbase inch	57
Seat height inch	30.5

Model	Electra-Glide
Code	74FL
Years	1966–69
No. cylinders	V-twin
Valves	ohv
Bore/stroke inch	3⁷⁄₁₆ x 3³¹⁄₃₂
Capacity cu in	73.66
Capacity cc	1,207
Ignition	coil
No of gears	4
Drive system	chain
Front suspension	teles
Rear suspension	s/a
Wheel type	wire
Wheel size inch	1⁵⁄₁₆
Brakes	drum
Wheelbase inch	60
Seat height inch	31

Below Left: Duo-Glide rear end, with suspension similar to Sportster. Garry Stuart

Bottom Left: Engine unit of the 1972 XLH Sportster V-twin with gearbox built in unit. Garry Stuart

Below: The Sportster for 1970. Garry Stuart

Bottom: A 1958 Duo-Glide, the big twin with front and rear suspension. Garry Stuart

Two-strokes and imports

Other events affected Harley-Davidson in the 1960s — beginning in 1961 with an association with the Italian firm, Aermacchi. This took place alongside an upgrade for the 164cc Hummer that became the Super 10 for 1960–61, and the 172cc Pacer for 1962–65. These road models were joined by the off-road 164cc Ranger model for 1962 only, and the 172cc Scat in 1962, this having a trail machine image. Both Scat and Pacer went from rigid frame to pivoted-fork rear suspension in 1963, using a system where the springs went under the engine unit. For 1966 the Pacer was replaced by the Bobcat that had glass-fiber for the seat base and rear fender.

From 1960 to 1965 this two-stroke line was joined by a scooter sold as the Topper. It used the 164cc engine with the cylinder laid down to point forward, and had a centrifugal clutch, a variable-ratio V-belt primary, and chain final drive. The front forks were long leading-links, there were 12in pressed-steel wheels and a glass-fiber body over the mechanics. It was not popular with traditional owners and arrived at a bad time as the scooter market in the United States was fading.

Below Left: Engine unit of the Sprint model built in Italy. Garry Stuart

Below: Road models with two-stroke engines came in this form as the SS250 or SS175. via Roy Bacon

The Aermacchi connection took over from the small domestic models, but the first sample was no two-stroke lightweight but the desirable 250 Sprint. This had a horizontal single cylinder, overhead valves, four-speed gearbox in unit with the engine, and a sound racing pedigree. Unfortunately, while the Sprint was a much wanted machine in Europe, it was less suited to the American view that preferred cubes for power, as this worked better in the land of vast distances and cheap gas. Also the Aermacchi electrics were prone to failure, build quality of the cycle parts varied, and the finish was often poor.

Other offerings proved even less successful with a 50cc Leggero model, soon replaced by one of 65cc, but finding few takers. For 1968 there was the 123cc Rapido, nice if conventional, and then the Baja 100 for racing with five speeds and an expansion chamber exhaust.

A 350 Sprint came in 1969 but the market had moved on so all these models were replaced by a new two-stroke line from 1973 on. All had single-cylinder engines and were offered in road and trail forms as 90, 125, 175, and 250 models, with the three larger listed up to 1977. All were conventional but soon found that the competition got better. A disc front brake was fitted to the 250 for its last year but made little difference.

Two-strokes and imports

Model	Super 10 & Ranger
Years	1960-61 & 1962
No. cylinders	1
Valves	t/s
Bore/stroke mm	60 x 58
Capacity cu in	10.0
Capacity cc	164
Ignition	flywheel magneto
No of gears	3
Drive system	chain
Front suspension	teles
Rear suspension	rigid
Wheel type	wire
Wheel size inch	19, Ranger-18
Brakes	drum
Wheelbase inch	50

Model	Topper
Years	1960–65
No. cylinders	1
Valves	t/s
Bore/stroke mm	60 x 58
Capacity cu in	10.0
Capacity cc	164
Ignition	flywheel magneto
No of gears	automatic
Drive system	belt/chain
Front suspension	leading link
Rear suspension	s/a
Wheel type	disc
Wheel size inch	1¾2
Brakes	drum

Model	Scat, Pacer & Bobcat
Years	1962–65, Bobcat-1966
No. cylinders	1
Valves	t/s
Bore/stroke mm	60 x 61
Capacity cu in	10.52
Capacity cc	172
Ignition	flywheel magneto
No of gears	3
Drive system	chain
Front suspension	teles
Rear suspension	rigid, 1963-s/a
Wheel type	wire
Wheel size inch	19, Pacer & Bobcat-18
Brakes	drum

Model	250 Sprint
Years	1961–67
No. cylinders	1
Valves	ohv
Bore/stroke mm	66 x 72
Capacity cu in	15.03
Capacity cc	246
Ignition	coil
No of gears	4
Drive system	gear/chain
Front suspension	teles
Rear suspension	s/a
Wheel type	wire
Wheel size inch	1⅞7
Brakes	drum
Wheelbase inch	51.2
Seat height inch	28.2

Model	350 Sprint
Years	1969–74
No. cylinders	1
Valves	ohv
Bore/stroke mm	74 x 80
Capacity cu in	21.0
Capacity cc	344
Ignition	coil
No of gears	4
Drive system	gear/chain
Front suspension	teles
Rear suspension	s/a
Wheel type	wire
Wheel size inch	1⅞7
Brakes	drum
Wheelbase inch	51.2
Seat height inch	28.2

Model	Leggero 50
Years	1965–66
No. cylinders	1
Valves	t/s
Bore/stroke mm	38.8 x 42
Capacity cu in	3.03
Capacity cc	49.7
No of gears	3
Drive system	gear/chain
Front suspension	teles
Rear suspension	s/a
Wheel type	wire
Brakes	drum

Model	Leggero 65
Years	1967–71
No. cylinders	1
Valves	t/s
Bore/stroke mm	44 x 42
Capacity cu in	3.9
Capacity cc	64
No of gears	3
Drive system	gear/chain

Front suspension ....teles
Rear suspension.................s/a
Wheel type ....wire
Brakes ....drum

Model........................**Rapido**
Years 1968–72
No. cylinders....................1
Valves...............................t/s
Bore/stroke mm ....56 x 50
Capacity cu in 7.51
Capacity cc 123
No of gears 4
Drive system.........gear/chain
Front suspension ....teles
Rear suspension.................s/a
Wheel type ....wire
Brakes ....drum

Model........................**Baja 100**
Years 1970–72
No. cylinders....................1
Valves...............................t/s
Bore/stroke mm ....50 x 50
Capacity cu in 6.0
Capacity cc 98
No of gears 5
Drive system.........gear/chain
Front suspension ....teles
Rear suspension.................s/a
Wheel type ....wire
Brakes ....drum

Code Z90
Years 1973–74
No. cylinders....................1
Valves...............................t/s
Bore/stroke mm ....48 x 49
Capacity cu in 5.41
Capacity cc 89
Ignition............................coil
No of gears 4
Drive system.........gear/chain
Front suspension ....teles
Rear suspension.................s/a
Wheel type ....wire
Wheel size inch 1⅞₆
Brakes ....drum
Wheelbase inch.................46.5
Seat height inch.................29.7

Code X90
Years 1973–74
No. cylinders....................1
Valves...............................t/s
Bore/stroke mm ....48 x 49
Capacity cu in 5.41
Capacity cc 89
Ignition......................magneto
No of gears 4

Drive system.........gear/chain
Front suspension ....teles
Rear suspension.................s/a
Wheel type ....disc
Wheel size inch 10/10
Brakes ....drum
Wheelbase inch.................40.7
Seat height inch.................26.8

Model........................**125**
Code ....SS, SX, SXT
Years 1973–77
No. cylinders....................1
Valves...............................t/s
Bore/stroke mm ....56 x 50
Capacity cu in 7.51
Capacity cc 123
Ignition....................electronic
No of gears 5
Drive system.........gear/chain
Front suspension ....teles
Rear suspension.................s/a
Wheel type ....wire
Wheel size inch 19/18
Brakes ....drum
Wheelbase inch.........SS-54, SX-49,
...............................SXT-53.5
Seat height inch..............SX-32,
...............................SXT-30.5

Model........................**175**
Code ....SS, SX
Years 1974–77
No. cylinders....................1
Valves...............................t/s

Bore/stroke mm ....61 x 59
Capacity cu in 10.52
Capacity cc 172
Ignition....................electronic
No of gears 5
Drive system.........gear/chain
Front suspension ....teles
Rear suspension.................s/a
Wheel type ....wire
Wheel size inch 19/18
Brakes ....drum
Wheelbase inch.....SS-56, SX-54
Seat height inch....SS-31.5, SX-32

Model........................**250**
Code ....SS, SX, SST
Years 1975–77
No. cylinders....................1
Valves...............................t/s
Bore/stroke mm ....72 x 59
Capacity cu in 14.66
Capacity cc 240
Ignition....................electronic
No of gears 5
Drive system.........gear/chain
Front suspension ....teles
Rear suspension.................s/a
Wheel type ....wire
Wheel size inch ......SS & SST-1⅞₈,
...............................SX-2ᵗ
Brakes ....drum
Wheelbase inch...........SS & SX-54,
...............................SST-56
Seat height inch......SS-30.5, SX-32,
...............................SST-32.5

The Topper

AMF and Super Glide

Back in 1969 Harley-Davidson was bought by American Machine & Foundry, AMF, which brought much plant investment. This lasted until 1981 when they sold it back to the family and others. The improved production facilities were of great benefit in the end, while progress with the product was slow but significant.

For 1970 the Electra-Glide changed from generator to alternator electrics with the ignition points moved into a cone-shaped boss on the timing chest. With this change the early engines became known as Generator Shovels and later ones as Alternator Shovels. The Sportster had the points moved into the timing cover for 1971, when the dry clutch was replaced by a wet one.

A new series was introduced for 1971 as the FX Super Glide to fit between the heavy, touring, Electra-Glide, and the Sportster that was in the sports image but beginning to fall back from the latest imports. So the FX was a mix, using the Alternator Shovel engine, and frame from the Glide along with its twin tanks, but with the XL forks and front wheel. The electric start was left off, but a

glass-fiber seat base and rear fender were used, albeit only for 1971.

The Super Glide sales performed well, so ran on with conventional rear styling for 1972, the year the Sportster models had their engines bored out to 1,000cc (the firm choosing not to refer to it as 61cu in for some time). A disc front brake went onto the Electra-Glide that year, and onto the Sportster in 1973 when the Super Glide changed to disc brakes front and rear.

A second Super Glide was added for 1974 as the FXE with an electric starter and proved more popular than the FX. In 1975 left-side footchange became mandatory, so the Sportsters had a linkage to cross from right to left and moved the brake pedal to the right. By 1977 the connection was internal and the range was joined by a new model in this series to herald the start of the expansion of the Harley-Davidson line up.

Unlike other firms, this was not done by adding new models in the usual sense, in fact the basis of all would remain the Shovelhead engine and the Sportster with its unit construction. What the firm did, however, was to dramatically increase the mix and match of new and old options to produce fresh models, each with its own style and variation.

Below Left: 1972 Electra Glide. Garry Stuart

Bottom Left: FLH from AMF period. Garry Stuart

Below: 1970s AMF FLH Shovelhead. Garry Stuart

Bottom: 1977 FX/FXE 1200 Super Glide. via Roy Bacon

AMF and Super Glide

Code	XLH & XLCH
Years	1972–85, 1972–79
No. cylinders	V-twin
Valves	ohv
Bore/stroke inch	$3\frac{3}{16}$ x $3\frac{13}{16}$
Capacity cu in	60.84
Capacity cc	997
Ignition	coil,
	1978-electronic
No of gears	4
Drive system	chain
Front suspension	teles
Rear suspension	s/a
Wheel type	wire
Wheel size inch	$1\frac{5}{8}$, 1980-$1\frac{9}{16}$
Front brake	drum, 1973-disc
Rear brake	drum, 1979-disc
Wheelbase inch	58.5, 1982-60
Seat height inch	29.5

Model	Electra-Glide
Code	74FLH
Years	1970–80
No. cylinders	V-twin
Valves	ohv
Bore/stroke inch	$3\frac{7}{16}$ x $3\frac{31}{32}$
Capacity cu in	73.66
Capacity cc	1207
Ignition	coil,
	1978-electronic
No of gears	4
Drive system	chain
Front suspension	teles
Rear suspension	s/a
Wheel type	wire
Wheel size inch	16/16
Brakes	drum, 1972-discs
Wheelbase inch	61.5
Seat height inch	33

Model	Super Glide
Code	FX, FXE
Years	1971–78, 1974–81
No. cylinders	V-twin
Valves	ohv
Bore/stroke inch	$3\frac{7}{16}$ x $3\frac{31}{32}$
Capacity cu in	73.66
Capacity cc	1207
Ignition	coil,
	1979-electronic
No of gears	4
Drive system	chain
Front suspension	teles
Rear suspension	s/a
Wheel type	wire
Wheel size inch	$1\frac{9}{16}$
Brakes	drum, 1973-discs
Wheelbase inch	62.7
Seat height inch	29

124

• *Harley-Davidson* •

Below Left: Generator Shovelhead.
Garry Stuart

*Below: AMF Super Glide with
alternator.* Garry Stuart

Low Rider

The 1977 model was the FXS Low Rider that was firmly based on the Super Glide but altered to give an image of toughness. This came from raked forks to move the front wheel out and increase the wheelbase, shorter suspension units and forks to reduce the ride height, a low seat so the rider was close to the ground even if the pillion remained on high, flat handlebars, cast-alloy wheels, and disc brakes front and rear. A special finish made the model stand out in the showroom and on the road with style.

The Low Rider was not the only new model for 1977 for the Sportster range also expanded with the XLT Touring and XLCR Café Racer. The first had a larger gas tank, deeper seat, lower bars, and raised gearing for more relaxed travel out on the road. The Café Racer was styled in that form with low bars, rear-sets, small fairing, and cast-alloy wheels with disc brakes. It also had a new frame. While neither model sold very well (both being listed for only two seasons), the frame was adopted by all Sportsters for 1978 as was electronic ignition.

The Electra-Glide had a needed capacity boost in 1978 to deal with its weight and the increasing emission controls. Both bore and stroke went up to give 82cu in and 1,340cc, although the enlarged engine was referred to as the 80 in company literature and machine markings. Both sizes went to electronic ignition and while the 74FLH ran on to 1980, it was the larger one that had the cast-alloy

wheels and disc brakes. Most continued with fairing, screen, big gas tank, panniers, and top box.

More new models arrived for 1979 including the FLHC Electra-Glide Classic with a special paint job and full equipment as standard. A further version with a sidecar was also listed and would continue on year after year, never in any great numbers but always appreciated by their owners. Some would go further and add a trailer to their full-dress Glide outfit and maybe a mini-bike bolted on that for beach transport.

In 1979 the Low Rider adopted the 82cu in engine and the Super Glide line changed to the electronic ignition. It was joined by the FXEF Fat Bob model that offered either engine size for that year, but only the larger from 1980. The model was mainly Low Rider but had the larger gas tank, hence "Fat," and cut-back, or bobbed, fenders, wire wheels, and high, pullback handlebars.

For the Sportster line the XLS replaced the XLT, being based on the standard XLH but in Low Rider format with extended forks and flat bars on risers, highway footrests, and its own paint style. As with the FXS, it sold well. For 1980 the XLS was named the Roadster and the XLH Sportster was also offered as the XLH Hugger with a lower seat and ride height.

The start of the new decade brought two new models in the Super Glide series, both using the 82cu in engine and four-speed gearbox. The first was the FXWG Wide Glide that was derived from the Fat Bob by fitting wider fork yokes to set the extended fork tubes further apart. The forks carried a 21in wheel and the machine had the big tank, highway footrests, well stepped seat, its own paint finish, and fixtures and fittings to suit the resulting chopper style.

The second new Super Glide was the FXB Sturgis, named after the famous rally. It was a Low Rider with one major difference in that it was fitted with belts for both primary and final drives. This was a radical move at the time but one that gave a smoother and quieter ride with few problems in the final drive, although the primary was less successful in use.

In time this led to all models using chain primary and belt final drives to get the best of both types.

For the Sturgis it was not a direct change as the belts were wider than the chains they replaced which affected the installation and the surrounding castings

Low Rider

Model .... **Tourer**
Code .... XLT
Years 1977–78
No. cylinders .... V-twin
Valves .... ohv
Bore/stroke inch .... 3³⁄₁₆ x 31³⁄₁₆
Capacity cu in 60.84
Capacity cc 997
Ignition .... coil,
.... 1978-electronic
No of gears 4
Drive system .... chain
Front suspension .... teles
Rear suspension .... s/a
Wheel type .... wire
Wheel size inch .... 1⁵⁄₈
Front brake .... disc
Rear brake .... drum
Wheelbase inch 58.5
Seat height inch 29

Model .... **Café Racer**
Code .... XLCR
Years 1977–78
No. cylinders .... V-twin
Valves .... ohv
Bore/stroke inch .... 3³⁄₁₆ x 31³⁄₁₆
Capacity cu in 60.84
Capacity cc 997
Ignition .... coil,
.... 1978-electronic
No of gears 4
Drive system .... chain
Front suspension .... teles
Rear suspension .... s/a
Wheel type .... cast-alloy
Wheel size inch .... 1⁵⁄₈
Front brake .... disc
Rear brake .... disc
Wheelbase inch 58.5
Seat height inch 31

Model .... **Roadster**
Code .... XLS
Years 1979–85
No. cylinders .... V-twin
Valves .... ohv
Bore/stroke inch .... 3³⁄₁₆ x 31³⁄₁₆
Capacity cu in 60.84
Capacity cc 997
Ignition .... electronic
No of gears 4
Drive system .... chain
Front suspension .... teles
Rear suspension .... s/a
Wheel type .... cast-alloy or
.... wire

Wheel size inch .... 1⁵⁄₁₆
Front brake .... disc
Rear brake .... disc
Wheelbase inch 58.5, 1982–60
Seat height inch 30

Model .... **Hugger**
Code .... XLH
Years 1980–85
No. cylinders .... V-twin
Valves .... ohv
Bore/stroke inch .... 3³⁄₁₆ x 31³⁄₁₆
Capacity cu in 60.84
Capacity cc 997
Ignition .... electronic
No of gears 4
Drive system .... chain
Front suspension .... teles
Rear suspension .... s/a
Wheel type .... cast-alloy
Wheel size inch 16/16
Front brake .... disc
Rear brake .... disc
Wheelbase inch 58.5, 1982–60

Model .... **Electra-Glide**
Code FLH80
Years 1978–84
No. cylinders .... V-twin
Valves .... ohv
Bore/stroke inch .... 3½ x 4¼
Capacity cu in 81.78
Capacity cc 1,340
Ignition .... electronic
No of gears 4
Drive system .... chain, 1983 belt
Front suspension .... teles
Rear suspension .... s/a
Wheel type .... cast alloy
Wheel size inch .... 1⁵⁄₁₆
Brakes .... discs
Wheelbase inch 61.5
Seat height inch 33

Model .... **Low Rider**
Code .... FXS
Years 1977–79
No. cylinders .... V-twin
Valves .... ohv
Bore/stroke inch .... 3⁷⁄₁₆ x 33½
Capacity cu in 73.66
Capacity cc 1207
Ignition .... coil,
.... 1979 electronic
No of gears 4
Drive system .... chain
Front suspension .... teles

Rear suspension .... s/a
Wheel type .... cast alloy
Wheel size inch .... 1⁵⁄₁₆
Brakes .... discs
Wheelbase inch 63.5
Seat height inch 27

Model .... **Fat Bob**
Code .... FXEF
Years 1979
No. cylinders .... V-twin
Valves .... ohv
Bore/stroke inch .... 3⁷⁄₁₆ x 33½
Capacity cu in 73.66
Capacity cc 1,207
Ignition .... electronic
No of gears 4
Drive system .... chain
Front suspension .... teles
Rear suspension .... s/a
Wheel type .... cast alloy or
.... wire
Wheel size inch 19/16
Brakes .... discs
Wheelbase inch 63.5
Seat height inch 27

Model .... **Low Rider**
Code FXS–80
Years 1979–82
No. cylinders .... V-twin
Valves .... ohv
Bore/stroke inch .... 3½ x 4¼
Capacity cu in 81.78
Capacity cc 1340
Ignition .... electronic
No of gears 4
Drive system .... chain
Front suspension .... teles
Rear suspension .... s/a
Wheel type .... cast alloy
Wheel size inch .... 1⁵⁄₁₆
Brakes .... discs
Wheelbase inch 63.5
Seat height inch 27

Model .... **Fat Bob**
Code .... FXEF
Years 1979–82
No. cylinders .... V-twin
Valves .... ohv
Bore/stroke inch .... 3½ x 4¼
Capacity cu in 81.78
Capacity cc 1340
Ignition .... electronic
No of gears 4
Drive system .... chain

Front suspension ....teles
Rear suspension................s/a
Wheel type ....cast alloy
Wheel size inch ....1⁹⁄₁₆
Brakes ....discs
Wheelbase inch.................63.5
Seat height inch................27

Model	Sturgis
Code	FXB
Years	1980–82
No. cylinders	V-twin
Valves	ohv
Bore/stroke inch	3½ x 4¼
Capacity cu in	81.78
Capacity cc	1340
Ignition	electronic
No of gears	4
Drive system	belts
Front suspension	teles
Rear suspension	s/a
Wheel type	cast alloy
Wheel size inch	1⁹⁄₁₆
Brakes	discs
Wheelbase inch	63.5
Seat height inch	27

Model	Wide Glide
Code	FXWG
Years	1980–86
No. cylinders	V-twin
Valves	ohv
Bore/stroke inch	3½ x 4¼
Capacity cu in	81.78
Capacity cc	1340
Ignition	electronic
No of gears	4
Drive system	chain,
	1984 chain/belt
Front suspension	teles
Rear suspension	s/a
Wheel type	cast alloy/wire,
	1985 wire
Wheel size inch	2¹⁵⁄₁₆
Brakes	discs
Wheelbase inch	65
Seat height inch	28

Above Right: XLS Roadster of 1982.
via Roy Bacon

Right: FXS Low Rider of 1982..
via Roy Bacon

Tour Glide

New for 1980 was the FLT Tour Glide that was much more than just another variant of the Electra-Glide. The engine was the faithful 82cu in Shovelhead but built as a single unit with the gearbox and carrying the pivoted rear fork as part of the assembly. This was then fitted to the frame with isolating mountings so that the engine vibration was concealed from the rider who no longer noticed it. The frame was new to suit the mounts and extended forward from the headstock to better support the fairing while the transmission had five speeds and an enclosed final-drive chain.

The Tour Glide was built as a whole for its job, rather than developed and evolved as in the past from an existing model. This removed many of the constraints and compromises in the design and the result was a much better machine for its task in every way. With it came the FLTC Tour Glide Classic with a special finish, while as the 74cu in engine was phased out, the FXE Super Glide changed to the 82cu in motor for 1981.

Tour Glide

Model	Tour Glide
Code	FLT80
Years	1980–83
No. cylinders	V-twin
Valves	ohv
Bore/stroke inch	3½ x 4¼
Capacity cu in	81.78
Capacity cc	1340
Ignition	electronic
No of gears	5
Drive system	chain
Front suspension	teles
Rear suspension	s/a
Wheel type	cast alloy
Wheel size inch	1‰
Brakes	discs
Wheelbase inch	60.6
Seat height inch	32

Model	Super Glide
Code	FXE
Years	1981–84
No. cylinders	V-twin
Valves	ohv
Bore/stroke inch	3½ x 4¼
Capacity cu in	81.78
Capacity cc	1340
Ignition	electronic
No of gears	4
Drive system	chain, 1984
	chain/belt
Front suspension	teles
Rear suspension	s/a
Wheel type	wire
Wheel size inch	1‰
Brakes	discs
Wheelbase inch	62.8
Seat height inch	26.6

Left: FXE Super Glide of c. 1983.
via Roy Bacon

*Overleaf: FXR Super Glide II of
c. 1983.* via Roy Bacon

Super Glide II

In 1982 a new series, code FXR, was launched and sold at first as the Super Glide II. It was built around the 82cu in engine unit of the Tour Glide with the isolating mounts and kept the five-speed gearbox. This went into a new frame with the rear suspension units well back and close to vertical, while the front forks were similar to those of the Super Glide and Sportster.

Two versions were offered: the FXR with wire wheels and the FXRS with cast ones, two-tone paint finish, and highway footrests. Both sold well and were much improved machines, as were the Sportster models that benefited from a new frame that same year.

A third model joined the new line for 1983 as the FXRT Sport Glide, taking this name despite being designed for touring as that name was already in use. To suit its purpose it kept the FXR 82cu in engine and five-speed gearbox, the latter dictating chain final drive as the belt width could not be accommodated at that time. However, the chain was enclosed as befitted a tourer and this aspect was further enhanced by air suspension, a fairing, and panniers. In all it worked well although the style did not shout Harley enough

• Harley-Davidson •

for marque fans but did worry some sales prospects who shied away from some aspects of the image. One of these was quality control, for that had deteriorated badly in the AMF period, but had been a top priority since 1981 and the buy-back.

There were two new Sportsters for 1983 with one, the XLX-61, that brought the famous capacity figure back. It was created as a price leader, having the base specification and minimum trim to get the retail down to pull buyers

into the showrooms where they could be encouraged to add extras to please both them and the dealer.

The second Sportster was the XR-1000 Café Racer that combined the basic engine with new barrels and light-alloy heads from the racing XR-750. With these came twin carburetors on the right and two waist-level exhaust systems on the left in the image of the racer. For the chassis the stock XLX frame and forks were used along with cast-alloy wheels and disc brakes front and rear. The

result was a fast motorcycle well able to win class events in competition — but also an expensive one that looked too similar to the base model to attract buyers. Furthermore, for those with Sportster experience, the extra money could be spent to better purpose with a greater return in performance.

Elsewhere for 1983 the Low Rider became the FXSB with belt primary and final drives plus extended forks, so the Sturgis was dropped. For the serious tourer the

• Harley-Davidson •

FLHT Electra Glide appeared in standard and classic form using the Tour Glide frame and engine isolating mounts, the five-speed gearbox, and chain final drive, as the belt was still not available with that number of gears. For the FLH Electra Glide, still with four speeds, there was belt final drive.

Super Glide II

Model	**Café Racer**
Code	XR1000
Years	1983–84
No. cylinders	V-twin
Valves	ohv
Bore/stroke inch	$3\frac{5}{16}$ x $3\frac{13}{16}$
Capacity cu in	60.84
Capacity cc	997
Ignition	electronic
No of gears	4
Drive system	chain
Front suspension	teles
Rear suspension	s/a
Wheel type	cast-alloy
Wheel size inch	$1\frac{9}{16}$
Front brake	disc
Rear brake	disc
Wheelbase inch	60
Seat height inch	28.7

Model	**Sportster**
Code	XLX-61
Years	1983–85
No. cylinders	V-twin
Valves	ohv
Bore/stroke inch	$3\frac{5}{16}$ x $3\frac{13}{16}$
Capacity cu in	60.84
Capacity cc	997
Ignition	electronic
No of gears	4
Drive system	chain
Front suspension	teles
Rear suspension	s/a
Wheel type	cast-alloy
Wheel size inch	$1\frac{9}{16}$
Front brake	disc
Rear brake	disc
Wheelbase inch	60
Seat height inch	28.5

Model	**Low Rider**
Code	FXSB
Years	1983–85
No. cylinders	V-twin
Valves	ohv
Bore/stroke inch	$3\frac{1}{2}$ x $4\frac{1}{4}$
Capacity cu in	81.78
Capacity cc	1,340
Ignition	electronic
No of gears	4
Drive system	belts, 1985
	chain/belt
Front suspension	teles
Rear suspension	s/a
Wheel type	cast alloy
Wheel size inch	$1\frac{9}{16}$
Brakes	discs
Wheelbase inch	63.5
Seat height inch	27

Model	**Super Glide II**
Code	FXR, FXRS
Years	1982–83
No. cylinders	V-twin
Valves	ohv
Bore/stroke inch	$3\frac{1}{2}$ x $4\frac{1}{4}$
Capacity cu in	81.78
Capacity cc	1340
Ignition	electronic
No of gears	5
Drive system	chain
Front suspension	teles
Rear suspension	s/a
Wheel type	FXR-wire,
	FXRS-cast alloy
Wheel size inch	$1\frac{9}{16}$
Brakes	discs
Wheelbase inch	64.7
Seat height inch	28.9

Model	**Sport Glide**
Code	FXRT
Year	1983
No. cylinders	V-twin
Valves	ohv
Bore/stroke inch	$3\frac{1}{2}$ x $4\frac{1}{4}$
Capacity cu in	81.78
Capacity cc	1340
Ignition	electronic
No of gears	5
Drive system	chain
Front suspension	teles
Rear suspension	s/a
Wheel type	cast alloy
Wheel size inch	$1\frac{9}{16}$
Brakes	discs
Wheelbase inch	64.7
Seat height inch	27.5

Left: XR1000. Garry Stuart

Evolution Engine

For 1984 Harley-Davidson introduced a new big twin — the V2 Evolution engine. As was usual for the firm it was not totally new — the lineage right back to 1936 and the Knucklehead was clear to see. Thus, it was still separate from the gearbox, had one camshaft, and kept the four pushrod tubes running up in splayed array to the rocker boxes.

The cylinders became light-alloy with iron liners, the alloy heads and rocker boxes were new, and the electronic ignition trigger remained within the cone, cast on the timing side. Internally, the valve included angle was reduced to give a more compact combustion chamber, better gas flow, and cleaner combustion. All added up to an engine that was as good as any, simply disguised to keep its traditional style that had close to half a century of service behind it.

Not all big twins fitted the new engine that year, the fortunate ones being the Electra and Tour Glide Classics, Sport Glide and Low Glide. During 1984 the older engine was phased out but had a last fling in two Electra Glide models, the FLHX de luxe and FLHS plain without the trimmings.

Two new models appeared with the V2 engine, one a limited edition Disc Glide coded FXRDG. This was based on the Low Glide model in that series but with a solid alloy disc rear wheel and a special paint job. The other was a further development into the chopper scene and listed as the Softail.

Right: 1984 Evo engine. via Roy Bacon

Evolution Engine

Model	Disc Glide
Code	FXRDG
Year	1984
No. cylinders	V-twin
Valves	ohv
Bore/stroke inch	3½ x 4¼
Capacity cu in	81.78
Capacity cc	1,340
Ignition	electronic
No of gears	5
Drive system	chain
Front suspension	teles
Rear suspension	s/a
Wheel type	wire/disc
Wheel size inch	1⁹⁄₁₆
Brakes	discs
Wheelbase inch	63.1
Seat height inch	26.8

Model	Low Glide
Code	FXRS
Years	1984–85
No. cylinders	V-twin
Valves	ohv
Bore/stroke inch	3½ x 4¼
Capacity cu in	81.78
Capacity cc	1,340
Ignition	electronic
No of gears	5
Drive system	chain, 1985
	chain/belt
Front suspension	teles
Rear suspension	s/a
Wheel type	cast alloy
Wheel size inch	1⁹⁄₁₆
Brakes	discs
Wheelbase inch	63.1
Seat height inch	26.8

Model	Sport Glide
Code	FXRT
Years	1984–92
No. cylinders	V-twin
Valves	ohv
Bore/stroke inch	3½ x 4¼
Capacity cu in	81.78
Capacity cc	1340
Ignition	electronic
No of gears	5
Drive system	chain, 1985
	chain/belt
Front suspension	teles
Rear suspension	s/a
Wheel type	cast alloy
Wheel size inch	1⁹⁄₁₆
Brakes	discs
Wheelbase inch	64.7
Seat height inch	27.7

Softail

The FXST Softail took its basis
from the Wide Glide with the
spaced out and extended forks,
21-inch wire front wheel and disc
brake, very stepped seating,
highway footrests and pull-back
handlebars. The engine was the
V2 driving a four-speed gearbox
but it was in the rear suspension
that the model was different. It
had a style line that suggested a
rigid frame. As with the Scat two-
stroke of the 1960s, this was done
by locating the suspension units
under the gearbox and linking
them to a pivoted structure that
held the wheel and was designed
to appear rigid. For all that, the
wheel had a disc brake.

During 1984 a further
important change was the
adoption of a diaphragm-spring
clutch. At one stroke this increased
the pressure and torque capacity of
the plates, greatly reduced the
effort needed to lift the clutch
and allowed it to run in the
primary chain oil, thus allowing
a move away from the belt which
had proved troublesome in that
location.

The new clutch went with
the V2 engine from mid-1984 and
was soon fitted to all big twins. It
also reached the Sportster later
that year for the 1985 line along

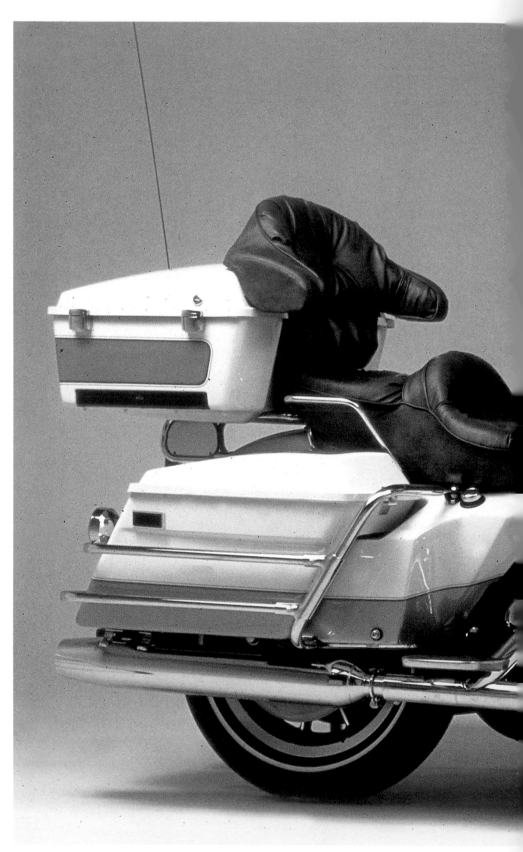

Softail

Softail

Model	Fat Bob
Code	FXEF
Years	1985
No. cylinders	V-twin
Valves	ohv
Bore/stroke inch	3½ x 4¼
Capacity cu in	81.78
Capacity cc	1,340
Ignition	electronic
No of gears	4
Drive system	chain/belt
Front suspension	teles
Rear suspension	s/a
Wheel type	cast alloy
Wheel size inch	19/16
Brakes	discs
Wheelbase inch	63.5
Seat height inch	27

Model	Low Glide Custom
Code	FXRC
Years	1985
No. cylinders	V-twin
Valves	ohv
Bore/stroke inch	3½ x 4¼
Capacity cu in	81.78
Capacity cc	1,340
Ignition	electronic
No of gears	5
Drive system	chain/belt
Front suspension	teles
Rear suspension	s/a
Wheel type	wire
Wheel size inch	19/16
Brakes	discs
Wheelbase inch	63.1
Seat height inch	26.8

Model	Low Rider
Code	FXRS
Years	1986–92
No. cylinders	V-twin
Valves	ohv
Bore/stroke inch	3½ x 4¼
Capacity cu in	81.78
Capacity cc	1,340
Ignition	electronic
No of gears	5
Drive system	chain/belt
Front suspension	teles
Rear suspension	s/a
Wheel type	cast alloy
Wheel size inch	19/16
Brakes	discs
Wheelbase inch	63.1
Seat height inch	26.5

Model	Low Rider Sport
Code	FXRS-SP
Years	1986-93
No. cylinders	V-twin
Valves	ohv
Bore/stroke inch	3½ x 4¼
Capacity cu in	81.78
Capacity cc	1,340
Ignition	electronic
No of gears	5
Drive system	chain/belt
Front suspension	teles
Rear suspension	s/a
Wheel type	cast alloy
Wheel size inch	19/16
Brakes	discs
Wheelbase inch	64.7
Seat height inch	27.5

Model	Super Glide
Code	FXR
Years	1986–94
No. cylinders	V-twin
Valves	ohv
Bore/stroke inch	3½ x 4¼
Capacity cu in	81.78
Capacity cc	1,340
Ignition	electronic
No of gears	5
Drive system	chain/belt
Front suspension	teles
Rear suspension	s/a
Wheel type	cast alloy, 1993-wire
Wheel size inch	19/16
Brakes	discs
Wheelbase inch	63.1
Seat height inch	26.5

Model	Softail
Code	FXST
Years	1984–90
No. cylinders	V-twin
Valves	ohv
Bore/stroke inch	3½ x 4¼
Capacity cu in	81.78
Capacity cc	1,340
Ignition	electronic
No of gears	4, 1985-5
Drive system	chain, 1985-chain/belt
Front suspension	teles
Rear suspension	s/a
Wheel type	wire
Wheel size inch	21/16
Brakes	discs
Wheelbase inch	66.3
Seat height inch	25.2

Model	Softail Custom
Code	FXST
Years	1986–98
No. cylinders	V-twin
Valves	ohv
Bore/stroke inch	3½ x 4¼
Capacity cu in	81.78
Capacity cc	1,340
Ignition	electronic
No of gears	5
Drive system	chain/belt
Front suspension	teles
Rear suspension	s/a
Wheel type	wire/disc
Wheel size inch	21/16
Brakes	discs
Wheelbase inch	66.3
Seat height inch	25.2

Models	1984–98, FLHTC, Electra Glide Classic 1985-87, FLHT, Electra Glide
No. cylinders	V-twin
Valves	ohv
Bore/stroke inch	3½ x 4¼
Capacity cu in	81.78
Capacity cc	1,340
Ignition	electronic
No of gears	5
Drive system	chain, 1985-chain/belt
Front suspension	teles
Rear suspension	s/a
Wheel type	cast alloy
Wheel size inch	19/16
Brakes	discs
Wheelbase	62.9
Seat height inch	28, Sport 27

Models	1984–91, FLTC, Tour Glide Classic
No. cylinders	V-twin
Valves	ohv
Bore/stroke inch	3½ x 4¼
Capacity cu in	81.78
Capacity cc	1,340
Ignition	electronic
No of gears	5
Drive system	chain, 1985-chain/belt
Front suspension	teles
Rear suspension	s/a
Wheel type	cast alloy
Wheel size inch	19/16
Brakes	discs
Wheelbase	62.9
Seat height inch	29.6

Below: 1986 FXSTC Softail custom.
Roy Bacon

with an alternator in place of the generator, a long overdue change.

Belt final drive went onto the Electra and Tour Glide models for 1985 as the new engine enabled this to be done while keeping the five-speed gearbox. In the same way the Super Glide models, Low Rider, Wide and Fat Bob went the same way and a Low Glide Custom joined the FXR line as a limited, one-year model with a 19-inch wire front wheel and special finish.

The Fat Bob and Low Rider were dropped from the 1986 line while the Low Glide became the Low Rider but kept the FXRS code. Additional versions were the FXRS-SP Low Rider Sport and the FXRD Sport Glide Tourer that was the FXRT plus top box and stereo sound system, both options for the basic Sport Glide model. The base FXR Super Glide was once again listed in its own right while a Softail Custom, coded FXSTC, joined the stock version using the solid rear wheel from the Disc Glide, the five-speed gearbox, belt final drive and a special finish with different paint and chrome.

Right: Heritage Softail. Simon Clay

Below: 1992 FXSTC Softail custom. via Roy Bacon

Evo Sportster

In 1986 Harley-Davidson introduced the Evolution Sportster
engine unit to bring that range up-
to-date in the same way as the V2
had done for the big twins. In fact,
the new unit had much more
changed although it kept the
existing style as far as possible
even if the mounting differed so
the new engine would not fit the
old frame.

Two engine sizes were
offered but with a common stroke
so that the bulk of the detail parts
went into both. The essence of the
past remained with each cylinder
flanked on the right by a pair of
parallel pushrod tubes running
up to the rocker box. However,
both cylinders and heads were in
aluminum, the latter very similar to
those of the V2 Evo engine, and
the included angle between
them stayed at the traditional
45-degrees, a Harley birthright.
Internally, the compact combustion chamber of the V2 was
repeated and the detail parts
modernized as required.

The engine castings were all
new, even if they looked much as
before, so the ignition trigger
remained in the cone-shaped boss
on the timing chest. The alternator
went in the primary drive case but
an oil filter was mounted in the old
generator position just ahead of
the front cylinder to keep the
familiar line. The gearbox continued with just four speeds but was
driven by the diaphragm spring
clutch. Final drive was by chain on
the right as usual.

The two models were the
XLH883 and, launched a few
weeks later, the XLH1100. They
shared a common frame and suspension, cast-alloy wheels and disc
brakes. The smaller was the loss
leader, priced right down to pull
people into the Harley showroom,

Evo Sportster

Below and Right: Evo Sportster.
Simon Clay

144

Evo Sportster

so the specification was basic. The larger had more equipment and a greater range of finishes and, just as always, all the extra items on the 1100 were options for the 883. Some appeared anyway on a De Luxe edition.

Once again the firm combined parts to create a new model in 1987, the FXLR Low Rider Custom. For this Harley took the FXR Super Glide with its fine chassis, V2 engine, five-speed gearbox and belt final drive. To this was added a 21-inch wire front wheel with disc brake and the solid rear wheel first seen on the Disc Glide, topped off with a small headlight as used elsewhere; suitable trim was added and the company had arrived at an older style with the latest engineering parts. It sold.

Another way back to the past and the retro market that year was the FLST Heritage Softail that was based on the Glide series, used the hidden rear suspension to give the rigid look, but had the V2 engine, belt drive and disc brakes front and rear. The style came from retaining the wire wheels with fat tires, big tank with its top panel, well-valanced front fender and a paint form and color that was reminiscent of the 1950s. To this was added a stepped seat with backrest and leather saddlebags

decorated with studs and tassels, a screen and a chrome finish for the fork tops, headlight and extra spotlights.

A classic version of the Heritage Softail was added for 1988 as the FLSTC, the year when the XLH883 was offered in a further form as the Hugger, with a lowered ride height and seat to attract the lady buyers. That year also saw the larger Sportster bored out further to become the XLH-1200 and thus the same size as the

old 74cu in models. An Electra Glide Sport with a screen in place of the usual fairing, less weight and a lower price was a further 1988 addition.

Below: Evo Sportster brake detail.
Simon Clay

Evo Sportster

Model ....Low Rider
....Custom
Code ....FXLR
Years 1987–94
No. cylinders....................V-twin
Valves..............................ohv
Bore/stroke inch.............3½ x 4¼
Capacity cu in 81.78
Capacity cc 1,340
Ignition............................electronic
No of gears 5
Drive system....................chain/belt
Front suspension ....teles
Rear suspension................s/a
Wheel type ....wire/disc
Wheel size inch 19/16
Brakes ....discs
Wheelbase inch.................63.2
Seat height inch................26.5

Model ....Heritage Softail
Code ....FLST
Years 1987–90
No. cylinders....................V twin
Valves..............................ohv
Bore/stroke inch.............3½ x 4¼
Capacity cu in 81.78
Capacity cc 1340
Ignition............................electronic
No of gears 5
Drive system....................chain/belt
Front suspension ....teles
Rear suspension................s/a
Wheel type ....wire
Wheel size inch ....1⁹⁄₁₆
Brakes ....discs
Wheelbase inch.................64.2
Seat height inch................26.5

Model ....Heritage Softail
....Classic
Code ....FLSTC
Years 1988–99
No. cylinders....................V-twin
Valves..............................ohv
Bore/stroke inch.............3½ x 4¼
Capacity cu in 81.78
Capacity cc 1,340
Ignition............................electronic
No of gears 5
Drive system....................chain/belt
Front suspension ....teles
Rear suspension................s/a

Wheel type ....wire
Wheel size inch ....1⁹⁄₁₆
Brakes ....discs
Wheelbase inch.................62.5
Seat height inch................26.5

Model ....Sportster
Code XLH883
Years 1986–99
No. cylinders....................V-twin
Valves..............................ohv
Bore/stroke inch.............3 x 3⁹⁄₁₆
Capacity cu in 53.90
Capacity cc 883
Ignition............................electronic
No of gears 4, 1991–95
Drive system....................chain
Front suspension ....teles
Rear suspension................s/a
Wheel type ....cast alloy,
1993-wire, 1995-cast alloy, 1996-wire
Wheel size inch ....1⁹⁄₁₆
Brakes ....discs
Wheelbase inch.................60.2
Seat height inch................28.5

Model ....De Luxe
Code XLH883
Years 1986–95
No. cylinders....................V-twin
Valves..............................ohv
Bore/stroke inch.............3 x 3⁹⁄₁₆
Capacity cu in 53.90
Capacity cc 883
Ignition............................electronic
No of gears 4, 1991-5
Drive system....................chain, 1991-
....chain/belt
Front suspension ....teles
Rear suspension................s/a
Wheel type ....wire
Wheel size inch ....1⁹⁄₁₆
Brakes ....discs
Wheelbase inch.................60.2
Seat height inch................28.5

Model ....Hugger
Code XLH883
Years 1988–99
No. cylinders....................V-twin
Valves..............................ohv
Bore/stroke inch.............3 x 3⁹⁄₁₆
Capacity cu in 53.90

Capacity cc 883
Ignition............................electronic
No of gears 4, 1991-5
Drive system....................chain, 1991-
....chain/belt
Front suspension ....teles
Rear suspension................s/a
Wheel type ....cast alloy,
1993-wire, 1995-cast alloy
Wheel size inch ....1⁹⁄₁₆
Brakes ....discs
Wheelbase inch.................59
Seat height inch................26

Model ....Sportster
Code XLH1100
Years 1986–87
No. cylinders....................V-twin
Valves..............................ohv
Bore/stroke inch.............3.35 x 3⁹⁄₁₆
Capacity cu in 67.21
Capacity cc 1,101
Ignition............................electronic
No of gears 4
Drive system....................chain
Front suspension ....teles
Rear suspension................s/a
Wheel type ....cast alloy
Wheel size inch ....1⁹⁄₁₆
Brakes ....discs
Wheelbase inch.................60.2
Seat height inch................28.5

Model ....Sportster
Code XLH1200
Years 1988–99
No. cylinders....................V-twin
Valves..............................ohv
Bore/stroke inch.............3½ x 3⁹⁄₁₆
Capacity cu in 73.36
Capacity cc 1,202
Ignition............................electronic
No of gears 4, 1991-5
Drive system....................chain, 1991-
....chain/belt
Front suspension ....teles
Rear suspension................s/a
Wheel type ....cast alloy,
1993-wire, 1995-cast alloy, 1998-wire
Wheel size inch ....1⁹⁄₁₆
Brakes ....discs
Wheelbase inch.................60.2
Seat height inch................29

Springer

The new model for 1988 was another look back into the past and appeared as the FXSTS Springer Softail. This went even further back for it began with the Softail, itself a facsimile of the rigid past, and added leading-link spring front forks in the style of the very early models and as used up to the late-1940s. While they kept the style of the past, they were brought up-to-date using modern technology to give adequate wheel travel, total stress and load capability, and a much improve brake. This was a disc with the caliper mounted on a link that ran from the axle up to a second link that connected back to the main fork strut. In this way the front brake reaction loads did not cause the suspension to rise when braking.

Ultra Classic versions of the Electra and Tour Glide models appeared for 1989 with the fullest equipment that could be installed for a full-dress tourer. The other new model that year was the FXRS-CN Low Rider Convertible. This was based on the FXR, to which a screen and saddlebags were attached by quick-release fasteners. Thus, it could be a tourer when required but easily altered for a sporting ride when the mood took.

Just one model was added for 1990, the FLSTF Fat Boy that was yet another version of the Super Glide. It had its own highly distinctive, rather conservative style with forks fitted with top shrouds as on the Glides, the Softail rear suspension, disc wheels front and rear, well-stepped seat and widely-spaced dual exhausts. It had a solid look about it with a paint finish to match and proved a popular model destined for a long life.

Springer

Model	Springer Softail
Code	FXSTS
Years	1988–99
No. cylinders	V-twin
Valves	ohv
Bore/stroke inch	3½ x 4¼
Capacity cu in	81.78
Capacity cc	1,340
Ignition	electronic
No of gears	5
Drive system	chain/belt
Front suspension	leading link
Rear suspension	s/a
Wheel type	wire
Wheel size inch	2¹⁵⁄₁₆
Brakes	discs
Wheelbase inch	64.5
Seat height inch	26.1

Model	Fat Boy
Code	FLSTF
Years	1990–99
No. cylinders	V-twin
Valves	ohv
Bore/stroke inch	3½ x 4¼
Capacity cu in	81.78
Capacity cc	1,340
Ignition	electronic
No of gears	5
Drive system	chain/belt
Front suspension	teles
Rear suspension	s/a
Wheel type	disc
Wheel size inch	1⁹⁄₁₆
Brakes	discs
Wheelbase inch	62.5
Seat height inch	26.5

Models	1988–93, FLHS, Electra Glide Sport; 1989–94, FLHTC ,Ultra Classic Electra Glide
No. cylinders	V-twin
Valves	ohv
Bore/stroke inch	3½ x 4¼
Capacity cu in	81.78
Capacity cc	1,340
Ignition	electronic
No of gears	5
Drive system	chain, 1985- chain/belt
Front suspension	teles
Rear suspension	s/a
Wheel type	cast alloy
Wheel size inch	1⁹⁄₁₆
Brakes	discs
Wheelbase	62.9
Seat height inch	28, Sport 27

Model	1989–93, FLTC, Ultra Classic Tour Glide
No. cylinders	V-twin
Valves	ohv
Bore/stroke inch	3½ x 4¼
Capacity cu in	81.78
Capacity cc	1,340
Ignition	electronic
No of gears	5
Drive system	chain, 1985- chain/belt
Front suspension	teles
Rear suspension	s/a
Wheel type	cast alloy
Wheel size inch	1⁹⁄₁₆
Brakes	discs
Wheelbase	62.9
Seat height inch	29.6

Above Right: Another view of the 1988 FXSTS Springer. via Roy Bacon

Below Right and Below: 1990 and 1992 Electra Glide Ultra Classic.
Both: Roy Bacon

Below: 1992 FLSTS Fat Boy. via Roy
Bacon

Bottom: 1990s FLHT. Roy Bacon

This spread: All round views of a superb Ultra Classic Electra Glide. All: Simon Clay

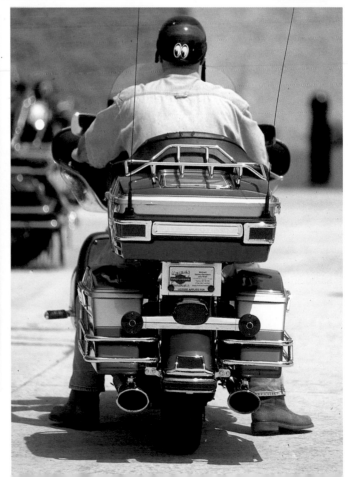

Dyna Glide

The Sturgis name returned to the line in 1991 for a model that incorporated a major step forward on the chassis side. Designed as a chopper and based on the FXR concepts, the new model had an improved isolating frame with a two-point mounting system at front and rear of the engine and gearbox assembly. The frame was based on a massive, square-section backbone with duplex downtubes that ran under the engine and then tucked in close to run up to the rear unit mountings. The result was a stiffer and better frame and a new name for any model using it, the Dyna Glide to emphasis how the engine vibration was damped down.

For the model, listed as the FXDB Dyna Glide Sturgis, there was the usual V2 engine, five-speed gearbox and belt final drive along with cast-alloy wheels and disc brakes. To suit the style the wheelbase was longer and the engine tilted back a few degrees to lower the headstock which aided stability at speed and gave the line a form sometimes known as muscle bike.

It was in 1991 that the Sportster line had a much needed improvement when the old four-speed gearbox was replaced by one with five speeds plus a new clutch. At the same time the De Luxe 883 and the 1200 went over to belt final drive, the more basic models keeping to chain but with the option of a kit from the factory to convert to belt.

• Harley-Davidson •

156

*Right: 1992 FXDC Dyna Glide
Custom.* via Roy Bacon

*Far Right: 1991 XLH883 Sportster —
the Hugger.* via Roy Bacon

In 1992 the Sturgis became the FXDB Dyna Glide Daytona, the name changed to highlight the half-century of racing at that venue. In the process it gained a second front disc brake, pullback handlebars and its own special finish as befitted a limited edition of just 1,700 machines. A further new model in the series for 1992 was the FXDC Dyna Glide Custom that was much as the Daytona but in silver and black. It was not a limited edition, but still sold out in the one year.

More versions of the new theme came for 1993 with the FXDL Dyna Low Rider and FXDWG Dyna Wide Glide, both carrying well known names of the past and recreating their style. The Low Rider was thus a custom machine with stepped seat, raked forks, cast-alloy wheels, the front 19-inch, and pullback handlebars. The Wide Glide was more extreme with ape hanger bars, higher seat level, wide-spaced front forks, bobbed rear fender and wire wheels, the front a 21-inch.

The third new model for 1993 was the FLSTN Heritage Softail Nostalgia. Despite the FL code it was based on the FXST Super Glide chassis with a touch of the Fat Boy style. However, it sported wire wheels, both of 16-inch, used the fatter FL style of front fork and had a well-stepped seat and the full retro style. For 1994 it became the Heritage Softail Special but kept the same code.

New for 1994 was the FXDS-CN Dyna Low Rider Convertible that replaced the existing model by one using the new frame but doing the same job. Also new was the FLHR Electra Glide Road King that was a tourer with the convertible attribute of being easy to amend to custom cruising by removing the screen and pillion pad. It had the traditional line of the early Electra Glide, so lost some of the weighty look of the full dresser, with this emphasized by the large, tank-mounted speedometer, wide bars and a big, chrome-plated headlamp nacelle. The fuel tank was similar to that of the Fat Bob but in one piece with a fuel gauge set in the left filler cap which was a dummy. However, the technology was there for the old style speedometer was electronic so had no need for a mechanical drive cable.

The flow of new models, variations on established themes, continued apace for 1995 with two of them taking their respective series back to basics. One was the FXD Dyna Super Glide and the other the FLHT Electra Glide Standard and both went back to their roots, not in the retro sense, but in the removal of all the extras

Dyna Glide

Dyna Glide

Model	Heritage Softail Nostalgia
Code	FLSTN
Years	1993
No. cylinders	V-twin
Valves	ohv
Bore/stroke inch	3½ x 4¼
Capacity cu in	81.78
Capacity cc	1,340
Ignition	electronic
No of gears	5
Drive system	chain/belt
Front suspension	teles
Rear suspension	s/a
Wheel type	wire
Wheel size inch	$1^{6}/_{16}$
Brakes	discs
Wheelbase inch	62.5
Seat height inch	26.5

Model	Heritage Softail Special
Code	FLSTN
Years	1994–96
No. cylinders	V-twin
Valves	ohv
Bore/stroke inch	3½ x 4¼
Capacity cu in	81.78
Capacity cc	1,340
Ignition	electronic
No of gears	5
Drive system	chain/belt
Front suspension	teles
Rear suspension	s/a
Wheel type	wire
Wheel size inch	$1^{6}/_{16}$
Brakes	discs
Wheelbase inch	62.5
Seat height inch	26.5

Model	Dyna Glide Sturgis & Daytona
Code	FXDB
Years	1991–92
No. cylinders	V-twin
Valves	ohv
Bore/stroke inch	3½ x 4¼
Capacity cu in	81.78
Capacity cc	1,340
Ignition	electronic
No of gears	5
Drive system	chain/belt
Front suspension	teles
Rear suspension	s/a
Wheel type	cast alloy
Wheel size inch	$1^{6}/_{16}$
Brakes	discs
Wheelbase	65.5
Seat height inch	26.6

Model	Dyna Glide Custom
Code	FXDC
Years	1992
No. cylinders	V-twin
Valves	ohv
Bore/stroke inch	3½ x 4¼
Capacity cu in	81.78
Capacity cc	1,340
Ignition	electronic
No of gears	5
Drive system	chain/belt
Front suspension	teles
Rear suspension	s/a
Wheel type	cast alloy
Wheel size inch	$1^{6}/_{16}$
Brakes	discs
Wheelbase	65.5
Seat height inch	26.6

Model	Dyna Wide Glide
Code	FXDWG
Years	1993-98
No. cylinders	V-twin
Valves	ohv
Bore/stroke inch	3½ x 4¼
Capacity cu in	81.78
Capacity cc	1,340
Ignition	electronic
No of gears	5
Drive system	chain/belt
Front suspension	teles
Rear suspension	s/a
Wheel type	wire
Wheel size inch	$2^{1}/_{16}$
Brakes	discs
Wheelbase	66.1
Seat height inch	29.7

Model	Dyna Low Rider
Code	FXDL
Years	1993–98
No. cylinders	V-twin
Valves	ohv
Bore/stroke inch	3½ x 4¼
Capacity cu in	81.78
Capacity cc	1,340
Ignition	electronic
No of gears	5
Drive system	chain/belt
Front suspension	teles
Rear suspension	s/a
Wheel type	cast alloy
Wheel size inch	$1^{6}/_{16}$
Brakes	discs
Wheelbase	65.4
Seat height inch	27, Convertible-30.6

Model	Dyna Super Glide
Code	FXD
Years	1995–98
No. cylinders	V-twin
Valves	ohv
Bore/stroke inch	3½ x 4¼
Capacity cu in	81.78
Capacity cc	1,340
Ignition	electronic
No of gears	5
Drive system	chain/belt
Front suspension	teles
Rear suspension	s/a
Wheel type	cast alloy
Wheel size inch	$1^{6}/_{16}$
Brakes	discs
Wheelbase	62.5
Seat height inch	27

that had been added. Thus, the Super Glide was just :no Low Rider, Wide Glide or Softail, simply the base of the series but with the Dyna frame.

It was the same with the Electra Glide that kept the essentials of screen plus panniers for touring, but lost the mass of extras of the full dresser without losing the technology. It was basic, but as well fitted out as when it first rolled out in 1965.

At the other end of the Glide scale came three real full dressers, the ones with it all fitted as standard. These were the FLHTCU Ultra Classic Electra Glide and the FLTCU Ultra Classic Tour Glide, the main difference the fork-mounted fairing of the Electra and the frame-mounted one on the Tour. Otherwise it was all there even though more trim and trinkets could be found in the option list.

Above Left: 1994 FLSTF Fat Boy.
via Roy Bacon

Left: 1994 Springer Softail FXSTS.
via Roy Bacon

Dyna Glide

This spread and Overleaf: Road King.
All: Simon Clay

164

This spread: Road King details. All: Simon Clay

• *Harley-Davidson* •

Below: Displaying its origins with pride,
an immaculate Dyna Glide.
All: Simon Clay

Below: 1998 Sportster XLH883.
via Roy Bacon

Bottom: 1998 FXSTC Softail Custom.
via Roy Bacon

Fuel injection

The third 1995 model was the FLHTCI Ultra Classic Electra Glide Anniversary to celebrate 30 years of Electra Glide production. It was in the usual form of a limited edition with the standard model given a special finish and, in this case, restricted to 2,000 being built. However, there was one essential difference in that the last letter of the model code highlighted that the engine had sequential port fuel injection in place of the normal single carburettor. A single round air cleaner continued to supply the engine so the appearance remained as the other models in the series.

The final new 1995 model was the FXSTSB Bad Boy based on the Springer Softail. This was mainly a styling exercise in trim and finish but with a change to a slotted disc rear wheel in place of the wire one. It made for a dramatic line.

For 1966 there were no Tour Glides but the Electra Glides in Road King, Classic and Ultra Classic forms were all offered with the fuel injection, plus the letter 'I' at the end of their model code, as an alternative to the carburettor. The other changes that year were to the larger Sportster which was offered in two further forms.

The XL1200S Sport was given flat handlebars, a more suitable seat, dual front disc brakes and an adjustable suspension system. This offered rear units with piggy-back reservoirs and cartridge front forks, both with adjustments for load and damping. For the XL1200C Custom the suspension was lowered along with the seat height and a 21-inch wire wheel fitted at the front.

In 1997 the FLSTS Heritage Springer combined the Softail rear and Springer front suspensions in a further form of the past. At the

front went a deeper fender carrying a chrome-plated auxiliary lamp, as first seen back in 1938, while from the same or earlier era came the horn that hung just under the headlight. The detail work continued this theme to the exhausts, saddle, rear light and wire wheels fitted with white-wall tyres.

This tyre type also appeared in 1998 on a Classic version of the Electra Glide Road King that replaced the original and was coded FLHRCI. It too had wire wheels, a change from cast-alloy, and a number of new trim items. It

Below: 1998 FXDL Dyna Low Rider.
via Roy Bacon

Bottom: 1998 FXDS Dyna Convertible.
via Roy Bacon

was also the year when two new models appeared, developed exclusively for the European market.

One of the new models was the FXSTB Night Train that was based on the Softail, but reduced to the bare minimum and only available in one black finish. At the front went a 21-inch wire wheel with single disc brake, while at the rear the suspension supported a disc wheel. The seat was stepped and slim, the handlebars on risers, the headlight small and tucked between the fork legs.

The second new 1998 model for Europe was the XL53C Custom 53. The number indicated

the engine displacement in cu ines but it remained the existing 883. For the custom style it had highway footrests and its own seat,

handlebars, headlight and detail fittings. These were set off by a 21-inch wire wheel at the front and a disc wheel at the rear.

Below Left: 1998 FLSTC Heritage Softail Classic. via Roy Bacon

Bottom Left: 1998 FLHR Road King. via Roy Bacon

Fuel injection

Model	Bad Boy
Code	FXSTSB
Years	1995-96
No. cylinders	V-twin
Valves	ohv
Bore/stroke inch	3½ x 4¼
Capacity cu in	81.78
Capacity cc	1340
Ignition	electronic
No of gears	5
Drive system	chain/belt
Front suspension	leading link
Rear suspension	s/a
Wheel type	wire/disc
Wheel size inch	21/16
Brakes	discs
Wheelbase inch	64.4
Seat height inch	26.1

Model	Heritage Springer
Code	FLSTS
Years	1997-99
No. cylinders	V-twin
Valves	ohv
Bore/stroke inch	3½ x 4¼
Capacity cu in	81.78
Capacity cc	1340
Ignition	electronic
No of gears	5
Drive system	chain/belt
Front suspension	leading link
Rear suspension	s/a
Wheel type	wire
Wheel size inch	16/16
Brakes	discs
Seat height inch	26.5

Model	Night Train
Code	FXSTB
Years	1998-99
No. cylinders	V-twin
Valves	ohv
Bore/stroke inch	3½ x 4¼
Capacity cu in	81.78
Capacity cc	1340
Ignition	electronic
No of gears	5
Drive system	chain/belt
Front suspension	teles
Rear suspension	s/a
Wheel type	wire/disc
Wheel size inch	21/16
Brakes	discs
Seat height inch	25.3

Model	1995, FLHT-CI, Ultra Classic Electra Glide Anniversary, 1995-96, FLHTCU, Ultra Classic Electra Glide, 1995-98, FLHT, Electra Glide Standard, 1996-98, FLHT-CI, Electra Glide Classic (injection), 1996-98, FLHTCUI, Ultra Classic Electra Glide (injection)
No. cylinders	V-twin
Valves	ohv
Bore/stroke inch	3½ x 4¼
Capacity cu in	81.78
Capacity cc	1340
Ignition	electronic
No of gears	5
Drive system	chain, 1985-chain/belt
Front suspension	teles
Rear suspension	s/a
Wheel type	cast alloy
Wheel size inch	16/16
Brakes	discs
Wheelbase	62.9
Seat height inch	28, Sport 27

Model	1994-98, FLHR, Electra Glide Road King, 1995, FLTCU, Ultra Classic Tour Glide, 1996-97, FLHRI, Electra Glide Road King (injection), 1998, FLHRCI, Electra Glide Road King Classic (injection)
No. cylinders	V-twin
Valves	ohv
Bore/stroke inch	3½ x 4¼
Capacity cu in	81.78
Capacity cc	1340
Ignition	electronic
No of gears	5
Drive system	chain, 1985-chain/belt
Front suspension	teles
Rear suspension	s/a
Wheel type	cast alloy
Wheel size inch	16/16
Brakes	discs
Wheelbase	62.9
Seat height inch	29.6

Model	Sportster Custom
Code	XL1200C
Years	1996-99
No. cylinders	V-twin
Valves	ohv
Bore/stroke inch	3½ x 313/16
Capacity cu in	73.36
Capacity cc	1202
Ignition	electronic
No of gears	5
Drive system	chain/belt
Front suspension	teles
Rear suspension	s/a
Wheel type	wire/disc
Wheel size inch	21/16
Brakes	discs
Wheelbase inch	59
Seat height inch	27.1

Model	Sportster Sport
Code	XL1200S
Years	1996-99
No. cylinders	V-twin
Valves	ohv
Bore/stroke inch	3½ x 313/16
Capacity cu in	73.36
Capacity cc	1202
Ignition	electronic
No of gears	5
Drive system	chain/belt
Front suspension	teles
Rear suspension	s/a
Wheel type	cast alloy
Wheel size inch	16/16
Brakes	discs
Wheelbase inch	60.2
Seat height inch	28.9

Model	Sportster Custom 53
Code	XL53C
Years	1998-99
No. cylinders	V-twin
Valves	ohv
Bore/stroke inch	3 x 313/16
Capacity cu in	53.90
Capacity cc	883
Ignition	electronic
No of gears	5
Drive system	chain/belt
Front suspension	teles
Rear suspension	s/a
Wheel type	wire/disc
Wheel size inch	2
Brakes	discs
Wheelbase inch	60
Seat height inch	27.5

Below Left: 1998 FLHRCI Road King Classic with ESPFI. via Roy Bacon

Bottom Left: 1998 FLTRI Road Glide with ESPFI. via Roy Bacon

Below: 1998 Electra Glide with ESPFI. via Roy Bacon

Bottom: 1998 FLHTCI Electra Glide 95th anniversary. via Roy Bacon

This spread: 1998 Bad Boy.
All: Simon Clay

This spread: Electra Glide details.
All: Simon Clay

• *Harley-Davidson* •

• *Harley-Davidson* •

This spread: Fat Boy details.
All: Simon Clay

Twin Cam 88

A major change came in 1999 with the introduction of a new engine, the Twin Cam 88, that went into the Dyna and Touring models. Other than for a few minor items, mainly screws, it was all new and took part of its name from its increased capacity of 88ci or 1448cc. This came from a bigger bore but shorter stroke that allowed bigger valves to be fitted and a more compact combustion chamber to be designed. The Twin Cam was something of a misnomer for there were no overhead camshafts, still valves opened by pushrods and rockers much as before. The one real difference was the camshaft drive that was by chain instead of gears. This helped to reduce noise and this, plus oil-tight joints, had been one of the aims. Power and torque were both up so the result was really more of the same Harley-Davidson tradition. A new five-speed gearbox went with the new engine and the attachment between the two was much improved to give unit construction in all but name.

• Harley-Davidson •

This spread: 88cu in Super Glide Sport details. All: Simon Clay

The Dyna models with the new engine comprised the Wide Glide, Low Rider and Super Glide which were joined by the FXDX Dyna Super Glide Sport. This featured the wire wheels and dual front disc brakes of the Low Rider, but with flat handlebars and the seat a little higher.

Among the touring models the Electra Glide Standard, Road King, Road King Classic and Ultra Classic Electra Glide all fitted the new engine, the last two retaining the sequential port fuel injection.

New was the FLTRI Road Glide with the 88 engine and fuel injection, and offered as a custom tourer fitted with the frame-mounted fairing that carried an enclosed twin-oval reflector optic headlight. It had a clean style, much as the basic Electra Glide, and the choice of wire or cast-alloy wheels.

Finally came an entry-level model as the FXST Softail Standard for that range that kept the Evo engine in all cases. It came with wire wheels, 21-inch at the front, and afforded a basis for the

purchaser who could add accessories and custom parts to choice.

As always from Harley-Davidson, the list of extras was enormous and went far beyond the machine into all manner of items. Clothing, jewellery, ornaments, tableware, the list seemed endless. For performance there was the Screamin' Eagle line brought right up-to-date with stage tuning kits for the new 88 engine.

Twin Cam 88

Model	Softail Standard
Code	FXST
Years	1999
No. cylinders	V-twin
Valves	ohv
Bore/stroke inch	3½ x 4¼
Capacity cu in	81.78
Capacity cc	1340
Ignition	electronic
No of gears	5
Drive system	chain/belt
Front suspension	teles
Rear suspension	s/a
Wheel type	wire
Wheel size inch	2¹⁄₁₆
Brakes	discs
Seat height inch	26.2

Model	1999, FLHT, 88ci Electra Glide Standard, 1999, FLHR, 88ci Road King, 1999, FLHRCI, 88ci Road King Classic (injection), 1999, FLTRI, 88ci Road Glide (injection), 1999, FLHTCUI, 88ci Ultra Classic Electra Glide (injection)
Years	1999
No. cylinders	V-twin
Valves	ohv
Bore/stroke inch	3½ x 4¼
Capacity cu in	81.78
Capacity cc	1340
Ignition	electronic
No of gears	5
Drive system	chain/belt
Front suspension	teles
Rear suspension	s/a
Wheel type	see below
Wheel size inch	1⁹⁄₁₆
Brakes	discs
Wheelbase	63.5
Seat height inch	27

wheels, FLHT & FLHRCI-wire, FLTRI & FLHTCUI-cast alloy, FLHR-either

Model	88ci Dyna Wide Glide
Code	FXDWG
Years	1999
No. cylinders	V-twin
Valves	ohv
Bore/stroke inch	3¾ x 4
Capacity cu in	88.36
Capacity cc	1448
Ignition	electronic

No of gears	5
Drive system	chain/belt
Front suspension	teles
Rear suspension	s/a
Wheel type	wire
Wheel size inch	2¹⁄₁₆
Brakes	discs
Wheelbase	66.1
Seat height inch	26.7

Model	88ci Dyna Low Rider
Code	FXDL
Years	1999
No. cylinders	V-twin
Valves	ohv
Bore/stroke inch	3¾ x 4
Capacity cu in	88.36
Capacity cc	1448
Ignition	electronic
No of gears	5
Drive system	chain/belt
Front suspension	teles
Rear suspension	s/a
Wheel type	wire
Wheel size inch	1⁹⁄₁₆
Brakes	discs
Wheelbase	65.5
Seat height inch	26.5

Model	88ci Dyna Super Glide
Code	FXD
Years	1999
No. cylinders	V-twin
Valves	ohv
Bore/stroke inch	3¾ x 4
Capacity cu in	88.36
Capacity cc	1448
Ignition	electronic
No of gears	5
Drive system	chain/belt
Front suspension	teles
Rear suspension	s/a
Wheel type	wire
Wheel size inch	1⁹⁄₁₆
Brakes	discs
Wheelbase	62.5
Seat height inch	26.5

Model	88ci Dyna Super Glide Sport
Code	FXDX
Years	1999
No. cylinders	V-twin
Valves	ohv
Bore/stroke inch	3¾ x 4

Capacity cu in	88.36
Capacity cc	1448
Ignition	electronic
No of gears	5
Drive system	chain/belt
Front suspension	teles
Rear suspension	s/a
Wheel type	wire
Wheel size inch	1⁹⁄₁₆
Brakes	discs
Wheelbase	63.9
Seat height inch	27

This spread: 1999 Road Glide.
Both: Simon Clay

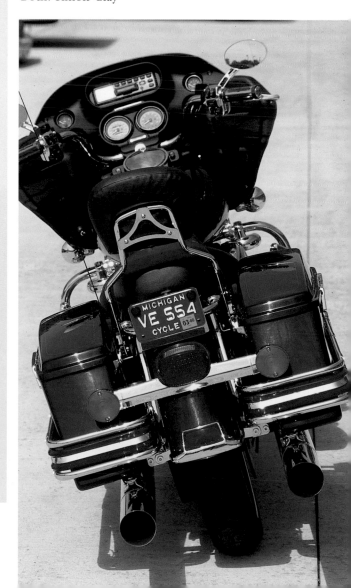

Buell

This is the name of machines built by Eric Buell who entered the market in 1987 with his RR1000 that used the Harley-Davidson XR1000 Sportster engine unit. This was rubber mounted to a stiff, light frame as a stressed member that had the rear suspension unit located under the engine and operating in tension as the wheel rose. From this came the RR1200 with the Evo Sportster engine in 1988 and the two-seat RS1200 the next year.

Five speeds arrived in 1991, a single-seat RSS1200 for the next year and by 1993 Harley-Davidson had a 49% stake in the Buell firm. By 1999 this had increased to 98% and a four-model range, all still with the under-engine rear-suspension unit was listed. The Sportster engine was tuned with either one carburettor or fuel injection, the transmission had five speeds and belt final drive was fitted.

The frame was a tubular perimeter type and the rear suspension fork in light alloy and controlled by a Showa unit. Forks from Showa went at the front and both 17-inch wheels were in cast alloy with three spokes. Single disc brakes were used, the front a massive 340mm with a six-piston caliper.

In all it offered a totally different machine but was all part of the Harley-Davidson all-encompassing range of models, performance, style and options.

Rught and Below: Motown Racing's Buell with front brake detail.
Both: Simon Clay

• *Harley-Davidson* •

*This spread: Motown Racing Buell
details. All: Simon Clay*

Left: Motown Racing logo. Simon Clay

*Below Left, Below and Right: Three
views of the Buell racer.*
All: via Roy Bacon

Harley-Davidson Models

SINGLES

1903		1st machine
1903-05		25cu in single
1906-08		27cu in single
1909-12		30cu in single, 1912 new frame
1913-18	5–35	35cu in single, mechanical inlet valve
1921-22	CD	37cu in single
1926-29	A/B	21cu in sv single
1926-29	AA/BA	21cu in ohv single
1930-34	C	30-50 sv single
1932-34	A/B	21cu in sv single

F-HEAD TWINS (ioe)

1903		1st machine
1903-05		25cu in single
1906-08		27cu in single
1909-12		30cu in single, 1912 new frame
1913-18	5–35	35cu in single, mechanical inlet valve
1921-22	CD	37cu in single
1926-29	A/B	21cu in sv single
1926-29	AA/BA	21cu in ohv single
1930-34	C	30-50 sv single
1932-34	A/B	21cu in sv single

F-HEAD TWINS (ioe)

1911-12		50cu in twin
1912		60cu in twin
1913		61cu in twin, 2 speed rear hub
1915-29		61cu in twin, 3 speed gearbox, oil pump
1921-29	F series	74cu in twin with magneto
1921-29	J series	74cu in twin with generator

FLAT HEAD TWINS (sv)

1919-23	WA	35 Sport, flat twin engine
1929-31	D series	45cu in sv twin
1930-36	V series	74cu in sv twin
1932-36	R series	45cu in sv twin
1932-74	G	45cu in sv Servi-Car
1935-36	V series	80cu in sv twin
1937-41	W series	45cu in sv twin
1937-41	U series	74cu in sv twin
1937-41	U series	80cu in sv twin
1945-48	U series	74cu in sv twin
1945-51	W series	45cu in sv twin
1952-53	K	45cu in twin
1954-56	KH	55cu in sv twin

Below: 1916 JE model twin.
Garry Stuart

Bottom: 1916 Model F twin.
Garry Stuart

Harley-Davidson Models

OVERHEAD-VALVE TWINS

1936-41	E series	61cu in ohv Knucklehead twin
1941	F	74cu in ohv Knucklehead twin
1945-47	61E series	61cu in ohv Knucklehead twin
1945-47	74F series	74cu in ohv Knucklehead twin
1948	61EL	61cu in ohv Panhead twin
1948	74FL	74cu in ohv Panhead twin
1949-52	61EL	61cu in Hydra-Glide Panhead twin
1949-57	74FL	74cu in Hydra-Glide Panhead twin
1958-64	74FL	Duo-Glide Panhead twin
1965	74FL	Electra Glide Panhead twin

SPORTSTER

1957-59	XL	55cu in Sportster
1958-71	XLH	55cu in Sportster
1958-71	XLCH	55cu in Sportster
1972-85	XLH	61cu in Sportster
1972-79	XLCH	61cu in Sportster
1977-78	XLT	61cu in Tourer
1977-78	XLCR	61cu in Cafe Racer
1979-85	XLS	61cu in Roadster
1980-85	XLH	61cu in Hugger
1983-84	XR1000	Café Racer
1983-85	XLX-61	61cu in Sportster

SHOVELHEAD TOURERS

1966-69	74FL	Electra Glide Shovelhead
1970-80	74FLH	Electra Glide Shovelhead (alternator)
1978-84	FLH80	80cu in Electra Glide
1979-82	FLHC80	80cu in Electra Glide Classic
1980-83	FLTC80	Tour Glide Classic
1980-83	FLT80	Tour Glide
1983	FLHTC	Electra Glide Classic
1984	FLHT	Electra Glide
1984	FLHX	Electra Glide
1984	FLHS	Electra Glide

Below: 1979 1,340cc FLH.
via Roy Bacon

Bottom Left: 1975 Sportster.
Garry Stuart

Bottom Right: 1959 XLCH.
Garry Stuart

Harley-Davidson Models

SUPER GLIDES

1971-78	FX	74cu in Super Glide
1974-81	FXE	74cu in Super Glide
1977-79	FXS	74cu in Low Rider
1979	FXEF	74cu in Fat Bob
1979-82	FXS	80cu in Low Rider
1979-82	FXEF	80cu in Fat Bob
1980-82	FXB	80cu in Sturgis
1980-84	FXWG	80cu in Wide Glide
1981-84	FXE	80cu in Super Glide
1983-84	FXSB	80cu in Low Rider (belt)
1985	FXSB	Low Rider (belt) (V2 engine)
1985	FXEF	80cu in Fat Bob (V2 engine)
1985-86	FXWG	Wide Glide (V2 engine)

FXR TWINS

1982-83	FXR	80cu in Super Glide II
1982-83	FXRS	80cu in Super Glide II De Luxe
1983	FXRT	Sport Glide
1984	FXRDG	80cu in Disc Glide (V2 engine)
1984-85	FXRS	80cu in Low Glide (V2 engine)
1984-92	FXRT	80cu in Sport Glide (V2 engine)
1985	FXRC	80cu in Low Glide Custom (V2 engine)
1986	FXRD	80cu in Sport Glide Tourer (V2 engine)
1986-92	FXRS	80cu in Low Rider (V2 engine)
1986-93	FXRS-SP	80cu in Low Rider Sport (V2 engine)
1986-94	FXR	80cu in Super Glide (V2 engine)
1987-94	FXLR	80cu in Low Rider Custom (V2 engine)
1989-93	FXRS-CN	80cu in Low Rider Convertible (V2 engine)

SOFTAIL

1984-90	FXST	80cu in Softail
1986-98	FXSTC	80cu in Softail Custom
1987-90	FLST	80cu in Heritage Softail
1988-99	FXSTS	80cu in Springer Softail
1988-99	FLSTC	80cu in Heritage Softail Classic
1990-99	FLSTF	80cu in Fat Boy
1993	FLSTN	Heritage Softail Nostalgia
1994-96	FLSTN	Heritage Softail Specu inal
1995-96	FXSTSB	Bad Boy
1997-99	FLSTS	Heritage Springer
1998-99	FXSTB	Night Train
1999	FXST	80cu in Softail Standard

Below: Duo-Glide. Garry Stuart

Bottom: 1975 Hydra-Glide. Ian Kerr

Harley-Davidson Models

V2 EVOLUTION TOURERS

1984-91	FLTC	Tour Glide Classic
1984-98	FLHTC	Electra Glide Classic
1985-87	FLHT	Electra Glide
1988-93	FLHS	Electra Glide Sport
1989-93	FLTC	Ultra Classic Tour Glide
1989-94	FLHTC	Ultra Classic Electra Glide
1994-98	FLHR	Electra Glide Road King
1995	FLHTCI	Ultra Classic Electra Glide Anniversary
1995	FLTCU	Ultra Classic Tour Glide
1995-96	FLHTCU	Ultra Classic Electra Glide
1995-98	FLHT	Electra Glide Standard
1996-97	FLHRI	Electra Glide Road King (injection)
1996-98	FLHTCI	Electra Glide Classic (injection)
1996-98	FLHTCUI	Ultra Classic Electra Glide (injection)
1998	FLHRCI	Electra Glide Road King Classic (injection)
1999	FLHT	88cu in Electra Glide Standard
1999	FLHR	88cu in Road King
1999	FLHRCI	88cu in Road King Classic (injection)
1999	FLTRI	88cu in Road Glide (injection)
1999	FLHTCUI	88cu in Ultra Classic Electra Glide (injection)

EVO SPORTSTER

1986-87	XLH1100	1100 Sportster
1986-95	XLH883	Sportster De Luxe
1986-99	XLH883	Evo Sportster
1988-99	XLH883	Hugger
1988-99	XLH1200	1200 Sportster
1996-99	XL1200C	1200 Sportster Custom
1996-99	XL1200S	1200 Sportster Sport
1998-99	XL53C	Sportster Custom 53

DYNA GLIDE

1991	FXDB	80cu in Dyna Glide Sturgis
1992	FXDB	80cu in Dyna Glide Daytona (1700 made)
1992	FXDC	80cu in Dyna Glide Custom
1993-98	FXDWG	80cu in Dyna Wide Glide
1993-98	FXDL	80cu in Dyna Low Rider
1994-98	FXDS-CN	80cu in Dyna Low Rider Convertible
1995-98	FXD	Dyna Super Glide, 80cu in
1999	FXDWG	88cu in Dyna Wide Glide
1999	FXDL	88cu in Dyna Low Rider
1999	FXD	88cu in Dyna Super Glide
1999	FXDX	88cu in Dyna Super Glide Sport

By Group

TWO-STROKES

1947-59	S	125cc Hummer two-stroke
1953-59	ST	165cc Hummer two-stroke
1960-61		165cc Super 10 two-stroke
1960-65		Topper 165cc two-stroke scooter
1962	165cc	Ranger two-stroke
1962-65		175cc Scat two-stroke
1962-65		175cc Pacer two-stroke
1966	175cc	Bobcat two-stroke

IMPORTS

1961-67	250 Aermacchi Sprint
1965-66	50cc Aermacchi Leggero
1967-71	65cc Aermacchi Leggero
1968-72	125cc Aermacchi Rapido
1969-74	350 Aermacchi Sprint
1970-72	100cc Aermacchi Baja
1973-74	90cc X90 and Z90 Aermacchi models
1973-77	125cc Aermacchi SS and SX models
1974-77	175cc Aermacchi SS and SX models
1975-77	250cc Aermacchi SS and SX models

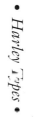

Harley-Davidson Models

1903		1st machine
1903-05		25cu in single
1906-08		27cu in single
1909-12		30cu in single, 1912 new frame
1911-12		50cu in twin
1912		60cu in twin
1913-18	5-35	35cu in single, mechanical inlet valve
1913	61cu in twin,	2 speed rear hub
1915-29	61cu in twin,	3 speed gearbox, oil pump
1916-21	16R	8-valve racu inng twin
1916-21	16S	4-valve racu inng single
1919-23	WA	35 Sport, flat twin engine
1921-29	F series	74cu in twin with magneto
1921-29	J series	74cu in twin with generator
1921-22	CD	37cu in single
1926-29	A/B	21cu in sv single
1926-29	AA/BA	21cu in ohv single
1926-36		21cu in ohv racer, Peashooter
1929-31	D series	45cu in sv twin
1930-34	C	30-50 sv single
1930-36	V series	74cu in sv twin
1932-34	A/B	21cu in sv single
1932-36	R series	45cu in sv twin
1932-74	G	45cu in sv Servi-Car
1935-36	V series	80cu in sv twin
1936-41	E series	61cu in ohv Knucklehead twin
1937-41	W series	45cu in sv twin
1937-41	U series	74cu in sv twin
1937-41	U series	80cu in sv twin
1941	F	74cu in ohv Knucklehead twin
1941	XA	45cu in flat twin engine, as BMW
1942-45	WLA	45cu in military
1942-45	WLC	45cu in military
1945-47	61E series	61cu in ohv Knucklehead twin
1945-47	74F series	74cu in ohv Knucklehead twin
1945-48	U series	74cu in sv twin
1945-51	W series	45cu in sv twin
1947-59	S	125cc Hummer two-stroke
1948	61EL	61cu in ohv Panhead twin
1948	74FL	74cu in ohv Panhead twin
1949-52	61EL	61cu in Hydra-Glide Panhead twin

By Year

Above Left: 1914 Single. Garry Stuart

Left: 1918 Single. Garry Stuart

Below: WA flat twin. Ian Kerr

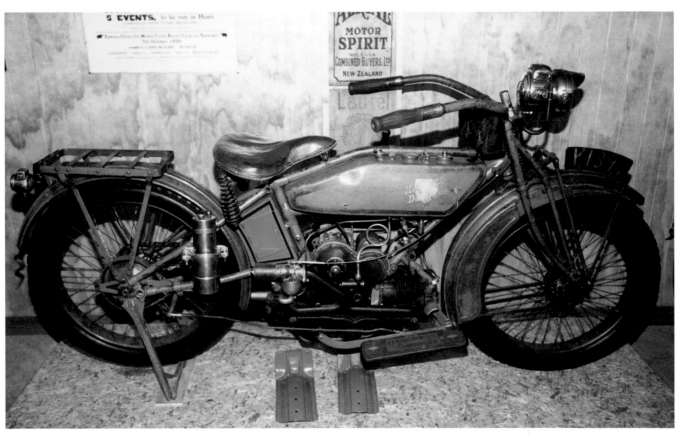

Harley-Davidson Models

1949-57	74FL	74cu in Hydra-Glide Panhead twin
1952-53	K	45cu in twin
1952-69	KR	45cu in racu inng model in various forms
1953-59	ST	165cc Hummer two-stroke
1954-56	KH	55cu in sv twin
1957-59	XL	55cu in Sportster
1958-64	74FL	Duo-Glide Panhead twin
1958-71	XLH	55cu in Sportster
1958-71	XLCH	55cu in Sportster
1960-61		165cc Super 10 two-stroke
1960-65		Topper 165cc two-stroke scooter
1961-67		250 Aermacchi Sprint
1962		165cc Ranger two-stroke
1962-65		175cc Scat two-stroke
1962-65		175cc Pacer two-stroke
1965	74FL	Electra Glide Panhead twin
1965-66		50cc Aermacchi Leggero
1966		175cc Bobcat two-stroke
1966-69	74FL	Electra Glide Shovelhead twin
1967-71		65cc Aermacchi Leggero
1968-72		125cc Aermacchi Rapido
1969-74		350 Aermacchi Sprint
1970-72		100cc Aermacchi Baja
1970-80	74FLH	Electra Glide Shovel with alternator
1971-78	FX	74cu in Super Glide
1972-85	XLH	61cu in Sportster
1972-79	XLCH	61cu in Sportster
1973-74		90cc X90 and Z90 Aermacchi models
1973-77		125cc Aermacchi SS and SX models
1974-77		175cc Aermacchi SS and SX models
1974-81	FXE	74cu in Super Glide
1975-77		250cc Aermacchi SS and SX models
1977-78	XLT	61cu in Tourer
1977-78	XLCR	61cu in Cafe Racer
1977-79	FXS	74cu in Low Rider
1978-84	FLH80	80cu in Electra Glide
1979	FXEF	74cu in Fat Bob
1979-82	FXEF	80cu in Fat Bob
1979-82	FLHC80	80cu in Electra Glide Classic
1979-82	FXS	80cu in Low Rider
1979-85	XLS	61cu in Roadster

Below: 1978 1200 Electra Glide for Harley's 75th anniversary. via Roy Bacon

Bottom: 1976 FL. via Roy Bacon

Harley-Davidson Models

1980-82	FXB	80cu in Sturgis
1980-84	FXWG	80cu in Wide Glide
1980-83	FLTC80	Tour Glide Classic
1980-83	FLT80	Tour Glide
1980-85	XLH	61cu in Hugger
1981-84	FXE	80cu in Super Glide
1982-83	FXR	80cu in Super Glide II
1982-83	FXRS	80cu in Super Glide II De Luxe
1983	FXRT	Sport Glide
1983	FLHTC	Electra Glide Classic
1983-84	FXSB	80cu in Low Rider (belt)
1983-84	XR1000	Cafe Racer
1983-85	XLX-61	61cu in Sportster
1984	FLHT	Electra Glide
1984	FLHX	Electra Glide
1984	FLHS	Electra Glide
1984	FXRDG	80cu in Disc Glide
1984-85	FXRS	80cu in Low Glide
1984-90	FXST	80cu in Softail
1984-91	FLTC	Tour Glide Classic
1984-92	FXRT	80cu in Sport Glide
1984-98	FLHTC	Electra Glide Classic
1985	FXSB	Low Rider (belt)
1985	FXEF	80cu in Fat Bob
1985	FXRC	80cu in Low Glide Custom
1985-86	FXWG	Wide Glide
1985-87	FLHT	Electra Glide
1986	FXRD	80cu in Sport Glide Tourer
1986-87	XLH1100	1100 Sportster
1986-92	FXRS	80cu in Low Rider
1986-93	FXRS-SP	80cu in Low Rider Sport
1986-94	FXR	80cu in Super Glide
1986-95	XLH883	Sportster De Luxe
1986-98	FXSTC	80cu in Softail Custom
1986-99	XLH883	Evo Sportster
1987-90	FLST	80cu in Heritage Softail
1987-94	FXLR	80cu in Low Rider Custom
1988-93	FLHS	Electra Glide Sport
1988-99	XLH883	Hugger
1988-99	XLH1200	1200 Sportster
1988-99	FXSTS	80cu in Springer Softail

Below: AA Electra Glide.
via Roy Bacon

Bottom: 1977 XLCR 1000.
via Roy Bacon

Harley-Davidson Models

1988-99	FLSTC	80cu in Heritage Softail Classic
1989-93	FLTC	Ultra Classic Tour Glide
1989-93	FXRS-CN	80cu in Low Rider Convertible
1989-94	FLHTC	Ultra Classic Electra Glide
1990-99	FLSTF	80cu in Fat Boy
1991	FXDB	80cu in Dyna Glide Sturgis
1992	FXDB	80cu in Dyna Glide Daytona (1700 made)
1992	FXDC	80cu in Dyna Glide Custom
1993	FLSTN	Heritage Softail Nostalgia
1993-98	FXDWG	80cu in Dyna Wide Glide
1993-98	FXDL	80cu in Dyna Low Rider
1994-96	FLSTN	Heritage Softail Specu inal
1994-98	FLHR	Electra Glide Road King
1994-98	FXDS-CN	80cu in Dyna Low Rider Convertible
1995	FLHTCI	Ultra Classic Electra Glide Anniversary
1995	FLTCU	Ultra Classic Tour Glide
1995-96	FXSTSB	Bad Boy
1995-96	FLHTCU	Ultra Classic Electra Glide
1995-98	FXD	Dyna Super Glide, 80cu in
1995-98	FLHT	Electra Glide Standard
1996-97	FLHRI	Electra Glide Road King (injection)
1996-98	FLHTCI	Electra Glide Classic (injection)
1996-98	FLHTCUI	Ultra Classic Electra Glide (injection)
1996-99	XL1200C	1200 Sportster Custom
1996-99	XL1200S	1200 Sportster Sport
1997-99	FLSTS	Heritage Springer
1998	FLHRCI	Electra Glide Road King Classic (injection)
1998-99	FXSTB	Night Train
1998-99	XL53C	Sportster Custom 53
1999	FXDX	88cu in Dyna Super Glide Sport
1999	FXST	80cu in Softail Standard
1999	FXDWG	88cu in Dyna Wide Glide
1999	FXDL	88cu in Dyna Low Rider
1999	FXD	88cu in Dyna Super Glide
1999	FLHR	88cu in Road King
1999	FLHRCI	88cu in Road King Classic (injection)
1999	FLHT	88cu in Electra Glide Standard
1999	FLHTCUI	88cu in Ultra Classic Electra Glide (injection)
1999	FLTRI	88cu in Road Glide (injection)

Below: 1989 Ultra Classic Tour Glide.
via Roy Bacon

By Year

Harley Types

207

Roadtests

Ian Kerr

FXDWDG
Dyna Wide Glide

Knocking Harleys is easy: most magazines do it on a regular basis, and it is almost a national pastime for riders in Great Britain. Similarly, in the States they knock anything Japanese and at some bike events they burn Japanese bikes to entertain the normally totally Harley riding crowd.

Knocking what we don't understand is a world-wide pastime. From a UK perspective the Harley is antiquated, hanging onto concepts and ideals that we buried with the British bike industry. However, with the exception of the "new" Triumph, our industry is dead and the American one is booming!

To look at just the bikes is missing the point; they are more than a bike they are part of a lifestyle, part of the American dream.

Talking to Willie G. Davidson at a press conference, he said very little about the bikes themselves, but launched straight into describing the concept and the lifestyle. And it's true: the more time you spend riding Harleys, the more you appreciate what people like Willie are about and why people just like riding them so much!

Now this is not a preamble to coming out of the closet and admitting to rushing out and buying one of Milwaukee's finest irons, it is just to point out that this test is not going to hammer the latest Dyna Wide Glide because it is not the quickest, smoothest thing through my favorite series of bends.

Neither is it the most comfortable mount available or the easiest bike to keep clean. What it is, is a living legend that you cannot help but appreciate and admire and riding one is not as bad or as slow as people would have you believe.

The minute you thumb the electric starter and the rich bellow barks out from the twin staggered "shorty" dural silencers on the offside of the bike you know you are Harley-mounted. Despite the modern mountings, the 45-degree V-twin Evolution engine still does its own thing within the confines of the tubular steel cradle frame.

Blip the throttle and the bike barks and people look around; grab the hefty clutch lever and clog the five-speed box into first and the world takes on a different perspective as the bike lumbers forward.

Despite the raked front end increasing the wheelbase way beyond other bikes, it is surprisingly easy to get round even tight

corners. A low centre of gravity helps the handling, achieved not only by sitting the engine low but also the rider.

You soon get used to sitting well within the confines of the bike on the sparsely padded stepped seat, feet pushed out forwards onto the highway pegs and foot controls, hands lifted slightly to meet the Ape hanger bars. It all sounds bad, but it is remarkably comfortable once you forget your prejudices and let the mind switch to another image whereby you just relax and enjoy life!

It is not all good, though, because you do have to watch the skinny front tyre, hugging the 21-inch spoked rim, in case it washes out on corners or meets some diesel. The riding position means it is a bit remote and the handlebars can feel like a tiller on a boat.

At the rear the laced hub is 16 inches in diameter and gets a pretty respectable 130/90 tyre that is more than capable of allowing some very good angles of lean on dry roads.

Right: What chucks out 1,340cc and makes people turn their heads? The 45-degree, V-twin Evo. Ian Kerr

208

• Harley-Davidson •

The "bob-tail" rear fender will keep most of the spray away from you or a pillion, and even the sparse-looking front item strung between the massively wide spaced front forks is better and more efficient than it has the right to be.

Similarly the small round "Bates" headlamp throws out a main and dipped beam that puts many sports and touring bikes to shame, especially considering its small diameter.

The suspension, on the other hand, could do with improvement. American roads are a lot better maintained than ours and although the front forks are both stiff enough not to flex or twist and supple enough to smooth out the ride, the back end needs improving.

The inclined twin shocks have pre-load but could do with some damping adjustments. Solo they work adequately, but when a pillion is added to the stepped seat with its padded sissy bar, they have a hard time and so do you!

The single front and rear discs are a vast improvement on Harleys of old. They are predictable and efficient and no longer does it need two hands on the lever or your full weight on the pedal to stop. Having said that, they are not one-finger jobs that will allow you to emulate GP

• Harley-Davidson •

Below: A factory picture showing the bike ex-works. However, few leave dealers in this condition, as they will already have had extras added.
via Roy Bacon

racers with their "stoppie" front-braking antics.

However, as I said right at the beginning, that's not what these bikes are about. Riding through the lanes or in town you never really feel the need to go fast or to find the bike's angles of lean.

None of them are slow though and it is quite easy to see three figures on the tank-mounted speedo, although unless you work out regularly, it is not something you want to keep up for long on this model. The bike is deceptively quick and you do end up enjoying the acceleration and torque that

1,340cc thump out in their distinctive way, and you have to keep a check on your right wrist.

Something you end up wanting to continue is the attention you get when out on a Harley. Despite the plethora of Japanese customs available, none attracts the same sort attention that a Harley does, especially from the non-motorcycling public. The name and the style are evocative.

In particular, the long low rider image that the Dyna Wide Glide gives, is of the style that started off the whole custom bike movement. It is in your face and far from

subtle, witness the color scheme and lashings of chrome. Not to everyone's taste, but what is?

Two weeks use of yet another Harley convinced me that the best marketing tool any manufacture could employ is to loan bikes out for decent long tests. You can never explain in print what a Harley is all about or why anybody would want to spend big money on a bike like this.

Ride it and you will know what the appeal is. One man's meat is another man's poison, and you can understand why people want the Harley antidote!

*Below Left:High rise bars and skinny front wheel are distinctive features of this model.*Ian Kerr

Below: Some things remain common to all no matter what the model or age, and that is the shape of the engine.
Ian Kerr

Harley-Davidson Road Glide

Harley's latest big touring mount is now the Road Glide; features everything you could want for long distance touring, including an excellent distortion free stereo to keep you entertained and informed!

This is located in a frame-mounted threequarter fairing that provides sufficient weather protection for the rider even with its low screen, but allows the engine to be seen in all its traditional V-twin glory. At the front of the fairing enclosed are two powerful head-lights that are good enough to light up even the remotest unlit roads ensuring a safe passage both day and night wherever you roam.

In 1998 I had a sneak preview and a few days' riding in Austria and Slovenia to find out what we would be getting in 1999. The open and almost deserted roads in the latter contrasted nicely with the tight twisty roads of the Tyrol and proved an ideal test location.

Like any Harley, the bike handles quite well provided it is properly set up for corners and you do not ask it to perform racing angles of lean.

You can maintain a high average speed thanks to the comfort factor and the generous tank range and you'll arrive at

Right: Photo shoot in Slovenia. Ian Kerr

Below: Clean dash with great sounds! Ian Kerr

your destination in a similar time to a sports bike rider who may well have gone faster, but had more stops!

One thing is for sure: you will be a lot more relaxed and less tired. Air adjustment on the rear suspension allows you a decent degree of fine-tuning to cope with luggage and pillions. Overall, though, this new addition to the Harley range is very comfortable with very little vibration ever making its presence felt.

Certainly these new Harley Evo motors do an excellent job in balancing tradition and modern attributes and are not the dinosaurs some may have you believe!

However, the bikes be on sale in 1999 have the all-new "Twin Cam 88" motors in them. These are claimed to be mechanically quieter, more reliable and have increased performance thanks to a lot of internal work on the combustion area. Increased rigidity

Previous Page: "The bike handles quite well provided it is properly set up for corners." Ian Kerr

Left: The all-new "Twin-Cam 88" motor. Ian Kerr

Above and Right: "The panniers just swallow luggage. Ian Kerr

will also help chassis stiffness as well.

As I have said before when testing Harleys, the brakes have come a long way, they are a lot better than ever before, but still need a little more in terms of feel and leverage, especially when the bike is fully laden.

Talking of which, the panniers just swallow luggage and any extra can be strapped on the rack between them, further increasing the capacity for a long tour. You will never run short of space at least!

Stereos on bikes — well you are either for or against, no middle ground seems to exist here, but the one that comes as standard is excellent! (You wouldn't accept a car without one, so what is the problem on a bike?)

Even without this, attracting attention was not a problem and even in deserted areas of Slovenia they all recognized the big V-twin from America and stopping was a time-consuming matter especially with the language difficulties!

The deep blue finish made the bike look classy and understated with just enough chrome and polished stainless to set things off. Should you want there are endless accessories to personalize the bike to your own taste. Personally I am quite happy with what comes as standard.

Below: "The deep blue finish made the bike look classy . . ." Ian Kerr

FXD
Dyna Super Glide

Unless you have been out of touch with the motorcycle world you cannot have failed to notice that 1998 was Harley Davidson's 95th Anniversary which makes them the world's oldest manufacturer of motorcycles. During their life they have become known as producers of big V-twin engines and around these built bikes of various types and styles.

The cynics will point out that during their existence little has changed and the "lifestyle" image has come about to cover lack of technical innovation. This, of course, is rubbish; the modern Harley is a long way from those that came from a 10 x 15 shed in Milwaukee, home of the Davidson brothers back in 1903.

All I would say, is try riding one of the latest American "Hogs" fitted with one of the new "Twin Cam 88" motors and then go and ride a model of ten years ago — chalk and cheese to say the least. After two weeks' use I can confidently say that the "88" is a very modern motor that delivers the goods and will take the company well into the millennium.

Harley-Davidson has taken all the points that have made the bikes a modern icon and incorporated them into a powerplant that delivers the punch that devotees have come to expect, but at the same time meets a lot of the criticism that has been leveled at the "Hog." Not an easy task, perhaps, but one which has been accomplished well.

Let's not get carried away: this increase in capacity to 1,450cc and various mods will not get you rubbing shoulders with R1 owners as you power out of bends, knee

on the deck at three figure speeds on track days. What it will give you is arm-wrenching torque that will allow a relaxed ride, but with sufficient response available when needed without recourse to shifting down a few cogs!

Gone is the vibro massage (that can cause discomfort), engine noise and clatter leaving just the pleasant potato sound at the end of the silencers to enjoy.

One of the benefits of the engine changes is a stiffer engine gearbox unit that increases chassis rigidity and improves handling. Added to this is a braking system that now inspires some confidence

and allows you to utilize the new engine to the full.

The bike I tried out was the 1999 specification FXD Dyna Super Glide. The original Dyna Glide made its debut in 1991 with a two-point rubber mounting system that has remained an integral part of the Dyna range and contributes to the comfortable ride.

The test bike is in fact the entry-level model of the range with a 28-degree fork rake, classic Fat Bob fuel tank, stepped seat and pull back bars. The latter will not be to everyone's taste, as the right wrist tends to turn in when opening the throttle.

You soon get used to it, the benefit being your arm position on long runs is very comfortable, even though your chest is exposed square onto the elements which leads to a little fatigue in blustery conditions. This more than anything will stop you finding the (estimated) 115mph top speed!

In keeping with its paucity of extras and gizmos the price reflects its basic specification, being very reasonable.

Below and Below Left: The engines now have a host of modern technology within.
Ian Kerr

Basic it may be but it is pure Harley, a slightly heavy cable-operated clutch, belt drive and a solid feel to everything.

There is, as always, a reasonable level of handling that will allow silencers to scrape once you become accustomed to the Dunlop Elite tyres fitted to 16-inch back and 19-inch front spoked rims that are actually extras in some parts of the world.

You do not, of course, have to touch anything down unless you want to, because the bike will, like all Harleys, hold a tight line through a bend providing you have set it up right at the offset.

Pillion passengers make no difference to performance or handling apart from the fact they will need to hang onto you if they are not to explore the cold comfort of the rear metal fender as they slide off the stepped seat on mild acceleration. (The rear shocks can be jacked up if required!)

Despite the 62.5-inch wheelbase the bike can make feet up turns on most roads and is very maneuverable in traffic; in fact, it is a very useful commuter mount.

The 4.9-gallon tank with its centrally-mounted fuel gauge will give over 150 miles before it needs replenishing with unleaded and is fitted with that rare item called a fuel tap, complete with reserve position!

Those short in inside leg inches will appreciate the 26-inch seat height and thanks to everything, including the centre of gravity, being kept low, the 700lb plus fully-fuelled weight will not cause problems.

The small round headlight once again questions the need for the twin-light units many sports bike have these days, as it throws a searchlight into the gloom that would be welcome on any lighthouse, automated or not.

Switchgear is standard and basic Harley, as is the instrumentation, which just about covers the actual bike and running gear — so what about the new engine?

Visually it still looks like the original 45-degree V-twin Harley first built in 1909. However, the rest of it is brand new with just 21 parts having moved across from the Evo engine, most of these being screws.

This is Harley's largest displacement engine and is the result of two million miles of road testing. The company is determined this latest unit will go down in history along with names like the Panhead, Shovelhead etc.

The bore has been increased to 3.75 inches to get the extra capacity, but the stroke has been shortened to just four inches. This allows for higher revs and smoother power delivery. Torque

on the Dyna is 106 at 2,900rpm. (It varies on different models)

The combustion chamber is a bathtub configuration to improve the combustion process, the compression ratio being 8.8 to 1. Staying at the top, the rocker arms get their own internal support, allowing the new two-piece covers to do just one job and become more oil tight.

Gaskets have also been redesigned for the same reason, while the head have deeper fins to improve cooling. A new nozzle in the crankcase sprays oil up onto the underside of the piston to provide added cooling and reduce wear. Ignition is a new single fire design.

The oil system in general is also changed with the pump running directly off the crank. This in turn has new forged flywheels and beefed up con rods to withstand the increase in torque. The common crankpin is also beefed up in case owners take advantage of the performance kits that are now offered.

For the same reason the crankcases have been increased in strength, but reduced in weight! The interface between the rear of

Previous Page and Right: The wet and greasy roads of the U.K. are not always kind to the chrome on bikes more used to warmer weather and salt free U.S. roads. Ian Kerr

the engine and the transmission has been made more rigid reducing inner primary loads.

The twin cam is chain-driven and the breathing system has been altered, all helping to reduce noise as well as increasing efficiency. The changes also make servicing a lot easier, which should help reduce the cost of ownership.

Visually it still looks good and the new oval air cleaner (increased volume) in front of the 40mm CV carb, almost goes unnoticed at a quick glance, so good is the styling. Just a point here, the fin area is up 50 percent on previous models, but overall the engine appears a neater unit!

In practice this all translates into pure Harley, but better. Grab a handful and the bike just growls and gets a move on with an urgency that will surprise a lot of people. If you just want to watch the world go by then it is happy to do so and eat up the miles in a mild mannered unflustered way. Vibration may be there, but it does not get to you, this is, relatively speaking, smooth!

As ever the gearbox contains just five ratios to cope with power output.

It is not mentioned in the specification whether any changes have been made to the shift mechanism, but the test bike never missed a shift up or down and felt smoother and more positive than ever before and will make clutchless changes when you get very lazy!

As already mentioned, the brakes now inspire a confidence (despite no claimed changes) the early items never could.

Should the standard engine package not be enough, Screamin' Eagle performance kits are available to fit straight from the crate. The Stage 1 kit for street use (there is a racing kit) includes a freer-flowing air filter and breather.

Then there is a stock bore calibration cartridge and ECU which increase torque through the rpm range by 10 percent at the peak. Not enough? Then there is a big bore kit to up the capacity to 95cu in and boost torque by 17 percent. These street applications do not affect the warranty if fitted by Harley dealers. (Racing versions may, of course, invalidate things, but do really get things motoring!)

If the test bike is anything to go by, these latest Harleys, like all their forebears, have what all the Japanese cruisers lack: presence, style and a name. Harley-Davidson has kept it all, but produced a bike capable of taking the company into the 21st century and for that they deserve a very big round of applause.

Metisse Harley

Ask most people what their ideal bike would be like and they begin to sketch out a ghost outline, taking bits from one bike and characteristics from another. If most of the designs ever saw the light of day as hard metal they would probably be real camels!

Motorcyclists of all ages are individuals with their own ideas; they ride because they want to, not because they have to! But having said that, they are all realists and accept that, like most things in life, bikes are a compromise and production techniques and costs invariably dictate the end product. Therefore, in the main, the bikes they buy tend to be what they are willing to accept, as opposed to what they really want.

Some people, though, are dogmatic enough to blaze their own trail and fight to get what they want. One such man is Adrian Pavey who at 34 years old has gone through some of the most desirable bikes from all corners of the globe in search of a bike to fulfil his needs and desires.

In reality his wants are not that complex. "I wanted a bike that had traditional values but was usable everyday so it had to have modern suspension, tyres and above all brakes that worked well at all speeds!"

Not a lot to ask, but where can you find such ideals in a showroom? Sure there are plenty of people making classic replicas, but that means, generally, that the brakes and suspension are period. On the other hand, Triumph is making modern bikes but the company are far from traditional.

The only option left is to build your own, which — as Adrian freely admits — has taken three years of toil and effort not to mention a lot of money. There was also a year off in between when diminished enthusiasm and cash caused a hiatus in the proceedings.

But the end result has been worthwhile, because the accolades have come from every branch of the motorcycle world. The custom riders love it, the specialist builders appreciate the skill and workmanship, the traditionalists admire it and the modern riders have to follow it through the lanes, which considering it's powered by a Harley motor is quite something!

Pavey's creation bears not his name but two legendary monikers from motorcycle history, Metisse and Harley-Davidson. The former seems somewhat appropriate in more ways than one because it is a French word meaning "mongrel."

The Rickman brothers originally chose it because the frames they built housed all different sorts of motors. When they sold out that part of their business to Pat French of MRD in 1983, he kept the name alive by producing the same beautifully brazed cradle frames to house all sorts of power plants. Some, such as the Harley, had never before graced the Rickman trellis.

The Harley name is on the tank because it belongs to the traditional V-twin motor that gives the bike the traditional feel that Adrian wanted so much. It is also there because the overall design of the bike owes a lot to the XR750 Harley flat trackers he has admired since his early teens.

How the bike came to fruition is a long and involved story but revolves around Pat French and his friendship with Pavey, who had conveyed his ideas to the frame builder on many occasion over a cup of tea. French was on holiday in the States visiting none other than Rob North (who built a few frames in his time) and found some brand new '82 Shovelhead iron-barreled XL-1000 engines still in their crates for sale in a dealership.

Below: Twin headlights give a totally different look to this flat track styled bike, but are still in keeping with the sleek minimalist lines. Ian Kerr

Below: Accolades have come from every branch of the motorcycle world for the Metisse Harley. Ian Kerr

On return to Blighty he passed the details of the shop onto Adrian who within a week had the motor delivered to French's Bristol workshop, a feat he points out would be hard to better with a company in this country! Next items to be sourced were forks and wheels to get the project into the realms of a rolling chassis.

Now, Harley may have provided the traditional power source but, as most will agree, parts from the American factory do not normally go hand in hand with the other design aims of handling, reliability and good brakes.

The forks originated from the land of the rising sun, but

actually journeyed to Bristol from south London. Formerly gracing the front end of well known racer Terry Rymer's Yamaha OWO1, the 43mm conventional (i.e. not inverted) items were surplus to requirements and sold off through the ad pages.

The wheels are 18-inch Dymag racing items that actually appeared on the market thanks to a long complicated insurance matter involving loss from aircraft companies and the like. The net result is that the wheels, originally destined for the USA, also appeared in the small ads to be snapped up for the Pavey special.

With the main ingredients now to hand, French made up a jig to hold the forks at the required angle (26 degrees) and the wheel spindles at the required distance apart (57.5 inches). These distances were decreed by Pavey on a very rough sketch (his words) but bear in mind this man is a trained aircraft mechanic and his ideas have experience and skill to back them up along with time spent on the drag strips of this country!

With lump sitting on the bench, Pat French then started to bend the high tensile chrome-moly steel around it within the "part" jig. Having got them into the required shape, they were then

brazed to give the integrity required allowing the oil for the engine to circulate freely within them.

A small sight-glass graces the left side and the oil is distributed from a neat block arrangement hidden beneath the tank. The advantages of utilizing the frame to cool oil are obvious — such as weight saving, space and, of course, better cooling of the 3.25 litres of oil thanks to the very large surface area. The iron block Harleys are hard on oil, so engine longevity will be an additional benefit with this set up as opposed to the stock system.

With the rolling chassis completed, the hard part of the job started — as anybody who has ever built a special will tell you, trying to make brackets, fittings etc. takes time and an awful lot of patience, and in some cases money.

Adrian is lucky in that he still has a lot of contacts in the aircraft world which means that what are throw away items in the ultra safety conscious world of flying make useful quality additions to two wheels. For instance, the bike is held together by Shearline nuts. The actual nut breaks off at a specified torque leaving the shank to hold the items together. Apart from looking good this saves weight.

Below: The best of the motorcycling cultures — a British frame with a an American engine full of torque.
Ian Kerr

Titanium was used for a lot of the brackets and all these small touches which add to the classy appearance, also help keep the weight down to 415lb including half a gallon of gas.

Adrian is quick to give credit to others for the help he received — such as Paul Hobbs of Hobbsport Earls who made all the braided steel hoses that appear all over the machine. Not only did he make and supply them, but then did a discount deal that saved an overdraft, just because he liked the bike so much!

The bike simply abounds with neat touches and quality items, not all of which are apparent or visible. For instance, the handlebars are filled with liquid rubber (normally used on planes as a sealing aid) to absorb some of the legendary Harley vibes. The top of the yokes were altered and re-welded to allow the use of the tubular bars, but you would never notice this until it is pointed out, such is the quality of the work!

A drag racing friend who trades under the name Boot Soop Racing made the wiring harness and managed to tuck the whole electrical system under the seat, including the massive battery necessary to spin the 45-degree lump into life.

Despite the assistance of friends, professionals have

occasionally been needed — such as with the petrol tank. This was hand-crafted by Pearsons in Swanscombe, Kent, and involved Adrian trailering the bike to the workshop and leaving it for a day, but as he points out the end result was well worth the effort.

The bike mirrors the minimalist appearance of the flat tracker that he kept in his mind, and the paintwork, a variation of traditional Harley colors, helps keep the theme going. Aesthetics are not my strong point, but apart from the twin headlamp set up at the front, everything about this bike looks right.

The problem with a lot of specials is that while they look good, they fail to translate the appearance of form into function. Not so with this bike. It goes even better than it looks!

Having let the owner gently warm the bike up, and thrown my leg across the tall saddle, my first few yards were spent at walking pace along an uneven alleyway. This immediately showed up a frame pedigree that encompasses all motorcycle sport disciplines including mud. The balance was superb and boded well for the twists and turns of the Wiltshire lanes.

The engine remains stock, even to the point of retaining the same final drive gearing, although this is maybe one area that will be

changed to drop the revs down when cruising at a legal seventy. The high level Stortz pipes have allowed the engine to breathe a little easier adding perhaps a couple of bhp to the standard 68, but there have been no other changes as yet.

Twin plugging of the heads is planned just to aid the combustion process rather than adding power, but otherwise the engine will be left alone. Quite honestly the motor has less weight to pull than it would have had and provides speeds up to and over the ton which is more than enough for our congested roads. The exposed riding position also tempers speeds despite being more than comfortable for normal use.

The motor pulls like you would expect and used sensibly in built up areas the bike attracts very little attention till you get to the lights, when heads turn and look. On the open road wind it up and let it go and the raucous bark is pure magic to those of us brought up on such sounds.

The gearbox will take short shifts or will allow the top of the rev range to be explored before changing up. There is a very large gap between third and fourth in the box and this is one of the reasons the gearing may be altered as it is almost impossible to engage fourth in 30mph limits without

Below: What all Harleys lack as standard is an effective braking system, but not on this bike! Ian Kerr

snatching taking place when opening the throttle.

The clutch is standard Harley and heavy in operation but whereas normally the right wrist would get similar exercise trying to stop the thing, on this bike one finger is all that is needed to caress the lever on the AP racing master cylinder. This brings into play a pair of four-pot Nissin racing calipers which bite hard on the 320mm rotors from PFM stopping the bike immediately!

Should you want to just steady the rear of the bike, a twin-pot Brembo caliper will grab a 220mm rotor at the back, but in normal use you can forget it and rely on the front to do the work.

Despite the bite of the brakes, there is little dive from the forks which are well set up, coping easily with the lighter machine than the one for which they were designed. Although firm enough not to dip under braking they are soft enough to track the road surface which was reassuring when being powered out of some of Wiltshire's less than billiard table smooth bends.

At the back, the bike now sports a pair of Swedish Ohlins set up by M&H racing after the original Fournales proved to be to difficult to set up thanks to the use of air as the springing medium. The twin shocks (in keeping with traditional values!) complement the front perfectly providing a level of comfort with surefootedness.

The steering damper helps keep the bike on course through the bends and you can actually deliberately bang the bars and find the bike self centres almost immediately such is the excellence of bike's geometry.

The Pirelli tyres fitted are no longer state-of-the-art and 18-inch diameters are also a bit old hat, but there is no way that you can complain about grip or ground clearance. The 110/80 front and 170/60 back will allow the bike to be canted over further than sensible use on the road will allow or for that matter more than most riders will ever want! Thanks to the hours of thought that have gone into this bike nothing will ever get close enough to dig in and cause any worrying moments.

However, one area where this has gone a little too far is the side stand. This item is so well tucked away that the only safe way of ensuring it is down and out is to do it by hand, which gets annoying after a while but I am sure you get used to it eventually.

Although I did not have the opportunity to try the bike at night, its owner states the lights are not as effective as they could be and is considering changing to a single more traditional unit.

This is a bike that is functional and, above all else, fun and very easy to ride hard and fast. One man's dream has become reality after a lot of hard work and effort, but the end result shows with pure quality. Careful listing of all monies spent puts the cost well above what you would spend on a modern bike (or, for that matter, a restored bike) but without the individuality of this machine.

MRD is now supplying frame kits to include swing arm, head bearings, fuel tank, seat, side panels and footrests for those who wish to go down the same route as Adrian Pavey. Even if people do, it is doubtful they will achieve the standard of this bike.

Mongrel it may be, but this has turned out a pure thoroughbred!

Right: Almost a case of tortured metal, but these pipes free the horses from within! Ian Kerr

Sundance Super XR — 1200 DT

Although Sundance are well known in Japan for their performance shops in Tokyo, world-wide they are known primarily for their racing exploits with the "Daytona Weapon," This all-black state-of-the-art racing bike is powered by a Harley-Davidson engine and has shown the Americans that their home-grown motors can run with the best from Japan. Run by 37-year-old Takehiko Shibazaki, the Sundance name has become synonymous with tuning and custom parts since he started the firm 13 years ago.

Now with two shops promoting his wares, he is using the experience gained in racing to good effect with a high performance XR type top-end conversation kit for Evolution Sportsters aimed primarily at the road rider.

To show how these motors can improve things, he has mounted two engines in two bikes that emulate the famous, very classic XR Flat Trackers and named them the "Springsteen Replica" and "Parker Replica" after two of America's most respected dirt track racers.

The engines in both bikes are Harley-Davidson 45-degree four stroke twins with a bore and stroke of 88.8mm x 96.8mm. The compression ratio is 12:1 but the heads are all Shibazaki's own work, and make all the difference, turning the bikes into engines that can run with the best of the modern world.

The combustion chambers have been reworked to become "Double A" specification. Staying with the alphabet designation, the exhaust ports are D-shaped, while the inlets are just plain oval. Combustible mixture feeds down these from two 41mm Keihn flat slide carbs, while a stainless 2 into 2 exhaust takes the spent gases away.

Primary drive is taken care of by a 42mm belt drive running in a billet case, this being a merge of Sundance and Tony Hayward parts. The clutch is a Barnett K-line Kevlar item to handle the extra ponies, before finally feeding the drive along a 520 O-ring chain to the rear wheel.

When you examine the work that has been put into the heads, you can see the care and attention to detail and the quality of workmanship, almost guaranteeing the extra power. Tested on a dynamometer the motors will top 100bhp with a racing exhaust, but still give well above 90bhp with a street-legal exhaust fitted.

In both replicas the motors are mounted in a Mule Chassis Kit from the States. Richard Pollock was already getting C&J Frames to make oil-carrying, twin/mono shock, frames to house the motors, based on their racing frames for his own projects. His company, Cycle Specialities, now sells the chrome-moly frames, swinging arm and battery box and engine mounts as a kit, and also provide a list of things you can fit, leaving the rest up to you!

It is for this reason that the two finished bikes differ in specification. The rake of both is the same at 27 degrees and the wheelbase is also the same despite the difference in cycle fittings. The "Springsteen" bike has 42mm forks from a Suzuki GSX-R and "Progressive" rear suspension shocks, whilst the other machine has 50mm White Power inverted forks and an Ohlins rear monoshock fitted.

However, both use the same braking set up. At the front 320mm discs taken from a Yamaha YZF 750 gripped by four-piston calipers from a Kawasaki ZX7 provide the retardation. At the rear, a four-piston Grimeca caliper grips a 250mm cast iron rotor from "Storz."

The bikes then deviate again in the wheel set up. Although both run 18-inch rims front and rear, on the "Parker" machine the wheels are magnesium cast items, with

old-fashioned spokes being used to good effect on the other machine. Tyre-wise they both run 120/80 fronts and 140/80 rears from Bridgestone.

Petrol is contained in aluminum tanks while fiberglass is used for the tailpiece. Interestingly, despite the differences in the running gear, both bikes weigh in with an identical 189kg or approximately 415lb.

Having watched the man himself build the engines and painstakingly put the bikes together in between fettling the "Weapon" at Daytona, I could not resist a quick ride to see if they went as well as their minimalist looks suggested.

Thumbing the button, the exhaust on the Parker version emitted a gorgeous bark as the bike warmed up, unfortunately showing an oil leak, which was later traced to an incorrect drilling on the motor. Heading out on to the smooth Florida roads, I went in search of some of those elusive bends they keep well hidden.

Despite the tightness of the new engine, throttle response was instant and the motor pulled hard

Right: Top performance in every respect from all around the world. Ian Kerr

even with the imposed rev limits for a new motor. There was no transmission snatch.

When the bends finally appeared I heeled the bike in without a second thought, the Bridgestone Batlax's gripping well without anything coming remotely close to touching the road surface as the bike tracked precisely through the corners. Going back though the tightening curves the other way, it was a similar story although it would have been nice to have had time to try a few adjustments to the suspension and dial things in to my liking.

Although 50 miles is not a lot to judge things by, the riding position was comfortable enough, although the upright stance may well get a bit blustery at high speeds on open roads. However, it seems to fit well with the idea that the bike should be equally at home in town doing some shopping or posing, as on the open road exploring both the motor's and the bike's handling limits.

The all-too-brief ride showed this was well above a stock motor in respect of response and urge. The power is constant throughout the rev range with

little in the way of steps (later confirmed by a dyno reading). Shibazaki certainly knows his stuff

Left: The man himself — Shibazaki hand building an engine. Ian Kerr

Below: Sundance at sunset. Ian Kerr

Road King

From the time you sit on the deep luxurious padded seat you know that you are on, or should it be in, a real Harley, not a Japanese copy. Thumb the electric start and feel the bike lazily come to life and you know this is one of Milwaukee's finest steeds.

As the bike takes time to warm up, being carburated rather than injected, you have to listen to that familiar "potato potato" sound they tried to copyright, coming from the long low silencers running each side of the bike. The 45 twin finally comes off the choke and you can heel or toe the five speed gearbox into first and slowly let the cable-operated clutch out and feel the kick as the motor powers you away to whatever destination you may choose.

In this case it was to be Faakar See in Austria just above the Italian border, nearly a thousand miles across Europe, but that is just what this bike is designed to do, cover ground. Like the other bikes in the party, including another Road King, these Harleys would cover more miles in ten days than many sports bikes cover in a year — all without a hitch.

The well-apportioned seat, the generous wide sweeping stainless bars and the slightly forward footboards all give an arm chair-like riding position that makes mile-munching fun. You also appreciate the whole depth of paint and chrome from this position.

No highway pegs are fitted to this touring frame, so it was case of using the optional crash bars as footrests when the need arose for a leg stretch as the miles tripped by on the tank-mounted speedo.

There is nothing new with this model, the all-black 1,338cc Evolution motor is rubber-mounted and apart from a gentle feeling of vibes coming from somewhere, vibration is not something to worry about. A laptop computer carried in the panniers and cameras carried on the back all survived 2,000 plus miles without having their performance impaired!

The mirrors with the now classic slogan about distance etched into them gave faultless rearward vision and allowed a weather eye to be kept on tailgating German drivers who seem to see bikes as a national sport, despite the fact they could come off worse should it ever turn into a Harley contact sport!

You cannot deny the size of the bike or the weight, at 670+lb ready to rumble, but size matters not. The bike is fleet of foot — or, rather, 16-inch wheels — once

under way, and anybody that followed us through the Austrian passes may well have thought the bikes they were following were anything but Harleys.

There is no doubt that in 95 years Harley has learned something, taken criticism on the jaw, and responded, and this is a bike that handles within its design parameters. Those who have never grounded out a bike will love roundabouts and tight bends which can shower onlookers with sparks if you really want to, but it is the confidence it inspires in its handling that makes you do it!

I really like the Road King; it feels like a big motorcycle should, it sounds like a bike and it relaxes me. Going fast on twisty roads is a challenge and keeps your concentration honed, but it cruises with ease on all of Europe's roads without being forced to sit behind very much .

You can't ignore the fact it is expensive, but then again the big Harleys do not depreciate much. It is not that fast, but with speed cameras getting ever more plentiful, is that such a bad thing?

One last point, it is a Harley, and it does attract an awful lot of attention; you seem to get waved at by every kid and his mother as you thunder down the road. What you don't get is waves from other riders on Japanese and European

Below: Heel and toe gear change.
Ian Kerr

Bottom: The bike showing that it handles bends as well as open roads. Ian Kerr

bikes — it seems there is still prejudice in the world!

I rode back in one go, just stopping for petrol and the 35-minute trip on Le Shuttle. After 950 miles of almost continuous riding I was still in good shape, with just general tiredness being the order of the day. Total riding time was just 15 hours. There are not many bikes you could do that on and say the same about, after covering considerably fewer miles!

Honda once said, that you meet the nicest people on their bikes, which is probably true, but you meet an awful lot more with a Harley!

Left: "I really like the Road King; it feels like a big motorcycle should." Ian Kerr

Below: Footboards are more comfortable than pegs. Ian Kerr

Bottom: The Road King takes to the fields complete with panniers. Ian Kerr

Buell S1 Lightning

The gospel according to Erik Buell consists of two words, innovation and simplicity — innovation to build sports bikes that ultimately become an extension of the rider and simplicity by using fewer parts.

Buell, a former road racer, has had these goals since he built his first bike back in 1983, a pure racing machine designed to

compete in the AMA Formula One Class. The RW750 was a two-stroke, square-four rotary-valve machine, which was clocked at 178mph on the track. A production version was released but only one sold before the class was scrapped.

As an engineer for Harley-Davidson, it seemed to make sense to use one of their engines for his next product. An XR1000 power-plant was put into the next bike with rubber mounts to absorb the vibes, although the engine was

actually a fully stressed (sic) member of the frame.

This bike was the first to feature his "Uniplaner" engine mounting system to channel vibes in a vertical direction. It also debuted a rear-suspension system with the shock absorber being mounted longitudinally beneath the engine and working in reverse of a conventional compression system, instead using tension. During the 1987/88 50 of these bikes were sold before the engine supplies started to dry up.

When the 1203 Evolution motor appeared he saw this as an opportunity to start tuning the motor to go with the finely tuned handling capabilities of his previous bikes.

The existing chassis was altered to take the new motor and the RR1200 model saw the light of day. Once again it was a small-specialized production run of 65 bikes. One year later, in 1989, he introduced a two-seater version with the code RS1200 for those who liked to share the Buell experience; 102 of these were sold.

When Harley moved to a five-speed gearbox in 1991 so did Buell, revising the engine mounting points and fine tuning the chassis still further. Inverted 40mm forks joined the ensemble along with a solitary six-pot calliper at the front. The same year he started

designing and producing his own bodywork.

Two new models followed the re-design although production was still small scale and suffering from lack of capital. This creates low volume and high prices — a vicious circle. At the start of 1993 Harley bought 49 % of the Buell company allowing things to move up a gear to provide capital, marketing expertise, and ease supply problems for components.

With the large corporation backing him he could not lose and moved from very small scale to producing bikes on a much larger scale without losing the individuality of his machines, but being able to drop prices.

The first bike to come out of the new East Troy (Wisconsin) was the S2 Thunderbolt a truly awesome machine that is now being used by some police forces as well as being raced in its own series. A panniered more touring version, the S2T machine soon joined it.

Last year saw the launch of the S1 Lightning a bike that is very different but is true to the Buell philosophy in every respect. It is unconventional, a sports bike, and it captures the spirit of motorcycling. How do I know about the latter, well they let me ride it!

Visually the bike is striking thanks to its abbreviated bodywork, large circular Halogen headlight and triangulated chrome moly frame. It is stark, apparently basic but eye catching. The lines it must be said are spoilt by the large airbox on the offside and the silencer beneath the engine.

This is the lightest bike ever produced by Buell, weighing in at 425lb dry. The bike's mass is centralized and as low as possible in the geodesic-perimeter frame which keeps the centre of gravity low to aid stability and responsiveness. The wheelbase is short and stubby at 55 inches adding to the responsive handling characteristics.

The heart of the bike, though, is the Harley 1203 motor but in a very different state of tune to the Thunderbolt. Utilizing the skill of Harley engine tuner Gary Stippich, new cylinder heads were cast which combine the 883 combustion chamber shape with the larger valves of the bigger engine. At the same time the compression ratio was raised from 9:1 to 10:1.

Standard internals were replaced by "Screamin' Eagle" parts, such as a longer duration cam. The inlet tracts were modified, the carb re-jetted and 3lb in weight was shaved from the flywheels.

As part of these tuning mods, independent specialists were used to design the airbox and exhaust systems so that the bike met noise and emission limits. They succeeded, although appearance was obviously not part of their skills or brief!

These mods have boosted the power to a claimed 91bhp which is 15 more than the Thuderbolt and a massive 50 percent more than a stock engine. The beauty is that it is all usable power, allowing the bike to pull all the way from tickover to the redline; this bike never lacks power!

Twist the throttle and the large airbox gulps in air; the exhaust note rises and the horizon comes up in a constant ratio to the noise. Come out of a bend and see the open road ahead, feed the power in and the bike kicks you hard in the small of the back and brings the next corner into focus ready to test out the handling capabilities.

Once again, the rubber mounts allow the engine to jump up and down in a vertical plane so as not to upset the balance of the bike. Set it up by reducing speed take an appropriate gear and drop the bike in knowing that it will track straight and true with the inverted multi-adjustable WP forks from Holland controlling any ripples at the front. At the back, or should it be below, the single shock in tension does a similarly reassuring job for the back wheel.

Should you be late and in a hurry, the motor can be spun hard towards the 6,300rpm redline giving performance akin to its moniker. Gear changes from the five-speed box are always precise and cannot be hurried but they never missed. There is also no transmission snatch from the kevlar belt drive.

The chassis just gets on with things in the same predictable manner, even when the bike is being pushed hard. At the other end of the scale relaxed riding is also possible although the heat getting through to the rider can get uncomfortable.

On the freeway legal speeds are fine but the upright riding position (thanks to the straight bars) gets tiring at three figures, especially towards the 130mph top speed. Petrol consumption suffers as one might expect if high speeds are maintained or a heavy right hand is the order of the day.

Hoever, the seat is painful at any speed; it is too sparse as is the room for one's legs. Pillions do not come into the equation unless their rear end will perch happily on a cent!

The open straight highway will at least allow you time to appreciate the quality of the bike, from the deep lustre of the petrol tank to the neat alloy housing for the clocks and sensible well-made switch gear and controls that are very un-Harley.

Operation of everything from the wet clutch through to the brakes is smooth and gives plenty of feedback. The front brake is superb: the six pistons gripping the 13.4-inch disc with enough power

Left: Belt drive adds to the clean looks of the rear wheel area. Ian Kerr

Below: Rider ready to roll as undercover cop! Ian Kerr

to slow a Mack truck but with the finesse of a silk worm. A single cast-iron disc takes care of the rear gripped by a Brembo caliper.

The 17-inch Marchesini cast alloy rims shod with Dunlop Sportmax tires are well suited and aid the sure-footed feel of the bike, whether in a straight line or through the few bends that exist in Florida.

It is difficult after an afternoon spent with the bike to judge how it behaves under all types of road conditions. It is easy to criticize the bike for being cramped, as shorter riders may well not experience my problems.

What I can say is that Buell has created a bike for riders who believe a ride's sensory experience is more important than the final destination. There are now 140 of the 400 Harley dealers in the United States stocking the Buell Lightning at around $10,000 which makes it cheaper than the S2 Thunderbolt.

This is like no other Harley; it goes like stink, handles well and more importantly stops! It has its faults; it isn't perfect. It is a fast rude, ride. Then again, so is life and I love them both!

Right: Only the exhaust spoils the looks, Note the inverted forks. Ian Kerr

Buell S2 Thunderbolt

Eric Buell is the 44-year old President and Chief Engineer of the company that bears his name. His early years were spent racing motorbikes, his employment as an engineer at the Harley factory assisting in his efforts to remove skin from his knees.

What little other time he had, he spent making bikes based on his racing experience, the aim to produce a sports bike that extolled all the virtues of a racing machine. The designs were radical and attracted attention, they were also expensive! All the bikes produced had Harley engines, as one might expect, and eventually the factory recognized his efforts and purchased a 49 percent stake in his firm.

That was in 1993 and marked a major step forward. The factory in Troy, Wisconsin, 40 miles southwest of Milwaukee, had just 18 employees at the time; it now has around 100. But there are no fully automated production lines, each bike is virtually handbuilt.

Thanks to direct access to Harley parts and component prices, as well as a lot of the parts being redesigned, the overall production costs were brought-down and a Buell dropped from $15,000 in 1993 to a mere $11,900 for a 1995 spec S2-Thunderbolt.

Heart of the bike despite the sports tag is a stock Harley Sportster motor. The 1,203cc air-cooled Evolution twin is standard and complete with belt drive to the rear wheel. Where things differ is the way it breathes and flows the gases.

Power is boosted by means of a 2 into 1 exhaust system, the silencer of which looks like a car exhaust. This is tucked beneath the engine and fed by reworked exhaust pies that twist down the right hand side of the bike. Thanks to this rerouting the standard air cleaner was junked in favor of Harley's own performance air cleaner (marketed under the Screamin' Eagle brand name) to stop debris entering the 40mm Keihn carburetor.

These simple changes led to better breathing and to a claimed increase of 15 percent in the power stakes. One American magazine dynoed their test machine getting readings of 65bhp, a stock sportster giving 51bhp at the rear wheel. Add this to the weight saving of some 27lb and things begin to look good.

Unlike the original Buell RR1000 the Thunderbolt does not hide everything beneath acres of fiberglass What little bodywork there is gives the bike its flowing lines, leaving the spectator in no doubt about the heritage of the machine.

The 45-degree V-twin engine is hung beneath a Ducati-style round moly tube lattice frame, weighing just 26lb. This is mated to a box section aluminum swinging arm controlled by a single shock absorber mounted beneath the engine. The Dutch White Power unit runs longitudinally along and beneath it, so the mass is kept low for good handling characteristics. As one might expect, both damping and spring pre-load are fully adjustable.

This is not the whole story as the shock works "backwards." As the wheel moves upwards as it hits a bump, the shock extends, the whole system acting directly on the shock without a system of linkages.

At the front end things are pretty conventional, with 40mm inverted forks giving 4.7 inches of travel. Damping once again is adjustable in both directions.

Vibration has always been a motorcycle's biggest problem or at least how to isolate it from the rider. Rubber mounting the engine, handlebars and footrests are just some of the solutions that have been tried.

Below: The large air box is necessary to meet legislation but it can reduce legroom. Note also the longitudinally mounted shock absorber. Ian Kerr

Right: Panniers and screen allow comforts both on and off the bike.
Ian Kerr

Buell has come up with a very clever idea employing tie rods. Called the "Uniplanar" system it uses three tie rods and rubber mounts spaced at 120 degrees around the engine. In essence, the front forks are firmly fixed to the frame, the engine is connected to the rear wheel. The engine can vibrate up and down thanks to the rubber mounts, but the rods prevent sideways movement. Thus the vibration is isolated from the rider, further helped of course by the belt drive.

Certainly as far as my test of the bike was concerned, vibration was not part of the equation even with the bike continually being taken to the redline. The engine could certainly be felt working away beneath me but it did not intrude on my comfort.

The seat and tank unit is striking in appearance and the dual seat is very comfortable, The riding position is more upright than it appears and your knees fit snugly into the cutouts on the tank sides. Foot controls are back and up but not to pure sports bike levels.

The fiberglass actually hides a plastic gas tank beneath and also the separate oil tank beneath the left side panel. This requires oil levels to be checked by means of a dipstick.

Carbon fibre is used in some areas like the air filter cover, the

rear wheel cover and belt guard, but that's about it in an effort to keep the costs down. Small narrow panniers are now available color-matched to the bike's basic primary colors, although the carrying capacity is not that great.

The Buell is full of contra-dictions. On approach, it looks sleek and sporty; sitting astride it, it feels like a large comfortable tourer; startg the bike and you feel you have stepped back in time with ignition switch and choke inacces-sible beneath the tank.

When it fires, your ears tell you are on a Harley, thanks to the gentle thud of the engine beneath you. Blip the throttle and it sounds as if you are on a race bike: it really does try and confuse you.

Leaning forward, your hands fall to the adjustable two piece tubular handlebars. These are different to the current trend but well placed. They do retain the stock HD switch gear and levers. These wide robust items are fine on a "Tour Glide" but a bit over the top on a sports bike. Pull the clutch in and you then know why they need to retain them.

The gear change for the five-speed box thuds in as each of the five ratios are employed to swing the bike up to the redline with consummate ease.

When you look at accelera-tion figures against other more sportier machines, its 0–60mph times are very much on a par, even quicker in some cases. It does lose out on outright top speed though, with 128mph being the limit.

Above 2,500 revs the "Uniplanar " system really does smooth things out and you can just enjoy the cacophony as the engine works away. Despite Florida being full of straight roads, I man-aged to find a series of testing bends through which to push the bike. There was not a hint of flex or squirm from the chassis and, after I got over my initial caution-ary runs through the twists and curves, I went harder and deeper into the bends without any worrys. The Marchesini 17-inch cast aluminum wheels were shod with some grippy Dunlop Sporstmax radials (120/70 front and 170/60 rear) and these were reassuring in their grip on the concrete road surface.

The suspension was set up with the factory recommended settings and, for me at least, it was OK. This was just as well because the close proximity of the silencer looked as though hands may get burnt if suspension adjustments were carried out on a hot motorcycle!

The low weight distribution gives the 450lb bike a much lighter feel and the 25 degrees of rake at the front end make it quick and responsive. The wheelbase at 55 inches is actually shorter than a Fireblade! Nothing touches down thanks to a ground clearance of just over five inches, everything being well tucked up and out of the away.

With America's low speed limits and the bikes willingness to accelerate, I had to constantly keep a wary eye on the white-faced speedo or risk a ticket, which somewhat spoiled the fun. This is a bike that enjoys to be ridden hard and I had to content myself with dropping a cog for an overtake and pulling smartly past before just rolling off the throttle and letting the engine braking bring the speed back down.

The occassional high speed on deserted roads showed the fairing could do with a higher screen to lift the airflow higher over my helmet. It also showed the bike got smoother the faster it went.

The offside of the front wheel sports probably the biggest disc brake rotor on a standard road bike at a whopping 340mm. It is gripped by a six-pot caliper made in-house while the back makes do with a 230mm disc gripped by a Brembo calliper. Both the rotors are cast iron and fully floating.

As you may expect just from the specs, they are more than capable of stopping the bike, but

the front is wooden in feel thanks mainly to the large brake lever.

Mileage between petrol stops should be in the region of 180 to 200 miles from the five gallon tank. The comfort of the bike will certainly allow that in standard trim. Higher screens, which for taller riders like myself would be a must, and optional legs shields would certainly add to the comfort levels. My test period was not long enough to give an every-day account of the bike in all sorts of conditions; however, the Buell has an awful lot going for it — top class handling, suspension, wheels tires and so on. It is let down by poor finish in some areas like the inside fairings, no tool kit, and awkward placing of the ignition and choke.

The main thing against it for a lot of people will be the fact that it doesn't quite know what it wants to be, a sports bike, or tourer, or even both. In my humble opinion it needs to jump down off the fence and go pure sports.

Having said that I loved it. Judging by the number seen at Daytona, so do a lot of other people.

Police Harleys

Denis Chorlton

Though it would be hard to prove, it seems likely that the sheer growth of American cities in the first two decades of the 20th century led to the first use of motorcycles for police duties in America. The days of a law enforcer on a horse were drawing to a close. Early on, certain large cities — such as New York — had serious congestion problems with horse-drawn vehicles despite the introduction of streetcars and elevated railway systems. Actual speeding in cars and racing against each other in public places was reported as early as 1904 in St. Louis. It seems that by 1907 the small size and good performance of the still fairly basic machines came to the attention of many city police authorities, not yet for chasing wrong doers in cars, but for what was then a real hazard on the city streets — runaway horses. This supposedly led to the idea, of fitting left-hand throttles to Harley-Davidsons, as the police rider of the motorcycle would try to catch the bridle or reins of the runaway horse with his right hand. Of course, he could also direct traffic or even use his pistol while keeping on the move.

Among the first city authorities to change over from horses to Harley-Davidsons was Pittsburg in 1909; these would have been the Harley-Davidson Model 5, a 500cc belt-driven, single speeder with pedals, good for nearly 45mph. Cincinnati was another city that bought its first Harley-Davidsons for their police department in 1913. Though the V-twin was available by then, it is more likely they had the trustworthy and serviceable Model 5–35 single, because they were $60 cheaper. Options on all models were improving, with the choice of belt or chain drive and the rear hub clutch. Among many others, police forces as far apart as Dodge City, Kansas (1915) and Omaha, Nebraska (1920) were now riding Harley-Davidsons.

Milwaukee was not slow to see the good publicity to be gained by portraying upholders of law and order mounted on their machines. Beneficial results were seen in a drop in accidents and fatalities in areas where motorcyle police were deployed.

While Europe licked its many wounds, America saw the most prosperous years ever after World War One. There was a big increase in the standard of living, and wages and expectations rose to new heights. This soon led to much increased ownership of cars, which had at last, thanks to the introduction of mass production methods, become a lot more affordable. In turn this led to a greater need for motorized law enforcement of speed limits and orderly conduct on the roads. Very often states simply had no laws regulating the use of motor vehicles, and needless to say no drivers' examination. The number of highway fatalities rose at an alarming rate, and a 1926 Harley-Davidson advertising publication announced "Harley-Davidson will curb this tragic traffic slaughter." The states had to respond with more motorized police units and highway patrols, and this, of course, was expensive if a police authority had thought to purchase fleets of cars. The obvious answer was the motorcycle, fast enough to catch the cars of the day, easy to fix, and cheaper to buy, especially after World War One when large numbers of excellent army surplus machines were released on to the market for several years. These often unused Harley-Davidson 61cu in Model J solos or sidecar outfits were ideal for police use in every respect. For what was good enough for the military was certainly good enough for police use. Recognizing the demand, Harley-Davidson opened a fleet sales office especially for law enforcement agencies in 1926. As the police forces themselves were going through a traumatic time

Right and throughout chapter: A Buell Lightning with panniers housing rear warning lights. Ian Kerr

Below: 1950s Servi-Car. This is a postal vehicle which accounts for the emphasis on the mailbox in the photograph. via Roy Bacon

Harley-Davidson

there were many enquiries. The period 1920 to 1935 witnessed an unprecedented crime wave in America, the principal cause of which was the passing of Prohibition, that provided opportunities for huge profits in liquor-running, or bootlegging, as it was popularly termed. Unfortunately the rural sheriff out on his Harley-Davidson Model J, who had the unenviable task of trying to stop the illicit liquor trade, often found that the boot-leggers were using Harley-Davidson's powerful new 74cu in

Model JD, introduced in 1921. With a top speed quoted at 60–70mph they could certainly outrun police patrols.

Like the World War One army despatch rider, the early motorcycle policeman had to be tough, and was expected to go out at all hours, in all weathers. If it rained, all he generally had was an everyday black raincoat; if a storm was really bad, a rider might find a farmer's barn to shelter in. There were no windshields or legshields and no standard issue wet weather clothing in those first years. Most

riders wore a stout pair of knee-length leather boots (or puttees) — which also protected the legs from engine heat and the total loss oil system — a pair of gloves, belt and holster, though hats varied from stetsons and peaked caps to the British-style police hats. If he worked in one of the northern states, a patrolman might still be expected to get back on a horse for several months in the winter if the snow was really deep. It is worth mentioning that, in the early days, there was no motorcycle training; you had to prove you could ride

when you joined. When Maine State Police was founded in 1925, taking on 40 troopers, a rider was paid $25 per week, and was issued with a regulation law book, a pistol and, best of all, a Harley-Davidson motorcycle. Uniforms varied a great deal and what a rider wore was often down to personal preference. Once he left his base, a rider was on his own, though several systems were tried where a petrol station or store would hang out a red flag on a patrolman's route if he was required to telephone his headquarters. Some cities had installed police call boxes before World War One, where a patrolman could ring in at regular intervals. A police force in Nebraska even tried small police garages, strategically placed, connected by telephone and just big enough to take a Harley-Davidson sidecar outfit and two patrolmen. They were then ready to respond to emergencies.

Eventually it became necessary to introduce some form of standardization, and motorcycle officers were expected to telephone as near to hourly as possible to get their messages. Of course, they also relied on passing motorists to tell them about problems or any accidents or requests for assistance that might require their presence.

Patrolling the main roads, of which extremely few were paved,

then, there was always the danger of breaking down or being run down by a reckless driver or a drunk, not to mention breaking an arm or a leg taking a spill when traveling at speed. As an officer of the law out in the rural areas, a patrolman had to be all things to all people; he was not there just to

Below: Frontal view of a Buell Lightning showing alternate red and blue lights that sit at driver's mirror height; also low mounted siren to help handling. Ian Kerr

hand out tickets, but had to deal with ordinary crime, disputes, turn mechanic, midwife or even priest.

This cherished independence was not going to last much longer for radio, in the form of one-way, receive-only sets, began to appear on Harley-Davidsons in the early 1930s. Initially they were expensive, unreliable and cumbersome, with a massive curved funnel speaker tube which snaked out from beneath the tank, up onto the area in front of the speedometer.

By the mid-1920s 1,400 county and city police departments were riding Harley-Davidsons, and by 1930 this had risen to nearer 3,000. The Harley-Davidson dealers themselves did not necessarily relish the police contracts, for although the initial publicity was good, with rows of gleaming new machines lined up outside their dealership, the police authorities as bulk buyers had tight budgets and often inserted machine servicing clauses and fixed buy-back options. The machines themselves were not much different to the machines the ordinary rider could buy. Not many civilian extras were offered by the factory, let alone anything related to police work. One essential for the police was the speedometer, of which two makes were available for fitting —a Corbin Brown or a Johns-Manville;

they fitted on the tank top and were driven from the back wheel. The riders themselves often took their basic machine and added the extras they wanted at their own expense. Items such as red lights, spotlights, claxton horns and later sirens, mirrors or leather saddle bags (literally straight off the horse) for carrying paperwork, were down to the patrolman himself. It is not until the early 1930s that we see Milwaukee producing fitments for police use, and an actual police model — the R.

Of course, Harley-Davidson had to share the market with old rivals Indian and Henderson, particularly because certain police and highway patrol units preferred the smoothness of the four-cylinder models they produced, a type of machine which Harley-Davidson did even contemplate making themselves for a while. In the mid-1920s motorcycle demand had dropped considerably; by the late 1920s there was almost one car for every five people, so the police market assumed greater importance for all the manufacturers.

The Eastern and Western areas of America had quite different speed laws. For example, in 1937 the New York State law stated that "A speed of over 50 mph for a distance of over a quarter of a mile is considered operating a vehicle in a manner not

careful and prudent." The heavily populated northeast always had lower speed limits than the rest of the country. In contrast the south-west — Nevada for instance — posted speed limits only within city confines in 1974.

One big user of motorcycles, and one of the most famous US police units, the California Highway Patrol was established in 1929, although there had been the California Association of Highway Patrolmen since 1920. In the mid-1920s the state's vehicle registrations exceeded one million. CHP's first batch of Harley-Davidsons, 30 new JD models all finished in white with gold lining, was delivered from the Sacramento dealership in 1929. From 1926 the Harley-Davidson factory had offered white (and cream) as a color option to the more usual olive green. The white color may have suited the California Police as it would have had a high visibility factor, and there wasn't so much mud around to mess it up, as the riders rode all year round in the better weather conditions, but riders were expected to keep their machines clean. By the mid-1930s other color options included police black and police silver and combinations thereof. In the mid-1930s CHP changed their color scheme from all white, to black and white. Gone were the days of simply

Below: Customising Guru Arlen Ness
used the police theme to good effect on his
aptly named "Ness Patrol" seen here at
Daytona. Ian Kerr

leaving the machine in its original factory olive green. The new JD model was introduced in 1925 complete with new styling, lower seat height and enhanced performance. Added to its legendary reliability, it was popular with law enforcement agencies, with or without a sidecar. The CHP also had the next machine to come from Milwaukee: the 1929 and 1930 twin-headlight Model D, the first of the side-valve motorcycles which were to be so very successful. When production of this model stopped 45 years later, it had served with distinction as a mail carrier, tow vehicle, racing machine, military mount and police machine. In 1933 the California Highway Patrol designated Harley-Davidson as their official motorcycle throughout the state.

Another new side-valve model had appeared in the shape of the 74cu in VL. Among the first forces to order these were Buffalo, New York Police, who had 17, and the Milwaukee County Police Squad who had 15. This model had a very shaky start — literally! — as at speeds over 50mph the vibration was numbing. It was also plagued with a weak clutch, frail flywheels, poor lubrication and a long list of faults. Milwaukee was commendably quick to cure these deficiencies, though orders and customers and even dealers were lost as a result of this failure. The cure was a redesigned engine in a slightly deeper frame loop, and all the early machines then had to be converted, an expensive exercise. In its revised form, with its detachable cylinder heads, interchangeable wheels, bigger

brakes and tires, lower seat height
and more ground clearance, it
eventually had the makings of a
good machine. By 1931 production at Harley-Davidson had
dropped as the effects of the Great
Depression arrived at Milwaukee.
In 1933, only 3,703 motorcycles
came out of the factory.

Another disturbing trend
that began in the mid-1930s also
saw many states such as Maine
State Police begin to phase out
motorcycles in favor of just having
patrol cars. By the end of the
1940s all its Harley-Davidsons had
been sold at public auctions and
the department never returned to
two wheels. Michigan was another
state where the police decided to
use more patrol cars and sold off
all their motorcycles. On the plus
side the factory had been
reasonably successful in selling to
foreign police forces and by 1935
the law enforcement agencies of
cities as far apart as Rotterdam and
Shanghai were riding Harley-
Davidsons. Exports were essential
in this difficult period and accounted for perhaps as much as 50
percent of production.

During 1930–32 we see
Harley-Davidson taking a bigger
interest in police contracts, as for

Right: FLHTP. Ian Kerr

the first time the Harley-Davidson motorcycle order form of 1930 has a Police Special Speedometer listed; in 1931 a siren was on offer too. After this time it was more common to see police machines with one or more sensible factory fitted extras. By 1934 safety guards and pursuit lamps were specified, and in 1935 the ordering had been split into sections with Police Group 1 including the following: safety guards: jiffy stand, speedometer and siren. The Deluxe Police Group included everything in Group 1, plus lug-

gage carrier, stop light, steering damper, ride control, first-aid kit, and fire extinguisher. 1935 also was the first time a police model was referred to as such.

Another safety feature for police motorcycles was promoted in 1935 — a new reflective paint called Safety Silver which supposedly made the machine more visible at night. No two forces seemed to go for the same paint scheme or accessories in those days. It was all down to the personal preference of the department heads. There was

supposedly also a system whereby a police department could have its older motorcycles updated to the latest specification at the Harley-Davidson factory; this would certainly be one way to make the budget go further.

With the smarter machines, the riders themselves were now expected to look more professional, and the typical uniform was now more formalized with jodhpur-style breeches, boots, thigh-length coat, John Brown leather belt, cross strap with holster positioned for right-hand

Below Left: FLHTP, note Motorola radio on back. Ian Kerr

Below: The "Ness Patrol" made use of the best-known police livery, Black and White, so much so that a quick glance you may think it is a genuine service machine. Ian Kerr

cross draw, white shirt with black tie and police cap.

This standard police cap was a bone of contention between riders and the authorities right from the start, until the crash helmet was introduced, for although the caps were alright walking the streets or in a patrol car, when riding a motorcycle it was not posible to stop them flying off! The patrolmen were, however, expected to wear them at all times. Although there was no practical way to do so, their superiors said that without the cap they didn't look like police officers. Chin straps were tried, but they pulled at the rider's neck as the caps tried to come off. If the wire inside was taken out they could be reshaped and made to fit tighter but there was really no solution. Being out in all weathers, a rider might be covered in dust or smothered in mud within a few miles. A popular addition out of the rider's own pocket was a rubberized rain suit which could be kept in the saddle bags. These were used particularly if a rider had a court appearance, but these suits were frowned upon.

Another role that was emerging was the involvement of motorcycle police at public functions and riding displays. This didn't take away from the fact that they were in the front line, and fatalities were not uncommon either from traffic accidents or in pursuit of bank robbers or bootleggers. As cars were getting faster, the roads began to improve, too, and the police rider couldn't always catch those speeding cars. The introduction of the Knucklehead went some way in redressing the balance, and the

California Highway Patrol was using these models in 1936. Most of the work still involved curbing speeding — something achieved just by making themselves visible, that was often enough to slow traffic right down. By then there were so few motorcycles on the road that if a motorist saw one in the distance, it was almost sure to be a patrolman. Patrol cars were still largely unmarked, so the motorcyclist was a very visible reminder of a police presence. The dull traffic and parking assignments slowly began to take precedence over the more exciting aspects of a motorcycle policeman's job, just as a practical new machine arrived from Harley-Davidson factory.

The world of urban motorcycle police work took a new and momentous turn in 1932 when Harley-Davidson introduced the three-wheeled Servi-Car. This was powered by the 45cu in side-valve and had a three-speed gearbox with a reverse gear, which made it very maneuverable. It was not initially designed for police use, but as a useful machine for garages (it was fitted with a tow bar) or for small commercial carriers using its big rear box. However, the police departments of America soon made it their own. A 1937 Harley-Davidson advertisement declares "Reduce traffic congestion with

Servi-Cars!" It shows a patrolman in Beaumont, Texas, marking tires with chalk, so he can come back later and book any cars which had been there over the allotted time. This had normally been done by several officers on foot or a two-man sidecar outfit, but with the easy-to-handle Servi-Car, a single officer could cover far more streets, quicker. Among many forces that took to this new design in 1936 were Denver, Colorado and Austin, Texas.

The Servi-Car design was quite simple, using the front forks and engine from a normal solo machine, with the addition to the rear frame of a fairly complex layout using both leaf and coil springs supporting the large metal carrying box. The rear carrying box was offered in several sizes. The forward opening lid could be upholstered to carry passengers, and twin grab handles were provided. Elegant rear lights and stylish rear chrome bumper were fitted. The back axle was a converted car design with chain drive through a differential to both rear wheels.

In 1935 a new constant-mesh gearbox was added and a strengthened axle. Early models had a single brake from the VL, but in 1937 brakes were fitted to each hub; at the same time a little restyling took place with an apron

Below: Fully equipped and ready to go the police Harley is a large and imposing machine by anybody's standards. This is a Milwaukee Police FXRP; note siren under fairing. Garry Stuart

Below: Chicago Police Servi-Car. This is a late-build version from thew 1960s with a fiberglass body. Many police Servi-Cars ended up doing parking patrols when they had finished active service. Garry Stuart

• Harley-Davidson •

extending from the bottom edge of the box to the rider's seatpost. Chromed hubcaps of a bigger size were added in 1938, as well as a larger and possibly more effective muffler, and the chain drive was enclosed. The company went so far as to offer the option of having the gear change on the right-hand side and the throttle on the left, to accommodate the police departments. This meant the police parking enforcement officers could mark tires with their chalk sticks right-handed and still keep moving. A great many accessories were eventually offered, one of the first fitments being the receive-only radio in 1936, and the front fender-mounted siren. Police agencies used the model without the tow bar which was designated the GA. The Servi-Car evolved steadily through the late 1930s into the 1940s, sharing many of the improvements made on the solo motorcycles. In fact some forces cut down their solo motorcycles and ordered more Servi-Cars.

In 1939 the rear body was offered in a larger size and the rear suspension was modified to reduce body roll; by 1940 Servi-Cars saw many detail changes — the rear axle was strengthened again with an increased thickness of metal around the chain opening to reduce the likelihood of damage should the chain break. The clearance of the chainguard was also increased, the rear brakes were redesigned with cast drums (instead of pressed) being introduced and a simpler method of brake adjustment. The battery box was moved to give more room for the clutch arm. Most

Overleaf: Chicago Police FL; note fiberglass windshield. Garry Stuart

importantly, in 1941 a new rear frame was introduced and the axle became welded tube rather than riveted tube; the front wheel and brake from the VL was fitted, tires were standardized at 5.00 x 16, and the compression ratio was increased to 4.75 to 1. Though production was never large, 1,159 Servi-Cars were built in 1941, the highest total so far. The figures then dropped because of war production, but picked up again after it was over. The police still continued to use sidecars alongside Servi-Cars.

Meanwhile, in another part of the Harley-Davidson factory, engineers were secretly working on prototypes of military Servi-Cars with shaft drive, and using the Knucklehead engine unit or the flat twin engine from the XA.

Though civilian production had been cut right back once the big military contracts were being worked on, the Servi-Car specification changed again in 1942 when bigger fenders were fitted along with new rear lights and some small detail changes, such as the shape of the rear grab handles. The smaller body option was discontinued. The bigger style of box had been particularly suitable for the police — for instance an accident investigation officer could easily carry all the

equipment he needed. The rear facing panel of the box was usually signwritten with the word "Police," and the lid had the easy-opening bar. Due to its tractability, it also started to be seen more on processions and ceremonial events.

The first installation of two-way police radios was in the mid-to late 1940s when two Wisconsin police departments had them fitted on their Servi-Cars. These installations were probably chosen because of the space available inside the box for the shock-mounted isolation these bulky units needed. It was jointly developed by Harley-Davidson and RCA. On the early models the speaker and controls were mounted by the rider's left hip, and if a call came through the officer had to stop and use the microphone in the box. Radios were almost universal on the Servi-Car by the 1960s, the later Motorola "DispatcherRadiophone" two-way radio being a popular option with speaker and microphone on the handlebars.

In the 1960s, police forces from Richmond, Virginia, to Omaha, Nebraska to Tampa, Florida, ordered the Servi-Car.

Since their invention in Oklahoma City in 1935, the parking meter had spread like a rash accross the US. These meters

needed constant attention to be checked and emptied regularly, and what better vehicle to do this job than the Harley-Davidson Servi-Car.

In 1951 the spoked rear wheels were exchanged for solid car type wheels with chrome hubcaps. Hydraulic brakes were also fitted to the two back wheels. The next year the Servi-Car become the only production model then powered by the venerable 45cu in (750 cc) side-valve engine. During 1958 the big twin springer forks were replaced with hydraulic ones fitted to the Hydra-Glide; these had been listed as an optional extra, for $10.25, since 1952. The box grab handles were deleted.

Another first; in 1964 the Servi-Car became the first Harley-Davidson to be fitted with an electric start (a year before the Electra-Glide was announced). The electric start machines were given the model designation GE, and made life a lot easier for the women officers now working as meter maids. Following on from this, in 1966, the generator went in favor of an alternator to handle the extra loads imposed by the electric start and all the electrically driven police fitments. By this time the police had virtually become the only customer for the Servi-Cars. The alternator was mounted on

the downtube of the frame and hidden in a metal pressing.

Further progress caught up with the Servi-Car in 1967 with introduction of the glassfibre box, made by the Tomahawk company, a practical move which molded the fenders into the whole, and lasted until the end of Servi-Car production in 1973. A special police speedometer was always an option on the later models, as were the twin red lights either side of the headlamp, which were the same as on the solo. The windshields with canvas aprons were a popular fitting, especially in the colder states; these were usually signwritten with the word "Police." Though most machines were delivered white or with the tank picked out in blue or black, the all-over police silver remained an option. They often had a rotating emergency beacon mounted on a telescopic tube plus extra rear facing lights. One of the final improvements was the fitting of the big twin disc brake on the front wheel, with the ugly "banana" type caliper.

Above all, being so stable, the Servi-Cars enjoyed a good safety record; officers of the Cincinnati Police Department won a national safety contest in 1958 for a full year's operation without accident. The last few Servi-Cars

were assembled in early 1974, they served on until the end of the 1970s.

To make the motorcycle truly useful to the police departments, it was essential to improve radio communication. Receive-only radios had been installed in squad cars as early as the end of the 1920s, and on motorcycles from the early 1930s. Price of course was always a factor; the first ones listed by Harley-Davidson in 1935 cost $75, and consisted of a large heavy receiver on the rear carrier. Bearing in mind the bumpy largely unpaved roads of the day and being fitted above the rear wheel of a vibrating motorcycle with no suspension at the rear, they were lucky to receive a signal at all. These early tube radios were both cumbersome and fragile, and it is not until after the war that we see the first really practical sets appearing on motorcycles.

Despite the early drawbacks, the California Highway Patrol took delivery of their first Harley-Davidson equipped with receive-only radio in October 1938. Manufactured by RCA, it was fitted as an extra and cost $135. The speaker, which was by now much smaller, fitted behind the headlight and looked like a spotlamp facing the wrong way. In this case it was tuned to 2,414 kilocycles to pick

up the Ventura, California, police bulletins. Michigan State Police riding Model 80 Harley-Davidsons, was another user from this period. However, there was no way the station could know if its message had been received, and inevitably there would be "dead spots" where nothing would be heard. The rider had to be within a certain distance of the transmitter, always depending on terrain and weather conditions. When they were about to send a message, a long tone signal would be transmitted by the station. Once the patrolman heard this he would pull in, turn off his engine, turn up the volume and wait for the message which would be repeated several times. If it were serious, he might look for a telephone. By 1940 earphones, clamped to the rider's head, had become an option

The only good thing to come out of wars are the technology leaps, and World War Two certainly brought improvements in radio communication. The first two-way radio for solo machines appeared in 1948; this was still rather large and weighed 27lb, fitting to the motorcycle in the position usually taken by the saddlebags, measuring 24in by 10in by 8in and held either side of the back fender in special steel frames which were shock-mounted

• Harley-Davidson •

with rubber isolators, which supported and protected the equipment like safety guards. The transmitter was on the right and the receiver on the left, with a small 18in whip antenna. The other antenna option was screen type which projected out horizontally over the rear light. The radio operated on the 152-megacycle band, or VHF Hi-band. A speaker box and squelch controls were mounted on the handlebars above the headlight, and a press to-talk microphone fitted next to it.

The main complaint about these radios was, of course, the loss of the carrying space on the motorcycles; for the rider had nowhere even to carry even a pair of gauntlets. He still kept his ticket book in the inside pocket of his leather jacket. There are photographs showing some forces with pannier bags fitted outside the radio fittings.

Certainly a big improvement on the earlier models, the new radios still had reliability problems, and transmission still tended to drain the six-volt system very quickly. To avoid flattening his battery the officer was forced to keep the engine running fast. This, of course, made his voice hard to hear. The power drain while receiving was also considerable, and it was recommended that the radio was turned off prior to

starting the engine. As it was a tube design, it took half a minute or so for the set to warm-up after it had been switched on before it was ready for use. Riders had to be aware of keeping the engine on fast idling when parked to make sure the battery was well charged in case they wanted to use the radio.

In 1949 the Harley-Davidson factory order form listed more police radio options, with models from General Electric, Motorola and RCA. Due to inflation the prices had started to rise

dramatically with the receive-only listed at $225, and the two-way Motorola Uni-Channel Sensicon at $530. This particular system had the speaker on the handlebars but the microphone on the petrol tank between the saddle and the ignition switch. Also listed for the police models was the Radio Application Kit, which consisted of the very necessary items such as radio interference suppressors, a special generator, a 44-amp battery, and special regulator for ensuring they got the best from their radio installations. These kits

were $92 for the solo and $43 for a Servi-Car. With the Knucklehead giving way to the Panhead in 1948, the prices of the machines themselves had recently risen by 30%. When you consider that the basic motorcycle itself, a 1949 FL, might be over $700; with full police equipment the total could double to as much as $1,500. Despite the costs, it was not long before nearly all police machines had a radio as standard.

For nearly ten years not much changed, Harley-Davidson listed another two-way radio by a firm called LinkVetric alongside the Motorola type, but the Link Vetric doesn't seem to have been used often. However, the transistor revolution was just starting, gradually replacing all the tube (valve) technology. Motorola launched their revolutionary "Dispatcher Radiophone" in June 1957, which instead of being an adapted car design, was specifically for motorcycle use. Because the FL Hydra-Glide models still had a rigid rear end, the new radio was initially designed to fit on the front forks. It was smaller and weighed half as much as the previous model, and because transistors do not use the power that the tubes did, it was not draining the motorcycles system as much; consequently more power was available, giving up to 50 percent more volume. This allowed good reception at speed, so the patrolman no longer had to stop. With the handlebar-mounted speaker with squelch and volume on the top and the press-to-talk microphone next to it, the new system was easy to use. This new design coincided with the almost universal adoption of wind

shields on police models, which was good for the rider and also kept the worst of the weather away from the unit. Wind noise was now greatly reduced and better weatherproofing had been developed for both the speaker and microphone. The "Dispatcher" cost $635, and was also fitted to the later Servi-Cars, utilizing space available in the rear box, with the speaker, controls and microphone on the handlebars in the same position as the solo.

The following year saw the arrival of the rear-sprung Duo-Glide that allowed the new Motorola in its weatherproof plastic box to be mounted on the rear rack over the rear mudguard — back where it started. Having freed the fender sides, streamlined plastic panniers were now offered in place of the traditional leather saddlebags, available in either black or white. The patrolman had storage space once more.

During 1966 Harley-Davidson ceased offering the option of radios fitted on its police machines; this now became the purchaser's responsibility, and radio equipment had to be ordered direct from the manufacturers. This coincided with the recent upgrade at Harley-Davidson to 12-volt electrics. The Motorola company produced a 6–12V conversion kit for the older models.

Today's radios are both smaller and lighter with far more power than their predecessors and have a multi-channel capability with scan. The rider has the boom microphone attached to his helmet and can conduct communication and receive broadcasts without taking his hands off the controls or his eye off the road.

During the war years 1941–45, production of civilian motorcycles was greatly reduced, fuel was rationed, speed limits were lowered to conserve fuel and rubber, even production of civilian cars and small trucks was curtailed. Certain metals — such as the nickel alloy Harley-Davidson used for engine cylinders — were impossible to get and substitutes had to be found. The models themselves saw virtually no changes in these years. Milwaukee limited the colors available to black, gray and silver, but by 1944 it was gray only, all optional chromed parts, such as wheels rims and safety bars, were painted.

Police contracts had now become a major part of Harley-Davidsons business, with well over 3,000 law enforcement agencies riding on Harley-Davidsons by 1940. They were not affected by the fuel rationing, anf if they had less traffic duty, their workload had increased elsewhere; some forces had to recruit more motorcycle patrolmen. Indeed, there were many extra duties — such as keeping an eye on military production plants and escorting convoys of munitions and war material in transit on the highways. In states such as California, police patrols were also expected to watch the coastline and were even provided with extra equipment in the form of an army steel helmet, gas mask and Thompson submachine gun. The Federal government had to allow small batches of Harley-Davidson police machines to be made, but only under special rules which required a great deal of paperwork. For once the dealer network was pleased to see the police contracts, as they could not get civilian machines to meet demand and the police contracts kept their workshops ticking over. In 1943, for instance, the War Production Board allowed 137 police departments to purchase new machines from Harley-Davidson.

After the war there was an understandably high demand for new machines, not only from the public but also from the law enforcement agencies. Again, the export market was wide open, with little competition and Harley-Davidson sold police machines to Canada (Royal Canadian Mounted Police) Mexico, South America and several other foreign countries.

Below: Another view of a Milwaukee Police FXRP. The street sign, slightly obscured, is for Janneau Avenue where the Harley-Davidson factory is situated.
Garry Stuart

The standard police machine of the period was the low-compression 74cu in FL, which had all the characteristics necessary for its duties: good low-speed handling with strong clutch and drive train, and a good top speed of 80mph even burdened with all its police fittings. Altogether it was a sturdy and dependable machine that could be driven many miles without much maintenance. Police fittings had not changed much in this period; they included safety bars back and front, pursuit lights, siren, first aid kit, fire extinguisher, front mudguard police sign, receive-only radio, windshield, special speedometer on which the rider could freeze the reading at the push of a button on the handlebars; and to suit some forces the hand gear change was often moved to the right-hand side.

By the end of the 1940s the Hydra-Glides models began to appear, heralding the first change in Harley-Davidson suspension in over 40 years — telescopic forks. For those like the police patrolman, who had to spend many hours in the saddle running traffic, the new forks plus the rubber-mounted handlebars, aided by the sprung seatpost and 5 x 16 inch tires, made the new model a popular choice from the comfort viewpoint. The very early ones were not without their problems,

however, and the forks leaked oil until the factory modified them.

The new forks vastly improved the look of the machine itself and were often chromed. Because of the new forks, attractive new streamlined one-piece fenders were fitted.

In 1952 the foot shift became a reality, though hand shift was still available, and was still favored for law enforcement use, as it left riders with a hand free to give traffic control signals if necessary. Hand shift remained available as late as 1976.

When the Indian factory closed in 1953, Harley-Davidson became the only major manufacturer of police specification motorcycles in the United States, althhough the 80cu in Indian Chiefs soldiered on for another ten years with some forces like the Pennsylvania State Police, until they were replaced by Duo-Glides in 1962–63.

There were new options for the 74cu in Panhead; these included a standard high compression for Highway usage or low compression engines and gearing

for city use. This model cost $1,015 in 1954, and a further option of chromed parts like the muffler, wheel rims and safety bars, etc, added another $75.75. A windshield — available in clear or tinted blue or red — would cost a further $23. Surprisingly, not all police motorcycles were delivered with radios, and it was not unusual to see the genuine Harley-Davidson accessory tooled leather saddlebags fitted to either side of the rear fender.

Evocative of police work in general, the rear wheel fitting siren

was the most popular with officers, as the front fender mounting tended to be just too close to the riders' ears for comfort, plus there were odd cases of them exploding! Problems were encountered if a siren were not adjusted to the correct tire condition or pressure; for instance, a new tire would expand during a long run at high speed, suddenly setting off the siren. The siren itself was operated by the rider's left heel on a cable-operating lever. This pivoted the siren until its drive shaft touched the rear tire, which started it spinning. To produce the characteristic "wailing" sound, the rider had to depress and release the foot lever. The rear mounting did have its drawbacks, however, as the siren could become inoperable when clogged with road dirt or snow, and could even freeze solid with ice in winter. At least fitted at the rear the siren wasn't so deafening for the rider should he have to respond to a code-three (emergency response) call. Electronic sirens which could be fitted above the headlamp or on the safety bars began to be seen in the mid-1970s, but they were not an official Harley-Davidson police option until around 1984.

The riders themselves started to get fiber safety helmets from 1954 onwards and the flyaway Garrison-style hat problem was

resolved at last. Members of the California Highway Patrol received theirs in 1956, and within a few years they became universal, greatly reducing head injuries.

Rider safety was becoming more of an issue; machines were inspected every day, and riders were expected to keep them clean. If an officer did drop his machine, this was treated as a traffic accident and a one-day suspension could be imposed in some forces. The biggest hazards for patrolmen were considered to be railroad tracks, big dogs and snow.

Patrol rider training became more organized in the 1950s and 1960s with many police forces instigating in-service training for new recruits to build up their rider skills. This meant practice runs accompanied by experienced officers over potentially dangerous surfaces such as railroad and streetcar tracks, cobblestones and brick paving. As well as this, there was slow speed maneuvering between cones to practise clutch control. As riders could be called upon not only to escort funerals in many areas, they might have to take part in slow-moving parades, riding at marching pace or less — stalling or dropping the machine in front of crowds of spectators was not an option. A new officer would be taught how to overtake a car, avoid a vehicle's blind spot and how to lay the bike down and slide on the safety bars to avoid an accident. After three years of riding a patrolman was considered experienced.

Another positive thing to come out of Harley-Davidson police motorcycle contracts were the display teams, and several large forces had very proficient drill

285

teams that could be called upon for special events or local Thanksgiving parades. Officers would wear smart dress uniforms, often with white gloves. The only technical problems for the drill teams were the slow riding, constant slipping of the clutch without wobbling, and not letting the engine backfire; this was practiced until the riders had perfected it.

The parades and drill teams presented a positive and popular image of the police to the public, and, by association, Harley-Davidson, whose machines they were riding. For example, Salt Lake City had a proficient drill team in the middle 1930s; Long Beach, California had one in the 1940s; Miami Beach had one in the 1950s; Louisville in the 1980s and there were many more across the country.

In 1958 the venerable FLH and FL models were fitted with rear suspension and re-christened the Duo-Glide. There had been some reported cases of high-mileage police FLs suffering breakages in luggage racks and the metal fittings needed to carry the police radio equipment. This was put down to the vibration inherent in the rigid rear end. In fact, the new hydraulically dampened coil springs, which would have worked

• Harley-Davidson •

Below: Michigan Police FLHTP.
Simon Clay

Overleaf: Another Sturgis scene — an FLHTP sits alongside a Kawasaki.
Simon Clay

more efficently in a vertical position, could be said to be fitted in such a way as to not hinder the pannier fitments which had become so popular with both the police and civilians. Not only did the new model have the swinging arm and rear shocks, it also had a new hydraulic rear brake, stronger transmission and clutch, and a police option of a new larger oil tank, though the downside was a weight penalty of 50lb.

Harley-Davidson still offered the police the chrome safety guards, the front one being a new one-piece design, and there are even a few photographs of police machines with the optional factory supplied white wall tires.

Despite being upholders of the law, patrolmen were well known for playing tricks on each other. If one rider should leave his machine unattended momentarily, his colleague would reach over and turn his radio up to full volume, so when the other rider returned and started his machine he would get a blast of sound. Another favorite when out riding was to creep into an unsuspecting colleague's blind spot, switch off the ignition for a moment, pump the throttle a few times and then turn the ignition back on. The resulting backfire would most certainly get the attention of the other rider!

In the mid-1960s there was a countrywide boom in motorcycle sales with Triumph, BSA and Norton expanding their dealerships and the Japanese manufacturers eager to sell their smaller machines. During 1965 the FLH and FL Duo-Glide models received electric starters, becoming the first of the Electra-Glides. This model was

immortalized as a police mount by Hollywood eight years later, in the film *Electra-Glide in Blue*, about a patrolman in Monument Valley.

The push-button starting meant a more powerful battery, which, in turn, necessitated the welcome change to a 12-volt system. A new aluminum primary casing now accommodated the starter, the oil tank was moved to the left side of the machine and there was a new frame to suit these changes.

The Harley-Davidson electric start was another positive step

for the police rider, who had long complained of the problem of making a fast getaway when in pursuit of speeding cars. Patrolmen who wanted to start their engines in a hurry tended not to bother if it did not start first kick.

As with earlier upgrades, the new model became substantially heavier than the previous one; more power was obviously needed as were better brakes to stop it. Significantly, it was nearly $150 more expensive, and price was always a factor with police contracts. The FLH was

approaching twice the price of a heavy duty police sedan, and this ultimately left the way open for the Japanese and Italian competition to challenge the Harley-Davidson police monopoly.

The 1965 Electra-Glide was the last year of the Panhead engine which had served faithfully for 18 years. For the next 18 years the power for the big twin was going to come from what was termed the Shovelhead — not an entirely new engine but at least a redesigned top end. This engine claimed to supply over 10 percent of the extra

289

power required, but riders had to wait until the early 1970s for a front 10-inch disc brake. Even so these brakes had trouble coping with police usage and had a bad reputation for fading and wearing out very quickly.

With the fully equipped police model now weighing a possible 800lb (363kg), the Electra-Glide was less than athletic, and it was just as well that actual high speed pursuit of offenders was becoming actively discouraged — it was safer to radio ahead. Police departments had entered the realm

of department liability, and the reality of high cost insurance and litigation and settlement. Police Harley-Davidsons were now used more for auto accident investigation, parking violations and ceremonial escort duties. In the 1960s it was considered a prestigious assignment to be a police motorcyclist, and there was even extra money in the form of hazardous duty pay from most forces. The larger customers, such as the California Highway Patrol, had over 400 motorcycles on their inventory in 1963.

Complacency was always a Harley-Davidson trait and little was done about the significant complaints regarding vibration, suspension and the control fittings, and by 1972 the California Highway Patrol was testing both Honda 750s and Moto Guzzi 850s. It was an indication of the very tough times ahead.

There were major changes coming with the acquisition of Harley-Davidson by American Machine and Foundry (AMF) in 1969, the growing challenge of foreign manufacturers daring to

• Harley-Davidson •

look at the traditional Harley-Davidson police market, let alone all the new government legislation regarding noise, emissions and safety. There were also serious questions being raised regarding the quality control at the factory and the growing reputation of Harley-Davidsons for breaking down and leaking oil. The image of the traditional Harley-Davidson rider had also taken a turn for the worse with publicity of some unsavory motorcycle gangs.

Milwaukee no longer seemed interested in the law enforcement contracts and the usual "take-it-or-leave-it attitude towards loyal police departments was beginning to wear very thin. They were going to need loyalty like theirs to survive.

Enter Kawasaki, who actually went to the California Highway Patrol in 1975 and asked them what sort of police motorcycle they would like, knowing that they were a tough customer. If they could satisfy them, other police forces would not be far behind. A plant was set up in Lincoln, Nebraska, from which came the Kawasaki KZp 1000 (61cu in) Police Special, which, after a few teething problems, developed into a first class police machine. It was light and powerful with superb acceleration from a five-speed gearbox up to

130mph, and significantly for Harley-Davidson needed far less maintenance, suiting the areas where machines were expected to do high mileages. With Kawasakis recording mileages of 40-50,000 miles before needing more than oil and plug changes, compared with the Harley-Davidson which required a full checkout after only 2,500 miles, the rising cost of maintenance was probably a deciding factor as police departments changed their allegiances.

Los Angeles Police Department chose the shaft drive Moto Guzzi 850 (52cu in) as their official police mount in 1974. To suit police requirements they were fitted with windshield, footboards, safety bars, chrome fenders, large comfortable saddle and the usual lights and siren etc. The Moto Guzzi also had an interesting integrated braking system which, when the foot brake was pressed, applied 70 percent braking to the rear brake and 30 to the front. Despite being popular with patrolmen throughout the 1970s they were replaced by the more powerful and reliable Kawasakis.

Police markets continued to be lost to foreign competition and natural wastage, as the trend towards more patrol cars continued. This was often seen by the authorities as an improvement as fewer officers were hurt in accidents and cars could be used in all weathers for various tasks. Many states had only used their motorcycles in the summer, the machines standing idle the rest of the time. Another factor was that the best use of a bike's capabilities was dependent on individual rider skill, not so much the case with cars.

• Harley-Davidson •

Below Left: Livonia Township WL of 1941. Note receive-only radio at rear and night-stick. Garry Stuart

Below: It wasn't only the regular police forces that used Harleys. This is a former Military Police WLA (see Military Harleys chapter. Garry Stuart

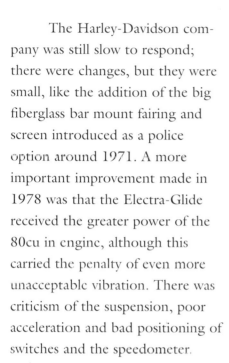

The Harley-Davidson company was still slow to respond; there were changes, but they were small, like the addition of the big fiberglass bar mount fairing and screen introduced as a police option around 1971. A more important improvement made in 1978 was that the Electra-Glide received the greater power of the 80cu in engine, although this carried the penalty of even more unacceptable vibration. There was criticism of the suspension, poor acceleration and bad positioning of switches and the speedometer.

Fortunately the Mid-West and, particularly, the Eastern police agencies where machines tended to cover smaller mileages remained loyal to Harley-Davidson and less open to Kawasaki.

The Harley-Davidson management buy-out from AMF in 1981 meant a new start for the company, but there was no let up in the complaints leveled at the cumbersome 80cu in police model compared to the popular Kawasaki. Towards the mid-1980s police sales were running at approximately 5 percent of Milwaukee

production, focusing on the FLH chain or belt, and the FLHT enclosed-chain models.

With a quarter of their police customers already gone, old lessons had to be relearned by the Harley-Davidson sales staff, in that police sales generated good publicity for civilian sales, and every patrolman mounted on a Harley-Davidson was an advertisement for the company. Sales staff encouraged the dealers to offer the police not only a straight-price bid for police contracts (which they were bound to lose) but also

leasing bids and a buy-back bid. This had the advantage of giving the dealer a good used bike for which there was always a market. Despite their money problems, Harley-Davidson had a new engine on the drawing board, one which would ultimately re-establish the company's prestige: the Evolution model.

At the same time, the police themselves were learning all over again about the attributes of motorcycles. As cities and urban areas became more congested with the sheer volume of traffic, the maneuverability of motorcycles put the police motorcyclist at a distinct advantage. The public began to ask questions about the response time of police cars; at least a patrolman on a motorcycle stood a good chance of getting to the scene of a crime or traffic problem in time to do something about it. With better response times the value of a motorcycle-mounted officer was once more becoming a viable proposition. Many forces that had disbanded their motorcylce units in previous years began to look closely at the figures of studies carried out on how cost-effective bikes could be. These figures showed that motorcycle units covered more miles faster, issued more tickets, investigated more accidents, were seen to be effective and were respected by the public.

Many forces that had completely disbanded their motorcycle squads eventually returned to motorcycles — such as St. Louis, Missouri, that had lost its motorcycles in 1958 and bought Harley-Davidsons again in the early 1970s or the Cincinnati Police Department which had last used motorcycles in 1961, and came back to on Harleys in 1993. The Michigan State Police did so after an even longer absence. It had stopped using motorcycles in 1941-42 and only climbed back on Harley-Davidsons in 1994, albeit in far smaller numbers.

That most crucial of police customers, the California Highway Patrol, was back testing Harley-Davidsons again in the mid-1980s, after an absence of nearly ten years. These were the Evolution-engined FXRP (Pursuit Glide) and the FLHTP (Electra-Glide), with the new rubber-mounted engine, belt final drive and five-speed transmission. The CHP was impressed at the many improvements, though there was still plenty of room for criticism, which had the positive affect of keeping the pressure on the Harley-Davidson designers. Ultimately the CHP purchased 183 FXRPs and though Harley-Davidson probably made a loss on this bid, it provided proof that the company was back in the game with a viable machine.

The riders themselves were pleased to have the choice once more of riding a real American machine, and the gamble paid off for Harley-Davidson. Orders from other departments such as Salt Lake City and Kansas City followed as a result. Gone were the days when a police Harley-Davidson could be considered unsuitable for police work, and by 1991 the improved FXRP model, with its distinctive fiberglass fairing, had a new frame and forks, engine mounting system, instruments, carburetor, seat, starter, alternator, clutch and exhaust system. The usual police fitments on the FXRP were still there, with a couple more sophisticated additions like the advent of the radar gun fitted behind the rider's right knee and the PA system with the microphone on the right side of the fairing. Machines could be fitted with extra strobe lights for better visibility and the rider also carried flares in the panniers. The FXRP model was discontinued in 1994. Meanwhile the FLHTP had the new adjustable air suspension back and front for comfort, with an anti-dive system on the front forks for safety. The front frame had been modified to improve steering and balance making the motorcycle as easy to handle as a much smaller machine, along with the solo-suspended air

Right: Flying the flag, but with all the extra lights this Harley look more like a Xmas tree. Milwaukee Police FLHTP. Garry Stuart

saddle and adjustable footboards that did much to reduce rider fatigue. Other additions were a larger battery and 5.2-gallon petrol tank, which gave extra range. The many instruments and controls were praised for being particularly well set out and accesible.

Although they have not changed as much as the machines, the riders themselves are a different breed from the patrolmen of the 1960s, let alone the 1930s. They are highly trained professionals who have a good level of education, and are expected to be expert at handling themselves and their machines in a wide variety of situations.

The next improvements came from Harley-Davidson in 1998 for the 1999 model year, with the introduction of the new Twin Cam 88cu in (1,450cc) engine — the first new engine for 15 years, but still a 45° V-twin, air-cooled push-rod unit, following in the tradition of the Knucklehead, Panhead, Shovelhead, and Evolution. It has more power, but is quieter, smoother and cleaner for the police models, the entry-level Road King FLHPI and the ultimate Electra-Glide FLHTPI, both of which have fuel injection or the option of a carburetor. With the changes, it can be said that Harley-Davidson has managed to close the gap with Kawasaki in both performance and maintenance, although there is also another contender for police contracts in the form of BMW.

The NYPD is the biggest Harley-Davidson customer in America, closely followed by New York State, and the company sells machines to police forces in every state. In the late 1990s the Police Fleet Sales Department at Milwaukee had been adding 200 new customers each year. By July 1999, when the company launches the model year 2000, it expects to have around 1,800 law enforcement agency customers. Export markets, too, have opened up with law enforcement agencies in 40 countries as far apart as Canada, Argentina, Korea and Australia riding Harley-Davidsons

For 1999 Harley-Davidson offered the Peace Officer Special Edition FLHTCUI, a machine aimed solely at serving or retired law enforcement officers for recreation use.

To buy this machine you have to prove your rank and badge number and provide a copy of police identification. This Ultra Classic Electra-Glide comes in two-tone police blue and is only available in North America. A carburated version, the FLFTC is also available.

Military Harleys

Denis Chorlton

On Sunday, June 28, 1914, a chauffeur mistakenly took a wrong turning in the Bosnian capital Sarejevo, with the unfortunate consequence that his passengers, Archduke Franz Ferdinand and his wife, were assassinated by a student. This was the hapless spark which ignited the conflagration that was to become, in August, the Great War of 1914–18.

The United States in general, and the American motorcycle industry in particular, took little interest initially; after all, with some 60 or so manufacturers fulfilling a home market that had been growing steadily since 1910, this was a busy period, and Europe was a long way away.

However, the effects of the European war were soon apparent: motorcycle output for 1914 was 10,000 machines lower than the previous year's total of over 70,000; motorcycle prices had inevitably risen because imports of many European components — such as magnetos and bearings — were curtailed when war was imminent. This started an inflationary effect which eventually touched other major manufacturing requirements, such as rubber and steel. On the positive side, foreign imports of complete motorcycles were now suspended,

— a boost for the domestic makers.

Perhaps most important of all, American manufacturers continued to be free to export around the world with considerably less competition. Up to this point Harley-Davidson motorcycles were not well known outside of America — the company had only opened a dealership in London until December 1913 — but all that was about to change. Harleys were going to war.

Another bonus for neutral America was the foreign war contracts that included motorcycles for military use. Harley-Davidson won at least two of these contracts; they supplied a number of solo machines to the Dutch military, and the Russian army was reported to have taken delivery of Harley-Davidson machine-gun carrying outfits and ambulance sidecar outfits in 1915. The latter were well designed and carried the standard army stretcher at saddle height held in place by four bolts with wing nuts. The same large Cee springs usually fitted to a sidecar body giving the casualty a fairly comfortable ride. These contracts no doubt added to the general confidence at Harley-Davidson, who for the first time, thanks to the new V-twin, could set its sights on expanding to challenge the two

big manufacturers, Indian and Excelsior. Building on its reputation for well-engineered, dependable machines and its recent racing achievements, the 1914–18 period was particularly crucial to the future development of Harley-Davidson.

Fortuitously, the company's first successful V-twin appeared in 1911, after the earlier failure of the 1909 Model 5D twin of which only 27 were made. The new model, called the 7D, of 49cu in (810cc) used the F head design from the singles with overhead mechanical inlet valves operated by long pushrods and rockers, and side exhaust valves. Unusually for the time, the controls were cable-operated, including the Bosch magneto which was fitted. Though it still had pedals and belt drive, it handled fairly well and was smoother and more powerful than the previous design.

The down side was the price, a rather expensive $300, which was more than most of its competitors. The 7D, however, heralded a new beginning and evolved, as we shall see, to be an excellent contribution to World War One and, ultimately, ensured Harley-Davidson's future. Considerable improvements to the V-twin followed in 1912 on what was designated the Model 8 (year eight). There were frame

Below: One of batch of sidecar combos destined for the Russian Front in 1915. Garry Stuart

Bottom: Model J in Europe c. 1915. National Motor Museum via Roy Bacon

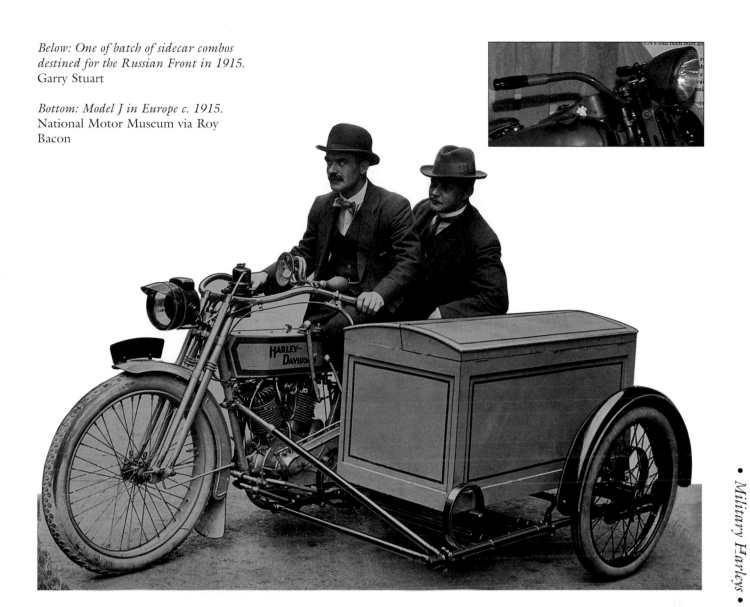

Below: Restored WLA; note holster and Harley-Davidson sidecar. Ian Kerr

Below Right: 1,000cc Model F of 1918. Note acetylene front headlight. Ian Kerr

alterations which lowered the saddle height to 29 inches and mounted the saddle itself (which had its own springs) on the centrally sprung saddle pillar giving four inches of travel for greater comfort; this was patented as the "Ful-Floteing" type. Comfort was always high on the priority list for the American rider. Handling was better with the rider now nearer to the centre of the machine, and the riding position was generally more acceptable.

Next came Harley-Davidson's first hub clutch (in the rear wheel) operated by a lever next to the fuel tank: if a clutch were specified, an X designation was added in front of the model number. For the first time the customer had a choice of chain with clutch (X8E) or belt drive with or without clutch (X8D or 8D). Internal improvements to the engine were that the big end and connecting rods were fitted with roller bearings for the first time, and a crankcase breather so arranged as to lubricate the primary chain. By popular demand from both dealers and riders the capacity became 61cu in (989cc) giving more power and bringing Harley-Davidson into line with the other major manufacturers as regards capacity. Small cosmetic changes to the shape of the petrol tank and mudguards also took place.

Though the single-cylinder machines still being made had benefited from the development work done on the twin and were still selling well, the focus of the company's effort was now switching to the V-twin type which actually outsold the single in 1912.

*Left and throughout chapter: WLC
detail.* Ian Kerr

*Right and throughout chapter: WLA
detail.* Ian Kerr

Despite the lack of interest shown in factory-sponsored racing by Arthur and Walter Davidson, who were perhaps the more conservative members of the company, Bill Harley and William Davidson started the company cautiously in racing, and recruited the experienced engineer Bill Ottaway. Before long his competition expertise began to show itself in the road machines.

An important transition was about to take place; Harley-Davidson was shedding its rather dull utility image and the publicity from the racing successes all added to nearly 13,000 machines being sold in 1913. During 1914, still riding on the general upsurge of interest in motorcyles, we see important additions — the now familiar folding footboards and their accompanying clutch and brake pedals; the two-speed transmission developed by Bill Harley and Bill Ottaway; and a step starter. Out of a production total of 16,500 machines over 13,000 were twins and nearly 8,000 were the 10F machines; the company's president, Walter Davidson, felt sure this could be bettered in the following year.

The Milwaukee factory had by now grown to employ a workforce of some 1,500 hands.

In 1915, the latest version of the two-speeder arrived in the form of the Model 11J with, according to the Harley-Davidson publicity, 98 improvements and refinements, the most important of which was probably that it was not a two-speeder! It was a three-speeder, with three-speed countershaft gearbox, and was also significant in that for the first time an electric headlight was offered. This new gearbox was made extra strong along contemporary car lines, and the new sturdy multiple-disc dry plate clutch was carried on the countershaft. This could be adjusted in a few seconds by simply turning a screw accessible through a hole in the chain case. A proper gate was now fitted for the gear change lever, in addition to an interlocking device on top of the gearbox which prevented the gear being changed while the clutch was engaged. The mechanical oil pump on the timing cover had a very simple screw method to regulate the oil supply and a small sight glass was incorporated to check visually on oil flow (a circulating pump was still 20 years away). Among the engine improvements was the fitting of a wider and enlarged diameter crank pin, and the engine breathing was

• Military Harleys •

greatly improved with larger ports and valves. The carburetor, the well-known Schebler, was now fitted with a shutter so that the air could be restricted to make starting easier. A dynamometer test of the engine showed that 15hp was developed at 2,500 revolutions and this was steadily increased to 3,500 revolutions without problems.

The three-speed gearbox meant that the engine's higher power could be better utilized, especially when pulling a sidecar. These were now as popular a choice with the motorcycling public as they were with the military. Again with sidecars in mind, the steering head was strengthened with thick steel webs and stronger drive chains were now specified. The great improvements in the Harley-Davidson twin became a serious concern to their rivals.

The Model 11J joined those similar heavyweight V-twins made by other American manufacturers such as Reading, Standard, Indian, Excelsior, Emblem, Dayton and others. It was tailored not only to the motorcyclist customer who wanted a strong reliable machine which could cope with long distances over largely unmade roads, but the needs of the military as well.

The years 1914–15 also marked the time of Harley-

Davidson seriously breaking into such markets as rural mail carriers and telephone companies. who were provided with special sign-written box sidecars and forecars (these replaced the front wheel and forks with steerable twin wheels with a large box in between). The US Post Office even produced a 10 cent stamp with a Harley-Davidson pictured on it; also nine federal departments were currently riding on Harley-Davidsons.

The listed Harley-Davidson sidecar chassis which was the one used for the Russian ambulances, featured a telescopic axle so that the width was variable from 44 to 56 inches. The fender was also very wide and substantial while the wheel was fitted with the usual 28 x 3 inch tire which was interchangeable with the ones on the motorcycle. The hub was said to be 100 percent over strength.

Another feature for strength was the diagonal member running from the extremity of the main rear member to the forward attachment point. Compensating ball joints were provided to the four main points of attachment, plus substantial leaf Cee springs for the choice of sidecar body.

Not before time, in 1916 the pedals finally disappeared from the Harley-Davidson twin as the popular folding kickstarter was fitted to the back of the gearbox.

The progress continued with the Model 16J (the prefix number now related to the year of manufacture). New front forks were stronger and wider, giving greater clearance to bigger, more curvaceous, fenders. The petrol tank lost its sharp edges and was given a more pleasing rounded shape and new larger filler caps, while new petrol taps were introduced underneath the tanks in place of the old needle valves. Large petrol filters were placed inside the tanks. In 1917 the 17J model (generator and battery system) would be the Harley-Davidson machine which would soon take Americans to war, mostly with a sidecar and fitted with lights. It was virtually identical to the civilian model apart from a little less bright nickel plating. Areas of further improvements included the oil pump, inlet manifold, rear brake, cam profiles, and strengthened valve gear, clutch, gearbox and kickstart.

In 1916 there was a brief, but well publicized, outing for Harley-Davidson, when their machines were used by the American military for the first time; this was during the hunt for the Mexican revolutionary General Pancho Villa. During the spring of that year Pancho Villa, on his own initiative, began raiding across the border into America and on one of these raids his followers killed 19

Below: 1943 WLA detail; note ammunition box and windshield. Ian Kerr

Americans in the town of Columbus, Arizona. The Mexican President, Francisco Madera, authorized the American army to enter Mexico in pursuit of Villa as he did not have enough forces of his own to deal with the problem. This led to President Woodrow Wilson sending a 20,000-man force led by General "Black Jack" Pershing in an unsuccessful attempt to capture him. The U.S. Army was already using other makes of motorcycles at this point but when the orders came, Harley-Davidson responded very quickly

in supplying machines. The Harley-Davidsons used by the military (almost certainly all V-twins) were both solos and the sidecar outfits carrying the Colt machine gun (capable of firing 480 rounds per minute). Between 20 and 30 machines were used by the army's First Aero Squadron on what was described as a "punitive expedition." The machines were standard civilian models, with lower gear ratios being the only concession to military use.

Unfortunately, they didn't catch their quarry, but the

newspaper coverage with photographs was very welcome publicity for the company.

This Mexican episode, in which the army deployed both aircraft and motorized units in operational conditions for the first time, did much to focus the motorcycle manufacturers' thoughts on military machines and military contracts, out of all proportion to the importance of the actual events.

However the Canadian Government, who had declared war on Germany shortly after

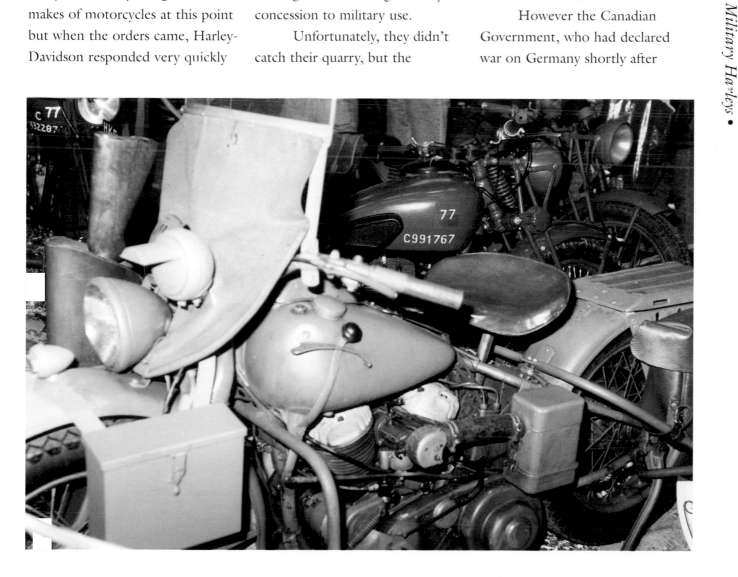

Great Britain, took small numbers of Harley Davidsons and Indians into real war for the first time with the CEF (Canadian Expeditionary Force) which landed in England in early October 1914. By the very part-time nature of the Canadian Army of the time, most often the motorcycles were the rider's own property, for which they received an allowance. Incredible though it may seem today, such was the patriotic feeling of the period on both sides of the Atlantic, that riders were known to buy new motorcycles at their own expense, when they enlisted, to take with them to war.

Problems regarding the supply of spare parts were soon encountered though, as the London War Office had no channels for dealing with American-made machines, and was reluctant to do so. Unfortunately this did lead to some bad feeling among the Canadian despatch riders. The use of private machines was stopped by 1916 as there were plenty of British models available; the Canadians, it would seem, took a liking to the "Trusty" Triumph Model H.

Meanwhile, back in America, the Milwaukee factory was

Right: Prewar publicity shot of WLA line-up. Note Thompson submachine-guns with magazines missing. via Roy Bacon

obviously interested in attracting military contracts, but Harley-Davidson was not about to forsake the commitment to its civilian customers and its growing dealer network. However, the latter part of 1916 saw the first official testing of Harley-Davidson machines by the American Government and the Procurement Department standardizing on heavyweight V-twin, 61cu in machines with three-speed gearboxes.

Harley-Davidson agreed to supply nearly half its annual production of some 7,000 standard J type machines, some solo, but mostly with the Chicago-built Rogers sidecar or stretcher carrier, all finished in olive green. This was the end of the light gray and earlier piano black paint schemes and the olive green color — described by the factory as olive drab but actually glossy — lasted with minor variations up until the early 1930s. It was a lasting reminder that the company's machines had been to war.

The US military authorities did not intend to be muddled with several types of motorcycle (though strangely they did have 200 of the Cleveland Model K two-stroke single) and introduced a sensible standardization. This made things easier for the army rider as well as the stores departments.

Throttle control was to be on the right twistgrip and spark control on the left; gear shift was on the left side of the petrol tank, with low gear in the forward position, high gear in the rear position. The clutch was to be foot-controlled on the left side of the machine with rear foot brake on

• Harley-Davidson •

Below Left: Standard wartime XA.
via Roy Bacon

Below: WLA with sidecar — note
"Liberator" nametag and ammunition
box with 2d Armored Division ("Hell
on Wheels") logo. Garry Stuart

the right side. Magnetos were to be of standard dimensions, spark plugs were metric fitting.

Oil grease cups were to be of a standard size as were all oil/petrol pipes and fittings. All chains were 5/8 x 3/8, with kick start ("motion starting device") on the right side of the machine. Tires were to be 28 x 3 and with 40 spokes front and rear to fit all wheels of all makes. Finally, there should be universal fitting head-lamp brackets. All these requirements were met by the Harley-Davidson Model J.

The military action in France during the first year of the war was far more fluid than in later years when the terrible trench stalemate took hold. Motorcycle despatch riders were very much able to prove their worth for the first time, and particularly their superiority over horses, runners or pigeons for delivering important messages, remembering that radio and field telephone communication were still in their infancy. Because of their rapid travel in the forward areas the motorcycle despatch riders usually had a much clearer

picture of the fast changing situation than the commanders, and were often called upon to make important decisions; invariably they were the only ones with up-to-date maps!

Among the hazards these first Canadian DR's faced on their Harley-Davidson's was riding near the front lines at night without lights, for although their motorcy-cles were fitted with acetylene lamps, if the lights were used when going toward the front, the bright glow made them an easy target. Of course, they often used them on

the return, though it was against army regulations. Many took up smoking as the red glow could be seen ahead in the dark and the engine heard by others on the road, so giving warning. If it rained, it was every man for himself.

The Harley-Davidson's riders soon found the sheer weight of their machines put them at a severe disadvantage compared to the much lighter British Triumph and Douglas machines, especially when negotiating the slippery high-crowned cobblestone "pave" roads so common in France, for if it rained any sort of grip was impossible to find, they just couldn't keep them on the road — not to mention sometimes bodily having to haul your machine through the deep mud caused by the war traffic! In fairness, problems caused by these conditions were not their fault; the machines were never designed to cope with this sort of environment. Thereafter, the larger heavier machines tended to be used on the better roads behind the front lines in England or Flanders, on longer runs and where reliability and sheer pulling power were an advantage.

In the roles to which they were suited, such as ambulance sidecar outfits, carrying officers and supplies, the Harley-Davidson's coped very well and were liked. They were soon to perform similar roles for the US Army.

Because of inflation in the cost of raw materials caused by the war, it was always hard for the company to make a large profit on these machines, though Harley-Davidson fared much better than rivals Indian, Cleveland and Excelsior who barely made any profit at all. Indian started its long decline from the end of 1918, suffering from the after effects of its larger under-priced war contracts, and its neglect of its dealer network during the war period.

Though President Woodrow Wilson had promised the country in his re-election campaign of 1916 to keep out of the war in Europe, the United States finally declared war on Germany in April 1917 following the public outrage over the sinking of the *Lusitania* in 1915, the continued predation on neutral shipping by the German submarines and the reported atrocities committed against Belgian civilians. The U.S. Army under General Pershing was still largely unprepared and had to be hastily enlarged and, where possible, mechanized. Appoximately 70,000 army motorcycles were ordered altogether, among which

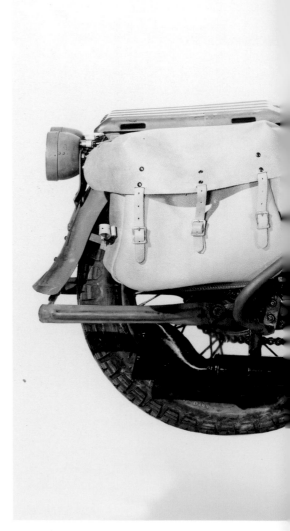

*Below: Factory shot of a WLA. Note
metal legshields — these were invariably
taken off in the field.* via Roy Bacon

were further contracts for Harley-Davidson, bringing the company's total for World War One to 26,486 machines, ordered through November 1, 1918. It seems the later contracts were negotiated under far more favorable terms, taking into account the wartime inflation in material costs.

The consensus of opinion indicates that about 7,000 of the Harley-Davidson military machines made were actually shipped to England or France and saw some active service. These would have been used in general service in the messenger carrying role, some scouting, also leading or escorting larger vehicles or convoys through to their destinations, though not of course in combat situations. Often unglamorous but essential work such as waiting at airfields for photo-reconnaisance aircraft to land was done by Harley-Davidson sidecar outfits; the rider would take the observer's exposed photographic plates to a field studio and then on to army headquarters for analysis. This is not forgetting the casualty evacuation of the ambulance sidecar outfits which performed very well in both England and France. A contemporary road test in July 1915 described an outing from London to Brighton for wounded allied soldiers, when a Harley-Davidson sidecar outfit (supplied by the London dealership) carried a wounded Belgian soldier at a steady pace of about 30mph on the open road. The driver initially found the clutch a little difficult but, once he had mastered it, found it most acceptable. Similar comments were made regarding the twist-grip throttle, though the

Harley-Davidson

automatic Schebler carburetor was praised for the controllability it afforded, as was the outfit's steering. The tester also thought the particular outfit used was rather too highly geared for sidecar work.

Beginning in July 1917, on the army's behalf, Harley-Davidson (along with the other major manufacturers) set up a training plan whereby enlisted men did an intensive three-week course at the Milwaukee factory on the repair and maintenance of military Harley-Davidson motorcycles. Starting with nine corporals from Fort Sam Houston, approximately 300 men had completed the course by the time the Armistice was signed in November 1918, though it is doubtful if any of them saw service in Europe, as the United States was not completely mobilized when hostilities ceased. These men, with the knowledge they had gained, must have subsequently been very useful to the dealer network. The war ended before this system realized its full potential for the military, but it was seen to be a success and adapted for future use in training of Harley-Davidson dealers and their staff.

Announced in late 1917 for 1918, there were several detail improvements to the Harley-Davidson range. There were five

models listed: these were the main model, the 18J, three-speed V-twin cylinder with battery and generator, the 18F model three-speed V-twin with Berling magneto and the 18E model, a V-twin which was geared direct. The two other machines were a single-cylinder three-speeder and a single-cylinder direct-drive. There was very good interchangeability of parts between these models apart from the engines.

Two striking improvements in the continuous process of refinement that was taking place, were undoubtedly the new lubrication system for the inlet valve rocker arm, and the double roller bearing used for the clutch. This new bearing of Harley-Davidson design replaced an earlier one which had caused a few clutch problems in the past due to lack of lubrication. It had been frequently necessary to remove the chaincase, and strip the clutch in order to pack the bearing with grease. The new design allowed the necessary lubrication with an oil-can through the center of the casing over the clutch. In the electrically equipped model fitted with the Remy mag-generator, several detail improvements had been made, including a heavier bracket for the electric horn.

Symbolic to the end of World War One was a picture

which appeared in many newspapers in America in the middle of November 1918. This showed an American corporal, Roy Holtz, who was photographed driving his army Harley-Davidson sidecar outfit inside Germany past retreating German soldiers. He was thereafter referred to as "The first Yank to enter Germany" (on November 11) after the cessation of hostilities. Very good publicity for Harley-Davidson, but how did he get there hours ahead of everyone else? It turned out that, with an officer passenger, they had got lost in bad weather, and strayed behind the German lines the day before, and had been captured. As the Armistice was signed the next morning, they were released and sent on their way to meet the allied advance, where the picture was taken.

With the termination of all War Department contracts in January 1919, the U.S. Army had approximately 14,600 Harley-Davidsons on its inventory, all but 300 sidecar-equipped. It was time to address the civilian market once more, where quite a few of the smaller motorcycle manufacturers had disappeared or were in difficulties. As the military models were almost no different to the civilian ones and Harley-Davidson had, in the form of the J type, almost a

one model range, available in approximately 1,000 dealerships, this did not pose too much of a problem. The J model continued to be built until 1929.

During the war years William Davidson had taken steps at the factory to improve its efficiency and quality control. The weaknesses in their competition had been carefully noted, advertising had been boosted and areas where the opposition (particularly Indian) appeared strongest, were targeted. The racing program was reactivated too.

This immediate postwar period was noted for its optimism in the motorcycle world, (Henry Ford's $300 Model T was still three years away) which found expression in the post-war Harley-Davidson factory expansion, with an investment of $3.5 million. This began at Milwaukee in late 1918 when the Harley-Davidson factory was considerably enlarged and re-equipped with the latest machinery. In 1920, after 17 years of manufacturing motorcycles, Harley-Davidson finally outstripped Indian and could claim to be the biggest motorcycle maker in the world.

There can be little doubt that the exposure the company received during World War 1 was essential for establishing the long

term reputation of the marque outside America. Not least were the machines themselves which were left behind and sold off as military surplus in France and England; these were well liked and continued to be used well into the 1930s. American army surplus machines were also bought by dealers and released onto the transport-hungry market. The stock kept by the military themselves lasted well into the 1920s and even 1930s in far-flung outposts, during which time very little was ordered, although in 1932 a batch of 100 R models was delivered to the US Army. In 1934, 312 VDS models (based on the civilian V and VL) fitted with the LT sidecar and nine of the RL model solos were delivered, followed by a few more of each in 1935. First mention of the WL model was made in 1937: this was a batch of 50 or so, again for the U.S. Army. Two years later, in 1939, the National Guard took delivery of 46 of this model.

This slow military procurement between the wars was more than offset, however, by the continuing demand for the company's police machines from various law enforcement agencies.

The troubled period before World War Two was characterized in America by the joke — "Boom,

bust and Roosevelt's "New Deal". The decade had started with the Wall Street stock market crash followed by the Great Depression and ended in September 1939 with the outbreak of another war in Europe. Unlike many companies, Harley-Davidson had survived the first two, and was now hoping for substantial military orders from the third.

Isolationalist America once more did not want to be involved in a war, but there were still eight million unemployed from the Depression years and it wasn't long before the trickle of foreign orders for armaments and equipment became a welcome flood, which eventually restored full employment.

By now Harley-Davidson's only competitor left in the American motorcycle market place was Indian, that was currently suffering from rather rundown plant and machinery, though surprisingly their production for 1939 and 1940 was slightly higher than Milwaukee's. Both companies were supplying motorcycles to the allied armies overseas but the real prize was who was going to be the major supplier to the U.S. Army. Indian had originally led the way with flatheads (side-valves) the military offerings being the early 45cu in (750 cc) Model 640,

which became the 30.50cu in (500cc) Model 741B (Scout) and the popular 74cu in (1,20 cc) model 340B (Chief). The small Indian didn't find favor with the U.S. Army that failed to order any of them, almost the entire production going for export under the Lend-Lease scheme. Although the U.S. Marines and the U.S. Navy did have a few.

At Juneau Avenue it was time to dust off the olive drab paint again, and consider the models suitable for development into military machines. Just before the Germans invaded Poland in August 1939 a pair of 45cu in side-valve models with the model designation WLA (A for Army) were sent to Fort Knox, Kentucky and Holabird QM Depot, Baltimore, for testing by the army.

Mainstays of the late 1930s had been the 45cu in (750cc) Models W and WL for solo work and the 74cu in (1,200cc) Models U and UL for sidecar pulling and commercial applications. When war became inevitable it was these two models, particularly the 45, that would find favor with the military. The army testing program, plus input from the bigger twins and the racing WLDR model, had produced big improvements in the 45; the clutch assembly grew stronger and smoother in operation, the gearbox was strengthened with

larger gears and an improved selection mechanism. The engine gained roller bearings in the lower end and one-piece cam gears. WLA models now had the new style tubular front forks, which had been lengthened by 2.75in to help with the ground clearance problem. Deep finned aluminum heads (from the WDLR) became standard for better cooling, bearing in mind all the slow convoy escort work that would be required. They also saved 5lb (2.27kg) weight, each! Another vital factor in keeping the engine cool was the oil pump, which was superb on the WLA, aided by the large 7.5-pint capacity of the oil tank. Engine lubrication was upgraded with the use of a centrifugal bypass valve. This valve opened at low speed to return much of the oil to the tank, as speed increased it closed, forcing more oil into the engine. Another very sensible feature on the WLA was the oil pressure indicator light on the tank top console. The "instant reserve" fuel valve was also fitted to the top left of the petrol tank, where it was easy for the rider to see and reach.

Practical considerations had seemed to point toward the side-valve machines, which were superbly tailored in quite a short timespan to be the most sturdy and reliable of military mounts.

Due to its low compression engine and restricted breathing, and loaded with all its military equipment, the WLA probably had a top speed in the mid-50s. Acceleration was also poor but there was loads of torque on tap when the going got tough. With its indestructible clutch and gearbox and over-engineered construction the WLA was ideal for the military. Not bad for the rider either, as comfort was good, thanks to the large pan saddle supported on its sprung pillar, combined with large tires and footboards. With its good stability and

ease of handling despite its obvious weight, the WLA was not expected to do much off-road work. With very little maintenance and often in appalling conditions, the WLA gave exceptional service.

The British had already gone the same route with their military motorcycles, using the tried and tested civilian models — the BSA M20 and Norton 16H side-valves 500cc singles — as a basis for their most popular machines.

The WLA was destined to be used by all the allied armies from America to Australia (even Russia and China) and by the Canadians and British as the WLC. Contracts issued to Harley-Davidson carried with them official authorisation to buy the necessary materials such as steel and aluminum to fulfill the orders. Production facilities at Milwaukee had been readied with considerable reorganization of working area and the workers' shift systems, so that the factory could work right around-the-clock. Extra personnel were recruited and additional plant space was leased nearby. At the same time the factory was also producing the UA and US model type military sidecar outfits in small quantities.

Along with foreign orders, Harley-Davidson were not disappointed by the response from their own army, for in January 1940 the American Army ordered 421 WLAs, followed by orders in September and December for a further 2,451. After this the (1942 style model) WLA was produced almost continuously until August 1945, with small variations. It is interesting to note that no WLA or WLC has a frame number; to date a machine you must look at the

engine number, and as the model year prefix '42' was used for all of these, even though they were made in 1943 or 1944, you have to look at the number itself. Also to conform to the licensing regulations in Great Britain, for instance, where a frame number is required to register a motorcycle, the engine number is often also found stamped on the frame. To confuse restorers even further, when overhauled at military Base Workshops in Europe during the war, the engine number was sometimes removed and replaced by the date of overhaul and workshop number.

From 1939 the Harley-Davidson service school at Milwaukee was back in business, turning out 50 mechanics every four weeks. In 1942 Harley-Davidson's civilian service training facility was altered to the Quartermaster School for teaching military mechanics. Needless to say the maintenance and repair of the WLA was still the top priority.

The differences between the civilian WL and the WLA were mostly the addition of a wide variety of military fittings, which also varied slightly from contract to contract. It is necessary to generalize and take the December 1941 main production onwards, as this is the machine with which most people will be familiar.

The WLA had a very substantial luggage rack over the rear mudguard; this was to take the weight, if necessary, of a 40lb army field radio (the SCR-300), and two cowhide saddle bags which usually hung from the rack. A very large steel bash plate fitted under the engine and gearbox, even extended to protect the lower run of the exhaust pipe/silencer and the rear chain. This had more to do with the ground clearance, or lack of it, and this plate was probably the biggest one fitted to any military motorcycle! Standard "Guide" blackout/convoy lights were fitted on the fenders — one at the front and two side by side at the rear. A "Guide" spotlamp with blackout mask (and switch) was often fitted next to the horn which was directly above the headlamp. The headlamp was not fitted with a blackout mask, and in combat areas the glass was usually painted over. A large cowhide scabbard, which could hold a Thompson sub-machine gun (or an automatic carbine) was fitted parallel to the offside front fork leg. This fitted into a flat steel frame which was bolted across the top of the front fender, continuing on to the nearside fork leg; this carried a small steel box to carry extra ammunition for the gun (not fitted to the WLC). The saddle itself was also different to the civilian pattern, in

having downturned edges held by three studs.

Bearing in mind the hostile desert conditions in which the machine might have to operate, a large oil bath air cleaner, usually made by Houde, was fitted. These came in two patterns, the early cylindrical one, and the later (far more common) pattern which was rectangular; stamped into the casing were the rider's "Daily Service" instructions. This filter was fitted below the saddle and connected to the carburetor intake by a two-inch diameter rubber hose. A small metal plate attached to the petrol tank gave lubrication, spark plug, and speed recommendations — "do not exceed 65mph" (unlikely), and a list of army publications which applied to the machine.

Crash bars front and rear were standard, as were a handlebar mirror and a sidestand (or Jiffy stand). To keep the rider's legs dry, large metal legshields were offered, but these were unpopular as their sheer size restricted the airflow around the engine, which led to overheating, not to mention that they also made minor adjustments on the engine impossible. However, one popular military option for weather protection was the windshield with apron, which came in several types, and was leatherette up until mid-1943 and

canvas thereafter. Military Police units liked these as they could be signwritten "Military Police" across the front in white paint. The MPs also often fitted a friction driven siren behind the nearside footboard which was operated by rubbing against the rear tyre; this could be engaged with the rider's left heel. Fenders were of the unvalenced wide-clearance type, so as to avoid getting clogged with mud. Obviously there was no chromium plating on the military models; many small fittings were parkerized or dull cadmium-plated. The exhaust system was painted black, but soon went rusty. Everything except the leather fittings was painted in olive drab synthetic enamel (lusterless flat). All these extras increased the machine's weight to approximately 560lb and cost the government between $370 and $395 each. Of the 60,437 WLA models produced, the U.S. Army received 26,275 units during the war period. It is worth mentioning that the WLA/WLC models were never fitted with a sidecar by the factory, though the Russians and the Australians (who had 4,200) were known to have fitted their own makes after delivery. The WLA resumed very limited production from 1949 until 1952, these being essentially the WL model with added military fittings from the

WLA series. During the four years the total of machines built would be approximately 1,000.

The role of the motorcycle despatch rider had not changed much since World War One, despite the big advances in telegraphy and radio communication. Radio in wartime had several big disadvantages; it could be intercepted, jammed or falsified. In the military mind there really was no substitute for having the original written copy in your hands, and that was most often delivered by motorcycle despatch rider,

especially early in the war. Still essentially non-combatant, if anything the motorcycle's roles had increased, with the normal daily despatches, reconnaisance, intelligence and military police duties, convoy escort, traffic control, emergency medical or parts delivery, even postman with the soldiers' mail. If a motorcycle broke down, the rider very often had to fix it himself; if he had an accident, he might cherish his independence, but he who rides alone, falls alone. There were more casualties among DRs resulting

from accidents than direct contact with the enemy. It was the nature of the job, dodging in and out of trucks and tanks while herding night time convoys over muddy, rough roads with only the glint of a blacked-out light to illuminate the way. For their own survival, riders had to become proficient at laying the bike down at speed and sliding the Harley-Davidson on its crash bars, even under a truck if necessary. There were also land mines, snipers, marauding Messerschmitts, shelling, wires across roads and booby traps to

MAKE: HARLEY-DAVIDSON
MODEL: 1942 WLA
SPEC: NORTH AFRICAN
CAMPAIGN.
8TH ARMY DESERT TRIM

RESTORED BY *Fred Warr 1998*

contend with, not to mention the weather, which included floods, snow and sandstorms if the action were in the desert. At least riding kit now included a steel helmet, goggles, kidney belt and proper waterproofs. The WLAs and WLCs came ashore with the allied invasion of Normandy in June 1944, the WLA eventually gaining the title "Liberator" in Holland. They were the preferred machines for convoy duty on the smoother roads; even with an enemy in retreat, the troops could only advance if transport was able to keep pace, which transport could only do if guided by the motorcycle DRs. Although the motorcycle, particularly the solo unit, was more maneuverable than other motorized units, the motorcycle's capabilities were far more dependent on rider skill. As World War Two neared its end, more and more of the traditional motorcycle work was done by four-wheeled vehicles, all but replacing the motorcycle sidecar unit, though the solos had a place until the end.

There were 18,182 Harley-Davidsons built for the Canadian National Defense as the WLC model, the first delivered in August 1941. Many parts were specified, especially in the early contracts, which made it different to the WLA. Most unusual was the provision of a hand-operated

Left: Excellent restored WLA showing leather scabbard, headlight and blockout light detail. Ian Kerr

Below: WLA instrument details. The speedo rated to 120mph appeared on all WLAs. Note plate giving lubrication details, oil and generator lights, oil (right) and petrol filler caps and brass ignition switch. Garry Stuart

clutch while still retaining the foot-operated system. So, in practice the Canadians and British riders simply used the hand clutch whenever possible, especially on tricky hill starts or turning left. The foot clutch was probably the most disliked feature among non-American riders in what was considered a practical, well thought out machine.

Though Indians also had a foot clutch, their's worked in the car manner; that is, you pushed forward and down to engage the clutch and let the clutch pedal come up to pull away. The Harley-Davidson clutch worked in the opposite manner and you had to push down and forward in an even manner to pull away. Another thing the Canadians did not like about the controls on the early pattern machines was having the throttle on the left grip. The idea behind this arrangement supposedly dates back to early police use of Harley-Davidsons where the rider was trained to shoot a pistol with his right hand. This sounds alright in theory, but how a soldier was supposed to manage the recoil of a revolver or submachine-gun while bouncing at speed over rutted and debris-covered roads was never explained.

Once issued it became normal practice for the riders, and then army workshops to change them over to right-hand throttle. Later pattern WLCs were equipped with a right-hand throttle before leaving the factory. On the early WLCs (up to mid-1941) the headlight was mounted higher up, above, rather than below, the electric horn, and a small auxilliary tool box was fitted onto the front

fender, on which was often painted
the machine's service number "CC
---" though usually this was painted on the petrol tank sides. The
extra toolbox required the small
front blackout light to be moved
to the very front edge of the
fender. The WLC had the civilian
pattern saddle. Headlights were
fitted with a blackout mask, which
allowed a little light out through
a slot three inches by a quarter of
an inch. The early WLCs did not
have the large rear rack or cowhide
bags, instead a pillion seat was
often bolted to the top of the
rear fender, the passenger being
provided with folding rear footpegs and a grab handle. These
were often removed, as the riders
found themselves called upon to
transport officers about if the seat
was there. Front crash bars with a
single bar fitted on the nearside to
protect the oil bath air cleaner
were fitted on the early models.
Later machines had the full set,
front and back as per the WLA.
Two patterns of blackout lights
were fitted on the fenders of the
WLC throughout the war, one at
the front and two at the rear.
The early ones were two inches
round and the later hexagon type
were one inch in diameter. The
combined ignition-light switch also
operated slightly differently, with
an extra position by turning the

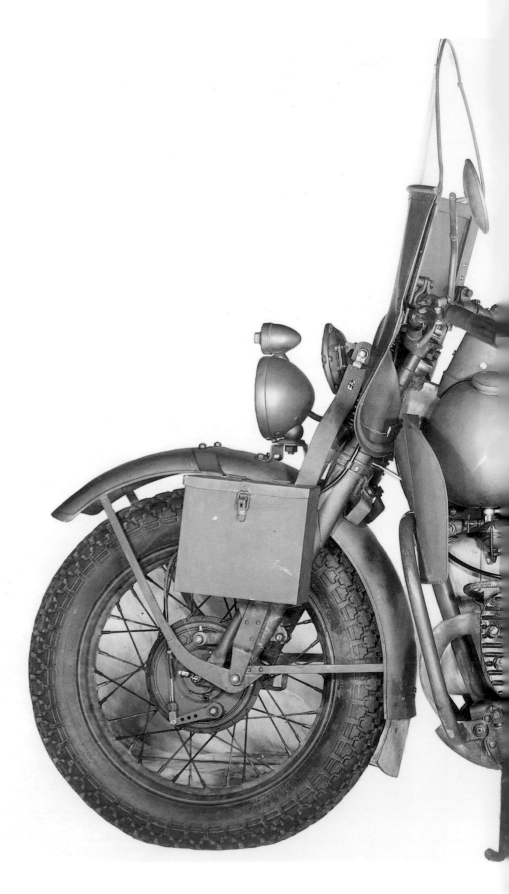

Below: Factory shot of the XA pilot model showing well the abbreviated rear bag and shortened leg shields. via Roy Bacon

switch to the left, where sidelights only could be turned on without the ignition, otherwise it was the same as the WLA. No handlebar mirror was fitted. Early WLCs had the folding kickstart pedal of the bicycle pedal rubber type, later ones had a bar with a tubular steel sleeve. On the Canadian model the wheels were interchangeable; this was facilitated by a substantial and no doubt very useful front wheel stand which was not fitted on the WLA. This in turn meant a different front wheel and brake which came from the "big twin" model.

On the later WLCs the D-shaped footboards were metal only with a pattern pressed in without the rubber mats. The windshields with apron were just as popular with the Canadians, especially in the winter; they didn't fit the legshields but did fit canvas covers over the front crash bars, which would have given the riders' legs some protection.

Some 10,000 of the WLC models were shipped for duties overseas, along with 44 ELC 61cu in OHV models fitted with the left hand (LLE) sidecar. The Canadian Army operated their

Harley-Davidsons successfully in North Africa, Italy and throughout Northern Europe after D-Day. When the war finished Canadian units continued to use their Harley-Davidsons, and there were some very smart WLCs in use with the Provost Corps (Military Police), both in Canada and with the occupation forces in Germany. These were painted white overall and seem to have often had windshields and an electric siren mounted on the front crash bar. They kept their Harley-Davidsons until they were replaced by the

• Harley-Davidson •

Below Left and Below: Left and right sides of an early WLC showing auxiliary tool kit mounted on front and roll bar at rear protecting the air cleaner.
Garry Stuart

Triumph TRW model from 1956 onwards. The Canadian Provost Corps Motorcycle display team was still using early pattern WLCs in 1955.

Less familiar than the military WLA/WLC's were their big brothers, the Harley-Davidson Models US and UA, 74cu in side-valves, of which over 4,000 were made for various customers. They were almost always fitted with a sidecar and the popular three-speed-and-reverse gearbox option. In 1938 the frame, brakes,clutch and transmission had all been strengthened and performance was good. Ordered by the the U.S. Army, 71 US models were delivered in 1938, and in 1939–40 a total of 884 UA models. These were the last motorcycle and side-car models purchased by the U.S. Army. The U.S. Navy had around 1,600 US models 1940–45 and the U.S. Marine Corps received a small number from the Navy. In 1941 the South African Union Defence Force ordered 156 US models along with 2,350 WL models (some of which were passed on to the Rhodesian Forces); they had a further 1,622 US models in 1942, and another 50 in 1944, all with sidecars fitted on the left. Australia also had 100 US solos in 1944. These export models would usually have had a front wheel stand, 5.00 x 16 inch tires and the big cylindrical oil bath air cleaner. Another peculiarity of the British Commonwealth models was their unusual silencers, being a hybrid of the WLA fishtail and the Big Twin silencer body. These 74s featured a low compression engine with iron heads, slightly lower gear ratios than the civilian model and

no chrome trim. All models used a Linkert carburetor, coil ignition and a substantial battery fed by Harley-Davidson's own design of generator. The improved oil system consisted of separate feed and scavenge pumps piped to the big oil tank mounted on the downtube under the saddle. Front forks were the lengthened type, the headlight was mounted above the horn (as the early WLA/WLC style). On the back fender there was either nothing at all, or a substantial pillion seat or rear rack but without the saddlebags. As the big

twins were not meant for frontline use there were almost no other military fittings. There was also the 1942 ELA army model with sidecar, five of which were built, based on the civilian EL model.

The U.S. Marine Corps used a small number of Harley-Davidsons (and Indians) during World War Two, these being primarily for messenger, convoy and military police duties. They had both solo machines and sidecar outfits. In fact, it could be said that they were the first Harley-Davidsons to see action in

American hands. Marine motorcycle units based at Camp Catlin at Pearl Harbor, Hawaii, came into action during the Japanese surprise air attack of Sunday, December 7, 1941; the attack of course, which brought America into the war. During the air raid which lasted one and three quarter hours, the motorcycle squad assigned to the 2nd Engineer Battalion was pressed into service in a variety of roles. They were equipped with Harley-Davidson Model US sidecar outfits, and were called upon to deliver ammunition, machine guns,

• Harley-Davidson •

first aid supplies, and to transport the wounded to hospital. They also escorted convoys of ammunition trucks carrying three-inch anti-aircraft shells from the Lualualei Depot to the air defence batteries. The Japanese lost 20 or so aircraft out of the 360 in the attack which sank or severely damaged 18 American warships including seven battleships, killing 2,403 Americans, and wounding another 1,178. President Franklin D Roosevelt had no option but to declare war on Japan the following day; three days later Germany and Italy declared war on the United States as they had a pact with Japan. Probably there were not more than 200 motorcycles used by the U.S. Marines 1941–45; records show these were scattered as far afield as Iceland and Western Samoa and, of course, at home bases in America. They differed only in color from the standard WLA or Model US, and were usually painted Marine Corps 34052 lusterless green. When not on garrison duty in the United States the engine would have been painted a dark color.

The advent of the Jeep meant that far fewer motorcycles were used by the U.S. Marine Corps later in the war. Several U.S. Army 74s were subsequently captured by the Japanese when

they took Wake Island and Bataan. Of course, the Japanese already had their own Harley-Davidsons, built under license in Japan from the mid-1930s as the Rikuo, or "King of the Road," and the much rarer Kuro Hagare, or "Black Iron." The U.S. Navy also had a few 61cu in OHV models for wartime Shore Patrol; these were the Navy model E.

In 1919 Harley-Davidson produced a model called the W Sport Twin, which was unlike any Harley-Davidson that had been made before: this was a flat twin with the engine lengthways in the frame, similar to the popular British machine the Douglas, 25,000 of which had served the Allied cause so well in World War One. As it was such a radical departure, the conservative American riders did not really welcome the model W, although Harley-Davidson made nearly 10,000 up until 1923, and many were exported. The U.S. Army also bought three for testing in 1920. This is worth mentioning because in January 1942 another very unusual flat twin model model emerged from the Milwaukee factory in the shape of the model XA (experimental army), which was built as an experimental war model. A contract was awarded in March 1941by the U.S. Army, who had been impressed by reports of the big BMW/Zundapp machines — flat twins with shaft drive — used so successfully by the German army in their European Blitzkrieg. With production of the WLC and WLA just getting under way, it seems that Harley-Davidson undertook this request somewhat

reluctantly. It is often suggested that the XA was a nut and bolt copy of the BMW R71 45cu in (750cc) side-valve flat twin, which had shaft drive, a four-speed gearbox and a hand clutch.

Although this was the XA specification, it would be fairer just to say that the XA design was closely based upon the R71, as no parts were actually interchangeable between the two machines. The Harley-Davidson engineers were said to have simply changed the metric measurements into inches. This is certainly born out in some of the really strange-sized threads and bearings in the XA engine.

Not that the Harley-Davidson copy was the first time this particular BMW model had been duplicated. When Germany and Russia were still allies in 1938, Germany exchanged new technology for Russian raw materials, and the BMW R71 motorcycle was supplied to the Russians under this scheme. BMW sold both the design and tooling and helped them set up a factory, where they produced an "official copy" of the R71, called the M72 Ural. This means that with the 27,000 Harley-Davidson WLAs supplied to the Russians, the two models would have served side by side with the Red Army during World War Two.

However, the story doesn't end there as the Russians sold off all the tooling five or six years after the war — to the Chinese where the "new" model was designated the Donghai Yangste. Meanwhile the Russians started making a BMW OHV Model R75 copy; this was still being made in Ekaterinberg at the end of the

1990s. Both the Russian OHV and the Chinese SV were still available world-wide at the end of the 1990s. The good news for owners of BMW R71s is that parts made in Russia and China are largely interchangeable with the BMW ones, though not the XA (with one exception — the cylinders and base gaskets). It is also worth noting that while the engineers at Harley-Davidson were following instructions and copying the (old) unit construction BMW engine and drive train, the German factory had moved on and developed the superlative military motorcycle sidecar machine — the OHV R75 model.

This had hydraulic brakes on the sidecar and rear wheel of the motorcycle, and a gearbox with not only a reverse gear but high and low ratios for first, second, third and reverse. They were often employed towing small anti-tank artillery pieces or trailers with stores or ammunition. The U.S. Army was particularly interested in the shaft drive concept, as drive chains were always a problem on motorcycles, and on the WLA it was one of the few regular adjustments that just had to be made.

On the XA (R71) even the primary drive and generator drive were by gears, so chains were eliminated altogether. The layout also had two other big advantages; first,

on a flat twin the cylinders are out in the airstream, the engine runs much cooler than a V-twin.

Second, there was the lack of vibration, a particularly well-known drawback of the V-twin design. In the opposed twin, the cylinders balance each other out, giving a quieter and smoother ride. On the XA this was further aided by the BMW-type frame with plunger rear suspension. Very few parts of the XA were interchangeable with any other Harley-Davidson model. The front forks are the long type similar to those fitted to the early WLC; they were often fitted with a hydraulic shock absorber on the offside fork leg, possibly for desert use. With offroad and deserts in mind, a few XAs were also fitted experimentally with 15-inch disc wheels. Many small items such as lights, horn, instrument console, toolbox, etc, came out of the general Harley-Davidson parts bin. The coil ignition unit fitted neatly in front of the engine between the duplex down tubes; the ignition system, which featured automatic advance and retard mechanism, was radio-shielded. There was only a very small weight advantage over the WLA, but the ground clearance was improved by two inches. The fenders were of the wide clearance type and, strangely, the XA was sometimes fitted with abbreviated leg shields (because of

the cylinders) and very shallow cowhide pannier bags (because of the rear suspension), which still attached to a modified version of the massive WLA rack. A large round oil bath air cleaner was fitted over the gearbox. Crash bars were standard back and front, the rear ones protecting the silencers. With the controls, the throttle was on the left twistgrip and the single-plate clutch worked by a lever operated by the right hand; the front brake was operated by the left-hand lever. The kickstart was as per normal BMW practice, on the nearside, and operated downwards at 90 degrees to the machine; the gear change was also on the left and made more difficult to use as Harley-Davidson fitted footboards and footpegs! The positive stop four-speed gearbox also had a short lever on the offside which could be used to change gear and was useful for finding neutral. There was a Linkert carburetor for each cylinder, stamped "L" and "R" for easy identification. Heatshields were provided behind each cylinder to stop the rider's feet getting too warm, and a large skid plate was fitted under the engine/gearbox unit. The engine's compression ratio was 5.7 to 1 compared to the WLA's more modest 5 to 1.

On the petrol tank the mandatory military plate was

mounted warning the rider not to exceed 65mph, and in the case of the XA they could easily do this.

The XAs were distributed to the U.S. Army for trials and testing; the Holabird Quartermaster Motor Base in Baltimore and the Fort Knox Armored Forces School in Kentucky being just two establishments that were asked to appraise the XA. As the third biggest purchasers of Harley-Davidson military motorcycles after Russia and the U.S. Army, the Canadian Army also had five XAs on test at their Barriefield Training Centre, Kingston, Ontario, during 1942. Canadian instructors thought the XA (and the Indian 841) unsuitable for military use because they were both too heavy and too complex. They were reportedly easy to ride in being nicely balanced, and the machines could be leaned right over when cornering, although the riding position came in for criticism as being uncomfortable, with the rider's legs too far back. As far as anyone knows the XA was never shipped overseas (until after the war) and therefore never saw any military action. However, film does exist of an XA leaving a landing craft purporting to be at the Normandy Beachhead in 1944; also, a very rusty XA wreck turned up in the South African bush in

the late 1970s. Unfortunately, the XA was not converted into a civilian model, though the last 1943 model was updated and tested with proper hydraulic forks, better saddle, front fender and heel and toe foot shift without the footboards.

The total number of the XAs made between 1941 and 1943 is quoted at 1,000 machines, which reportedly cost the military nearly $900 each, over twice the unit cost of the WLA. In fairness, this price included all tooling, design and development work required for what was, in comparison to the WLA, a very short production run. The surviving XA machines were sold off surplus when the war was finally over, at $500 each. Luckily some XAs have found their way into the hands of motorcycle enthusiasts and museums.

There is some photographic evidence of a Servi-Car three-wheeler, the Model K, which utilized the XA engine and shaft drive; this was probably a one-off prototype. Other proposed uses were for an XA-engined portable generator, and also using the XA engine to power a type of small cross-country vehicle, to be made

Right: Close-up of WLC engine. Garry Stuart

by Willys: neither of these came to anything.

The Jeep had now found favor with the military and put an end to large military spending on motorcycles in the future, in the same way that the VW Kübelwagen (German equivilant of the Jeep) pushed out the BMWs and Zundapps. As the German military had primarily used their BMWs with sidecars which had a differential sidecar drive, it was also suggested by the army that Harley-Davidson should explore this route. In 1942 this became the Model XAS though it did not get past the prototype stage; it featured a large bulbous sidecar fitted on the right. While still on the subject of military prototypes, there are three more wartime Harley-Davidson projects worth a mention. The first of these was a 45 motorcycle with sidecar, designated the WRS, one of which was built in 1944 with special forks, frame and sidecar. The second was a completely different idea, with the mating of two Knucklehead OHV engines into a power unit to propel a proposed Canadian mini-tank, but this idea again only reached the prototype stage. Last was an 1940–41 U.S. Army contract to design and build 16 shaft-drive Knucklehead-powered Servi-Cars with disc wheels; this was the model TA.

The first prototype was sent to Camp Holabird for testing, but with disappointing results. The handling, engine vibration, weight distribution and leaking oil were listed as unsatisfactory. Another prototype was built addressing the problems of the first. This was delivered to the army in August 1940 and was cautiously approved, though the contract went no further.

Indian was also asked to produce an experimental machine to the same military request as the XA; this became the model 841, which featured shaft drive, four-speed gearbox, rear suspension and an entirely new unit construction engine of their own design. A thousand were made, and a few still survive. The Indian engine unit did see active service as an auxiliary power unit in the Boeing B-29 Superfortress bomber.

In recognition of the Harley-Davidson Company's phenomenal motorcycle production as its contribution to the U.S. war effort, the company was awarded the U.S. Army-Navy production award, known as the "E" award for excellence, for both 1943 and 1945.

This award was accepted by the company president, William H. Davidson, on behalf of all the company employees. The final production total for all the contracts and all models built

1940–45 was over 88,000 machines (plus considerable spares). The profit margins for Harley-Davidson on the wartime production were pretty narrow; they are quoted as cost plus 10%. Nor was the government, it seems, prepared to honor the total cost of the spares produced by Harley-Davidson.

As was the case at the end of World War One, much of the wartime motorcycle production never actually reached the front-line forces. When all the military motorcycle contracts were terminated by the U.S. War Department in February 1944, it signaled the release onto the civilian market of many thousands of the WLA model, at a price fixed by the government of $450 each. The first batch, including 2,500 Harley-Davidsons, appeared in early spring, with another release of 1,750 coming on to the market in August 1944. The summer of 1945 saw a further 15,000 ex-military Harley-Davidsons for sale, most of which would have been bought by dealers. The military thinking was that they had enough machines in store for the European theater and, as motorcycles were unsuitable for the island hopping and jungle terrain predominant in the Pacific war, production could safely be stopped. No doubt the Jeep,

Harley-Davidson •

which was now performing many of the duties originally assigned to motorcycles, was also part of the equation. For in August 1943 the combined monthly Jeep production from Willys and Ford reached its 16,000 maximum. As a matter of interest the total World War Two production of the Jeep in its many guises from all manufacturers was nearly 660,000, against total combined Harley-Davidson and Indian motorcycle production of approximately 130,000.

A war had once again increased the awareness of another generation to motorcycle riding, and many young GIs had been trained by the military to ride motorcycles and, of course, trained to fix them. As there had been twice as many Harley-Davidsons in military service as Indians, the chances were pretty good they had ridden a Harley-Davidson, and had been impressed. On returning to civilian life these ex-servicemen could well be be looking to buy a motorcycle; hopefully this would be one of the new F-series Knuckleheads, though wartime shortages were still apparent in 1945–46 in the lack of paint options and chrome trim. 1946 was the first full year of civilian production and the following year 20,000 machines were manufactured.

Again, as in 1917–18, the global conflict had meant many more countries had come into contact with the Harley-Davidson motorcycles. Ex-military machines were sold off surplus after the war in most European countries, plus more far-flung places like South Africa and Australia. This could only have a positive influence on civilian export markets and overseas sales in the future. In England the vast majority of the surplus models were WLCs left behind by the Canadians or part of the small number used by most of the British services, but particularly popular with the Royal Air Force. Many U.S. Army surplus WLAs were bought after the war by American dealers, refurbished and sold to countries like Greece whose army had several thousand.

Bearing in mind the success that Harley-Davidson had enjoyed during World War Two it was to be a long 18 years before they would win another U.S. military contract. This was for 418 machines of the XLA model, which was a Sportster fitted with fiberglass panniers and a wind-shield. These machines were primarily for Military Police and Shore Patrol units. The last were delivered in 1963 and they marked the last true Harley-Davidson to be used by the American military services. There was no significant

use of military motorcycles in the Korean or subsequent Vietnam conflict.

A different sort of military contract came along in 1983 when Harley-Davidson started making metal racks for transporting U.S. Air Force bombs, this turned out to be extremely profitable.

Back to motorcycles, in 1987 Harley-Davidson purchased the world manufacturing rights to the British Armstrong company and its successful product, the MT500, which was a lightweight military trail bike, with an engine made by the Rotax company in Austria.

This was a development of the Canadian Can-Am Bombardier 250cc design, built 1977–85, which had finally dragged military motorcycles beyond World War Two technology. They were used extensively by the armies of Britain, Canada, Uganda and Belgium. Light and powerful, they were extremely popular with the servicemen who rode them.

In 1995 the British Ministry of Defence placed a contract with Harley-Davidson for 1,450 of these machines. They were delivered but the project was cancelled in 1998, and remaining stock sold through dealers to civilians. Meanwhile the American military were buying over-the-counter Kawasakis where necessary.

Road Test

Ian Kerr

Sanrisha

At the beginning of the 1930s the Japanese started to develop the motor tricycle as a commercial freight carrier. Many of them still exist, with engines varying in capacity from 350 to 1,000cc. Some of the lighter types have chain drive to the axle, there being no differential used, but the larger capacity variants have either a double chain or shaft drive to the axle through a differential.

Virtually all of them used a three-speed transmission plus reverse and the gearing was always on the low side to enable loads as large as 1,000lb to be carried. When the war came round, these machines were used extensively by the army although no real standard machine appears to have existed; virtually anything that was available being pressed into military service.

This posed the biggest problem for New Zealand business man Bruce Henderson when he found two of these utility machines rotting away in a disused cotton mill on the Pacific island of Vanuatu. The other problem he had was that the engine that powered the bike was a Harley-Davidson made in Japan!

Henderson took the two bikes along with other items of interest back to NZ. Due to their very strict health laws (not forgetting the nuclear activity in the area from which they had come), it took a lot of time and effort to get them cleaned and cleared. Officials actually suggested the scrap heap might be an appropriate place to deposit them such was their condition.

Undeterred by such remarks Henderson's friend, retired panel beater Graeme Cantwell, set about the mechanical restoration, while Garth Sims started collecting information on the bike. The file is now thick and sources all over the world have contributed, but things are still very sketchy.

The Japanese motorcycle industry, which has a history dating back to the turn of the century, nearly died in the 1920s, but due to the military expansion recovered in the early 1930s This was a time of recession the world over and the civilian bikes still suffered, but the military side of things was good.

They had been using HD's since WW1 and wanted to continue doing so. Sankyo a Japanese firm handled all the sales of the US built machines, and due to a drop in the value of the dollar against the yen in 1929, an agreement was struck for the bikes to be built under licence in Japan. Harley-Davidson provided blueprints of the 45, 30, 50 and 21cu in models for $3,000 each set. In addition royalties were to be paid on all machines built and a percentage of US made parts would be used.

By 1935 however, the whole bike was made in Japan and two years later they were called Rikuo. Further political changes saw Harley-Davidson pulling out of the equation all together and the Japan Internal Combustion Engine Company took over manufacture.

Records such as they are show that in the Rikuo guise some 18,000 machines in all variations from solos to sidecars to trikes

• *Harley-Davidson* •

were made. Engine capacities also varied.

Around this time as well there were also other Japanese manufacturers with various copies of machines and engines from all over the world. One firm built a machine called the Toyo Kogyo, which was a bike as far as the rear of the seat then it was attached to a chassis with a platform on it for carrying loads.

Harley in America were unable to help Sims and some other sources, one may well have expected to come up trumps were also surprisingly lacking in information on the bikes sitting in Cantwell's workshop. It would appear that the bike came from Guadalcanal from where it was salvaged after the war and was used for a period in the New Hebrides before lying disused for 40 years.

Sims meticulously recorded each scrap of information and the puzzle became more interesting and complex. Even now his task is far from over, as slowly more items of interest surface.

Cantwell meanwhile had worked six plus hours a day on the two wrecks and one machine is now up and running being a combination of the two.

When Cantwell stripped the machines he had a strong steel chassis that housed a motorcycle engine at the front, but the rear of the frame carried an axle mounted on leaf springs. The forks were blade type girder forks similar to European machines at the time.

All three wheels (or four counting the spare) were solid rims

All photographs: Ian Kerr

345

Military Harleys

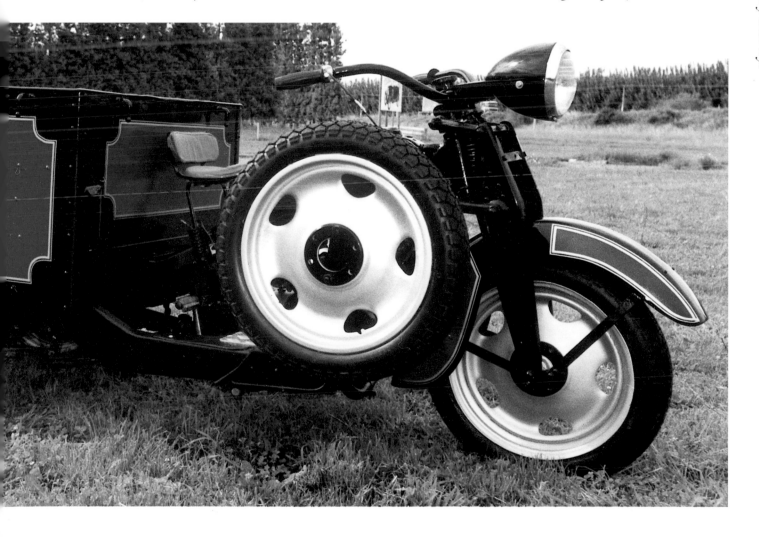

with cut outs, but had conventional inflatable, as opposed to solid, tires.

All the 18-inch wheels were interchangeable for obvious reasons. All these parts were sound and reusable, but Cantwell needed the expertise of his former trade to make mudguards, along with side panels for the back. Carpentry skills were called for to make a floor for the load space.

On the mechanical front, the 750 engine was seized and a lot of time a patience was required to free it off, but fortunately parts were not too hard to come by being pretty standard Harley-Davidson. Interestingly the crankcases have the addition of Japanese hieroglyphics that form part of the actual casting as well as stamped in numbers identifying the type, bore and stroke.

The engine is mounted across the bike rather than in line with the tank and is mated to a three forward and one reverse car type gearbox. A long lever comes up on the left of the single saddle seat to select ratios. Drive to the rear axle complete with differential is by shaft.

There is no brake on the front wheel but both rear wheels have internal expanding drum brakes and they are operated by a right hand foot pedal and a rod linkage. A foot pedal mirrors the brake one the left side of the machine and operates the diaphragm clutch. On the outer edge of the left of the bike a ratchet-operated parking brake stops it running away whilst it is being loaded, quite useful if the payload is bombs!

The only other controls are a twist grip in the conventional place and a hand operated oil pump on top of the tank. Although the engine has a mechanical pump it was apparently felt that additional oil might be helpful at high speeds. The bike is geared for 35mph flat out so this seems somewhat unnecessary.

The bike was repainted mostly in black but with panels of blue lined with two gold lines similar to contemporary machines of the time. Nobody seems quite sure why it was not done in military colors!

Some items are not finished due to the lack of information, like the lighting system. Despite the large Lucas light sitting at the front it is not connected and there are no rear lights fitted. The bike was reassembled as it came once again due to lack of a definitive specification.

Having got the bike running and to a reasonably complete condition, it has been placed in the Te Puke car museum just outside Tauranga on the north island in the hope that more information may come to light. Due to the museum being very much a working one as opposed to a mausoleum, I was given the privilege of a quick spin on the machine.

Sitting on the bike it is very comfortable, the wide bars coming almost back to you, whilst your feet sit flat on the footboards on either side. The saddle is separately sprung from the rest of the bike.

It is just a case of turning on the petrol and oil, pulling up the ignition switch on the tank top and swinging down on the bicycle crank that is the kick-start. Several kicks and the bike fired into life and sat chuffing quietly away through the long exhaust that exits below the rear platform.

The clutch freed easily and the gear slipped in silently and the bike pulled cleanly away without fuss. Gear changes were also fuss free and the bike felt faster than the tank-mounted speedo suggested. Cornering was easy; in fact, apart from not having to balance the thing; it was just like riding a bike.

Surprisingly the suspension, which was presumably designed to take great weights, was supple enough to absorb the undulations, even with just a rider on board.

My brief test was over far too quickly but as to date, only

one other of this type of machine is known, everyone understandably was being careful with this one. Its rarity is such that the Japanese government is interested in acquiring it as part of a historical display. Until then it will remain at the museum in the hope that more information comes to light to document this interesting machine still further.

Harley Racing

Richard Fleury

Strange though it might seem given Harley-Davidson's later motorsports successes, the company's founders were reluctant racers.

For the first few years, the fledgling marque kept its distance from the dollar-hungry world of motorsport. But before long, the snowballing competition success of rival manufacturers finally forced Milwaukee's hand.

Conservative men by nature, only William Harley believed in the power of sporting accomplishment to sell road machines. As a result, Harley-Davidson continued to steer clear of racing, even after Walter Davidson turned out to be a gifted competition rider.

Walter was 30 years old when in 1907 he entered a two-day, 400-mile endurance run from Chicago to Kokomo, Indiana, and back. He was one of only three riders to complete the event with a perfect score.

Just one year later Walter was feted by the motorcycling press following an prestigious competition win aboard a belt-driven single-cylinder Model 4.

He achieved a perfect 1,000-point score in the Federation of American Motorcyclists' national endurance run, a 175-mile event from Catskill, New York, to New York City.

The triumph worked wonders for Harley-Davidson's public image and sales tripled to 3,100 machines the following year.

By 1909 the American motorcycle racing scene was thriving. Riders competed at fairground tracks as a kind of motorized rodeo attraction, hill-climbs were catching on fast and board track motordromes were appearing all over the U.S.

Despite his own personal successes Walter, like Arthur Davidson, took a more skeptical view when it came to the merits of factory-supported racing. Consequently Harley-Davidson's early forays into competition were tentative, low-key affairs. A handful of race bikes were built for privateer racers in 1910 but it wasn't until a year later, when the company's sworn rival Indian scored a well-publicized hat-trick at the Isle of Man races that Milwaukee was forced to take its own sporting endeavors seriously.

A works race department wouldn't materialize for several years yet, but the company began taking an active interest in the competition successes of privateer-run Harley-Davidson machines. These famously included a victory in the San Jose road race, won on a 61cu in X8E which led the field by a 17-mile margin.

It may not have been ready to race officially, but that didn't stop Harley-Davidson bragging about privateer wins in its advertising. An expedient strategy, this allowed the company to bask in the reflected glory of competition successes while disassociating itself from high-profile failures such as the comprehensive trouncing of a pair of non-works bikes in the 1913 San Diego–Phoenix Desert Race.

Meanwhile, as stronger and more powerful versions of Harley's V-twin engine were developed, the factory prepared its assault on motorcycle sport. Milwaukee finally took the plunge in 1913 and decided to field a factory team to take the battle to Indian. The famous Harley "Wrecking Crew" was born.

The Crew made its debut at the Dodge City 300-mile race in 1914. They came home without a single win but despite this inauspicious start, Harley-Davidson's racing glory years were about to begin.

Before the end of 1914, the Crew had claimed one national championship win at Birmingham, Alabama. But the fight for track supremacy began in earnest at the start of the 1915 season. The Dodge City and Venice, California, road races both fell to Harley works rider Otto Walker, much to

• Harley-Davidson •

the chagrin of Indian and Excelsior's team chiefs.

Soon the Wrecking Crew was living up to its name, demolishing the competition at dirt-track and board-track racing across the country. By 1921, Milwaukee's domination of U.S. motorcycle sport was almost total and the speed and reliablitity of Milwaukee metal was established beyond all doubt.

The decade 1915–25 proved a golden era for US motorcycle racing and Milwaukee was right there in the thick of it.

While the World War One raged in Europe, the Harley Wrecking Crew's overwhelming success made national sporting celebrities of men such as Eddie Brinck, "Red" Parkhurst and Jim Davis and secured a place in racing history for the Crew's legendary race manager Bill Ottaway. Victory followed victory, boosting Milwaukee's credibility and proving machines such as the K model and eight-valve racers — both based on the 61cu in (1,000cc) twin.

Although crude by today's standards, board-tracker bikes were fast. The eight-valver kicked out 20hp on a good day and routinely lapped at over the ton, thundering around a steeply banked circuit surfaced with wooden boards.

Ferociously quick and incredibly dangerous, board racing was a popular spectacle in its heyday. Despite the high speeds, the bikes had skinny tyres, no brakes and riders wore only lace-up boots, a leather helmet, goggles and a sweater for protection. If they lost control, the consequences could be brutal — and often fatal. The speeds may have been lower, but compared with modern GP and Superbike racing, board-track was a grisly bloodbath.

The sport was dominated by professional teams. The Harley-Davidson race bikes of the time, such as the Peashooter, a light-weight 350cc ohv single, and the multiple-valve 61cu in twins were specialist sports tools either not available to ordinary road rider or amateur racer or too expensive.

At the same time, however, Harley riders were making their mark in point-to-point racing — timed, long-distance endurance contests held on America's rapidly expanding road network. Earl Hadfield, for instance, rode more than 3,000 miles between New York and Los Angeles in under 78 hours. And with Hap Sherer in the saddle, a Harley-Davidson sport twin made it from Denver to Chicago in 48 hours. Sherer also won the Three Flags Run from Canada to Mexico on the same bike.

Despite an impressive track record, a postwar sales slump led Harley-Davidson to rethink its race spending and the factory temporarily withdrew from motorsport in 1921 — the same year a Harley-Davidson became the first motorcycle to win a race at an average speed above 100mph. Never fully convinced of the benefits of racing, a nonplussed Walter Davidson was said to have pulled the plug after Dodge City's police force continued to buy Indians even after the Harley-Davidson team had won the

town's famous 300-mile race four years running.

But the popularity of bike racing continued to grow in the U.S. — Harley or no Harley — and the American Motorcyclist Association was established as the official regulatory body in 1924.

After a few years of watching on the sidelines as racing honors fell to Indian and Excelsior riders — some of them ex-Wrecking Crew stars — Milwaukee took up the racing challenge again. The factory's most stylish comeback win came in 1925 when the young

• Harley Racing •

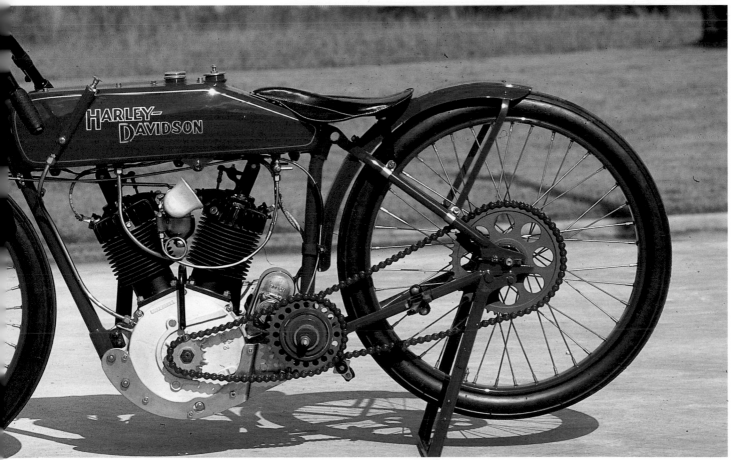

Joe Petrali vanquished all-comers at Altoona board track in Pennsylvania riding a twin-cam Harley.

During the late 1920s and 1930s, Harley hero Joe Petrali was racing's undisputed king. A motorcycle prodigy, Petrali was born in Sacramento, California, in 1904. He learned to ride while barely into his teens and by the tender age of 16 was taking on experienced, hardcase board racers and winning.

Petrali began his career riding Indian singles, got his big break at the age of 21, thanks to an exceptional piece of chutzpah. A virtual unknown, he rolled up at a Pennsylvania race meeting without a bike and somehow talked the Harley works team into giving him a ride. Amazingly, they let him race the bike of injured factory rider Ralph Hepburn. Even more amazingly, Petrali won . . . and did it in tremendous style. Spectators gaped in disbelief as the mystery youth annihilated every one of the big name professional riders around him, averaging a blistering 100mph-plus over the 100-mile race. By the time he crossed the finish line, Petrali was already a legend.

Right: Freddie Dixon on an eight-valve Harley in the early 1920s. National Motor museum via Roy Bacon

• *Harley-Davidson* •

This explosive debut set the scene for his entire track career. From that moment onward, Petrali was near-untouchable. When he raced, no one else got a look in and his freehold on the chequered flag continued for more than a decade.

Not content with being crowned hillclimb National Champion for five consecutive years from 1932, in 1935 he took first place in every single National Championship dirt track race of the season, knocking off five separate wins in a single day at one American Motorcyclist Association event in New York. And two years later he took a streamliner version of Harley-Davidson's new 61 ohv Knucklehead twin to a new world record speed of 136.183mph on the sands at Daytona Beach.

Yet despite his towering achievements riding Harley-Davidson machinery — notably the 21cu in Peashooter single — in the 1930s, Petrali received very little help from the factory. With America in the grip of the Great Depression, racing budgets dwindled away as Harley-Davidson, like other motorcycle manufacturers, grew more concerned with survival — and the looming threat of World War Two — than track glory.

While Petrali continued his reign, board-track racing was slowly dying. Always a risky undertaking, by the end of the "Roaring" Twenties it was becoming near-suicidal. The V-twin bikes were getting faster but the board circuits weren't getting any bigger. In an attempt to reduce mortality rates, smaller capacity classes were introduced. But it was too late, board track's heyday was over.

Below Left: Flathead racer from about 1921, probably at Brooklands racetrack, England. National Motor museum via Roy Bacon

Below: Dixon on an eight-valve Harley in 1923. National Motor museum via Roy Bacon

As the Depression struck America, bike racing drifted into the doldrums. In a much-needed attempt to breathe new life into the scene, the American Motorcyclist Association introduced Class C racing in 1934. Designed to woo amateur enthusiasts back into racing, Class C rules limited machinery to the more affordable 750cc standard production motorcycles offered by the big U.S. manufacturers, notably Harley-Davidson and Indian.

A long-overdue alternative to the closed shop of factory-dominated professional racing, Class C was a huge success, particularly on dirt or "flat" tracks. Factory-supported Class A professional racing continued of course, but very soon every medium-sized town in America would soon have its own flat oval track. Dirt track had arrived.

As American as cowboys and Indians, Ma's apple pie, Ronald McDonald and drive-by shootings, dirt track or "oval" racing is the original Stateside bike sport. It has existed in one form or another for almost as long as the motorcycle itself. And as long as riders have raced on dirt, they've done it on Harley-Davidson mounts.

Also known as flat-track racing, dirt track has been at the heart of the U.S. bike racing scene since board track's decline. Once a smalltown, spit'n'sawdust fairground sideshow, today it's a national institution and an established training ground for America's many 500 GP heroes. Greats such as Eddie Lawson and Wayne Rainey came up through the dirt-track scene, developing nerves of steel and learning the

black art of rear-wheel steering along the way.

There's no real European equivalent to this most gung-ho, hairy-chested brand of bike racing. If you think speedway looks dangerous, recalibrate your gray matter and try to imagine the something similar, only fought out at speeds topping 130mph, on mile-long tracks, with a pack of 16 desperate lunatics slithering sideways as they casually hurl agriculturally heavy 750cc, 100bhp V-twin monsters around each corner in a wild series of extravagant, full-lock broadsides. If their bikes begin to step out of line mid-slide, riders calmly reach down and adjust the steering damper with one hand while drifting across the track

at a ton-plus. The word insanity doesn't begin to describe these intense, shoulder-to-shoulder clashes.

Dirt tracker bikes were not even equipped with brakes until 1970, when officials conceded that rear brakes were an acceptable accessory. Until then, throwing your bike into a kamikaze tailslide was the only way to scrub off speed. Front brakes are still conspicuously absent on today's dirt irons . . .

Flat track racing began as America's grassroots, "people's" bike sport, with unofficial outlaw races springing up all over the country until it went legit in 1946, when the national championship was founded by the American Motorcycle Association. Since then

Below Left: Part of Harley's Museum collection. Ian Kerr

Below: Harley racing legend Al Knapps' 1940 750 in the pits at Daytona waiting to take to the banking in the classic race series. Ian Kerr

Below Right: Close-up of 1949 engine.
Ian Kerr

Below: 1949 racing Harley complete with modern steering damper seen in the pits at Daytona in 1998. Ian Kerr

• *Harley-Davidson* •

it's remained an integral part of the US motorcycle racing land-scape. Until very recently the AMA championship was decided not just in road racing competition but in five different racing arenas, dirt track included.

Only in 1986 was a separate road racing series created. Before than, the winner of the AMA Number One plate had to prove his supremacy on one mile and half-mile dirt ovals, as well as tarmac. The championship also included two other forms of racing. These were short track and the crowds' favourite — the Tourist Trophy steeplechase or TT. An adrenalin-charged mix of dirt track and motocross, TT races (nothing to do with the historic Isle of Man event) incorporated a dramatic 40ft jump midway through each lap. In the 1960s, up-and-coming Tourist Trophy stars included a young gun by the name of Evel Knievel, who was reputedly so quick he had to be handicapped by starting races behind the rest of the field facing in the wrong direction. The young motorcycle daredevil still managed to win, more often than not.

Sponsored for several years by Harley-Davidson, Knievel later used modified XR750 racers for many of his famous death-defying leaps.

Dirt-track racing has changed little since the bike sport boom triggered by the AMA's introduction of Class C racing in the 1930s. In 1941, Harley-Davidson launched its WR side-valve (or "flathead") racer. A hopped-up variant of the WL road bike, the WR flat tracker had race-spec valve gear, magneto ignition and a lightened frame.

Its successor arrived in 1952, in the shape of the Model KR 750cc flathead racer, a rigid-framed purpose-built dirt-tracker.

Riding WRs and KRs, fearless Harley team racers such as Joe Leonard, Carroll Resweber, Jimmy Chann and Bart Markel dominated America's oval dirt tracks between 1947 and 1961. Talented Texan Resweber won the national title four years running between 1958–62.

Bart Markel's aggressive, hell-for-leather attitude won him a loyal following as well as three

championship titles. The fans loved his hard-charging riding style which frequently saw him colliding with crash barriers and other racers.

Markel's technique didn't translate well to tarmac events, however, and his reluctance to brake for corners led to a string of spectacular tumbles. Against the odds he survived an impressively long 23-year career between 1957 and 1980.

By the late 1960s, more power was required and a replacement for the KR became an urgent priority for Milwaukee. It arrived in 1970, in the shapely form of the XR750. The functional, stripped-out XR, with its oversized air filters, minimal seat, compact teardrop fuel tank and complex tangle of pipework was to become a motorcycling icon and considered by many present-day Harley-Davidson afficianados to be the coolest-looking Harley ever created, bar none.

It performed, too, on the dirt at least. On the ovals, against BSAs, Triumphs and Nortons, the 130mph XR750 achieved much more than it would ever manage in its less competitive road-racing form against the latest Japanese tarmac rockets.

Of course, this dirt-track dominance was due in no small part to the AMA's protectionist tactic of handicapping un-American machinery. Bikes powered by overhead-valved engines (i.e. European machines) were limited to 500cc while side-valvers (i.e. Harleys) could go up to 750cc. Subtle it wasn't but the strategy kept Milwaukee in the points.

Above Right: KR 750. Garry Stuart

Below Right: K model dirt-tracker at Delmar, California. Ian Kerr

Below: 1948 Harley racer offered for sale at Daytona. Ian Kerr

The XR750's early dirt track triumphs came courtesy of Mark Brelsford and Gary Scott, before Kenny Roberts' fearsomely unpredictable Yamaha TZ750 snatched the AMA Grand National title in 1973 and 1974.

The following season, XR750 jockey Gary Scott won back the championship for Harley-Davidson and between 1976 and 1978 Jay "Springer" Springsteen cemented the XR's reputation by handing the Number One plate to Milwaukee for three years running. One of American bike sport's best-

loved stars, Springer has been plagued by a mysterious illness throughout his long career, although his health problems have not stopped him competing in almost every different class of dirt and road racing.

The venerable alloy-engined XR750 is still delivering the goods today, with only minor changes to the original design. Almost 30 years after its launch, Harley's most famous race tool is still mixing it with latter-day dirt stars such as Steve Eklund, Ricky Graham and Scott Parker in the saddle.

The single most successful rider in the history of dirt track, Scott Parker has stamped his authority on the sport like no one before. Parker, who was just 13 when he competed in his first race, has ruled the roost for more than a decade. His first championship title came in 1988, setting the scene for a dazzling career which, to date, has earned him a staggering nine AMA Number One plates.

Like Bart Markel and Jay Springsteen, the supremely gifted Parker hails from Flint, Michigan, the appropriately-named town

Left: Fully faired racing KR bears the name of Harley legendary rider George Roeder. Garry Stuart

Below: A stripped down KR-engined racer contrasts strongly with the fully faired bike at left. Ian Kerr

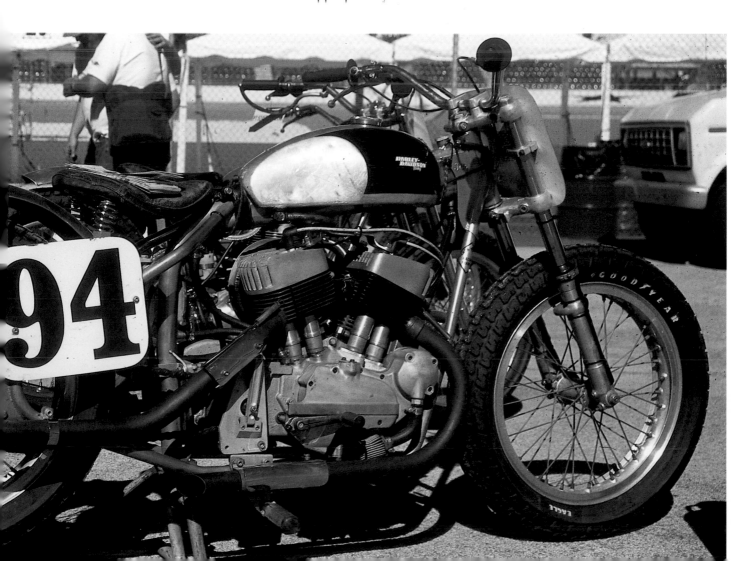

which seems to breed rock-hard dirt track daredevils.

In 1991, he became only the second rider ever to win four championships in a row. Harley-Davidson team mate Chris Carr took the title the following year, then in 1993 it went to Ricky Graham. Parker returned to reclaim his throne in 1994 and refused to give it up again for the next five seasons.

Despite being outgunned by the Honda RS750 during the 1980s, the XR750 remains a dirt track favorite today. And with almost 100bhp on tap and a top speed of around 135mph, it should stick around for a few years to come.

Recent changes to the AMA race rules, however, could soon see Harley's old warhorse competing against a new crop of rivals and finally end its lengthy dirt track reign. A planned 1,000cc ceiling in some dirt racing classes may soon see the XR battling against faster bikes powered by big-bore Harley engines. Even Ducati or Suzuki sportsbike powerplants are being tested in experimental one-off dirt trackers.

Milwaukee may have been a driving force in dirt track but the Harley-Davidson name never made quite the same impact in the world of road racing.

Even with world-class talent such as the late, great Cal Rayborn

pushing Milwaukee-built race machinery to the limit and beyond, the factory team has traditionally struggled to gain an edge over other marques.

As far as Harley-Davidson was concerned, modern road-racing began in 1937 at the Daytona 200 — the first time the classic American road race was held. Then, as now, Harley-Davidson tarmac racers had a tough fight on their hands every time they took to the track.

Harley's 45cu in sports bike, the WLDR, was heavier and less agile than its Indian counterpart. But the bulletproof side-valve motor was more reliable and, thanks to tuning wizard Tom Sifton, a San Jose Harley-Davidson dealer, it was soon winning races in the hands of racer Sam Arena.

Sifton's breathing and lubrication tweaks found their way into subsequent machines including the WR racer introduced in 1941.

Early skirmishes with old adversary Indian would soon give way to battles against British opponents on faster, lighter kit. During the 1940s and early 1950s, Harley's WR 45 race bike struggled against rivals including the Indian Scout 45cu in racers and the latest British bikes, notably the reliable and extremely rapid Featherbed Manx Norton.

Below: 1996 photo of a 1955 KR 750.
This shot clearly shows the rudimentary
layout including the hand gear change
that riders had to battle with during
races — not the most comfortable of
rides. Roy Bacon

Right: Vastly modified Harley-powered Hillclimber complete with chains and lengthened swinging arm to help get the power down and prevent the bike looping on the ascent. Ian Kerr

Below Right: 1972 Harley in full racing trim decked out in traditional racing colors. Ian Kerr

Below: Night-time action at the Municipal Stadium, Daytona, shows a short-track machine powered by a V-twin as opposed to the more common road tax single-engined bikes bearing the Harley name. Ian Kerr

Milwaukee suspended race bike production briefly when the United States entered World War Two but Class C racing resumed at Daytona in 1947. Honors fell to Indian rider Johnny Spiegelhoff in the season-opening Daytona 200 that year and former Harley racer Floyd Emde won in 1948, again on an Indian.

By 1952, Harley's WR TT (the road racing version of the side-valve WR) was well off the pace. Fortunately, its long-awaited replacement, the KR TT, was waiting in the wings. This side-valve 750cc engine was the most radical makeover yet of Harley's long-serving V-twin but it was still heavier and slower than most of the British equivalents.

The new bike finally gave Harley-Davidson the chance to trounce the Brits in 1953, with Paul Goldsmith's win at the Daytona 200-mile race on a 37hp KR. Milwaukee breathed a sigh of relief. It was the first time Harley had won Daytona, the quintessential American road race, since the war.

Harley's Daytona glory was short-lived as BSA took the race the following year. But the British victory proved just as temporary. Harley's secret weapon, tuner Tom Sifton, had discovered some new tricks which would transform the KR's lacklustre performance.

As the 1954 season unfolded, racer Joe Leonard took his Sifton-tuned KR to no fewer than eight AMA race victories, clinching the national championship in the process.

Sifton's tweaks must have been something very special because the very same bike went on to win the 1955 Daytona

Left: Many dealers use racing to promote their dealership and become almost as well known as Harley. Shown here is one of Bartels' short-track machines on display at Harley's exhibition at Daytona in 1995. Ian Kerr

Below Left: Alastair Quaid's XR750, seen in 1994. Roy Bacon

Below: Jay Springsteen's 883 Sportster racing at Daytona. Garry Stuart

200-miler in the hands of 19-year-old rookie by the name of Brad Andres. By the end of the season Andres had won the national title and become the only "first-timer" ever to claim the coveted Number One plate.

Harley's successes led to new regulations intended to slow the KRs down and give other makes a fighting chance, but the KR still scooped all seven AMA title rounds in 1956. And in 1957, both Daytona victory and the championship title fell to Joe Leonard, with rising Harley-Davidson star Carroll Resweber coming in fourth at Daytona. The following season Resweber cleaned up. Furthermore, he remained champion for four consecutive years (1958–61), an achievement which earned him a place in the record books. Alongside the seemingly unstoppable Resweber, Harley's other big hitters at this time included dirt demon "Black" Bart Markel and Roger Reiman, both of whom later became AMA champions.

Resweber's reign — and sadly, his track career — came to an abrupt end during the 1962 season when he was involved in an appalling crash with two other racers during a practice session in Illinois. Resweber, who was leading the championship at the time, smashed a leg. One of the other riders, Jack Goulson, was killed. The tragedy allowed Bart Markel to take the title in 1962 but BSA and Matchless rider Dick Mann took the AMA crown from Harley-Davidson the following year.

Roger Reiman reclaimed the AMA championship for Harley-Davidson in 1964, with Bart

Markel taking the top spot in 1965 and 1966.

Meanwhile, Harley-Davidson's 1960s tie-up with Italy's Aermacchi opened up new racing possibilities with the Aermacchi/Harley-Davidson Sprint putting in creditable performances in 250cc AMA and Grand Prix races. Another lightweight Aermacchi/Harley race bike, the twin-cylinder RR250 later carried Walter Villa to three 250 World Championships and one world 350cc title in 1974–76. To this day they remain the only world championship titles won on Harleys.

By the mid-1960s, the side-valve KR racer was growing long in the tooth and only the Milwaukee-friendly AMA regulations, which pitted the 750cc flathead against smaller 500cc ohv Brit irons, kept the Harley-Davidson competitive alongside the likes of Triumph and Matchless. That said, the KR did notch up a dozen Daytona wins between 1955 and 1969 — not bad for a design deemed outclassed in its first season's racing.

As Harley engineers kept looking for more performance, Californian Lance Weil campaigned an experimental race bike at circuits around Britain in 1967. The one-off 883cc ohv-engined machine stirred up plenty of excitement by winning a brace of 1,000cc races.

• *Harley-Davidson* •

Below: One of the many dealer-sponsored machines in the 883 series which proved so popular with American racing fans thanks to the bike's being kept close to stock specification. Ian Kerr

Below, Below Right and Bottom Right: These machines show the diversiity of engine styles used by Harley. V-twin powers short track racer No 9; single powers road-based Aermacchi-Harley-Davidson racer at right; watercooled-twin from the AMF days. Roy Bacon, Ian Kerr, via Roy Bacon

But Weil's one-man transatlantic invasion wasn't just an attempt to wind up the Limeys. His bike's lowered chassis became the backbone of the faster, revamped KR on which Cal Rayborn whipped the opposition to win 1968's Daytona 200-miler. Rayborn, from Spring Valley, California, won Daytona just as convincingly in 1969, while the AMA title fell to Harley team mate Mert Lawwill.

Two years later, Rayborn piloted an XLR-engined Harley-Davidson streamliner to a new world speed record of 265mph at Bonneville Salt Flats.

In February 1970 Harley proudly unveiled its new race tool, the iron-engined XR750, at the Houston Astrodome. Trumpeted as an all-new design, it was in fact based on a hybrid of old KR cycle parts and the engine adapted from the XL Sportster production bike.

In flat-track guise, the XR750 eventually proved a winner for Harley-Davidson. But in tarmac trim it was blighted with design problems which would prove catastrophic out on the circuit. It was swift enough, but reliability was a nightmare and the bike's notorious fragility and overheating problems quickly earned it the nickname the "Waffle Iron."

The dismal 1970 AMA season saw the Harley racers thrashed by Honda-riding Dick Mann and produced the Harley-Davidson works team's poorest-ever showing in the national championship. Mert Lawwill's sixth place was the best result.

Lumbered with the XR750, the Harley-Davidson team fared badly in the 1971 season too,

again losing to Mann, this time aboard a BSA. Yet, despite his machine's glaring inadequacies, it was during this unhappy period that XR750 pilot Cal Rayborn revealed his brilliance as a racer. If it didn't break down on him, Rayborn worked miracles with the infamous "Waffle Iron."

Desperate to claw back some credibility, Milwaukee rushed out a new alloy-engined XR750 in time for the 1972 season. It was a great improvement. The alloy cylinders and head proved a more rugged design and Harley-Davidson's

young Grand National hopeful Mark Brelsford won the AMA title by a healthy margin. The same year, Cal Rayborn took a factory XR750 to the UK (his idea, not the factory's) to compete in the Transatlantic Match Races. The bike was clearly outclassed by British and Japanese hardware, but that didn't faze master-rider Rayborn, who, against the odds, floored the opposition with a virtuoso performance.

The 1973 saw the team dogged by disastrous luck once again. A terrible high speed crash

at Daytona saw reigning champ Brelsford's bike engulfed in flames. The accident broke both his legs, finishing his season. A seized engine downed the great Cal Rayborn in the same race, breaking his collarbone in the process.

A demoralized Rayborn left Harley-Davidson at the end of the season. Tragically, he was killed soon afterwards on his first non-Harley-Davidson outing. He was piloting a 500cc Suzuki two-stroke around the Auckland circuit in New Zealand when it seized, slamming him into the crash barrier.

A natural-born, road racing genius and natural heir to the great Joe Petrali, Rayborn had already earned the respect of the entire bike racing community when he died at the age of 33. Often cited as the man who blazed a trail for his countrymen Kenny Roberts, Wayne Rainey and Randy Mamola, he notched up 11 AMA race wins including two at Daytona. He was never crowned champion but is nevertheless widely regarded as one of the finest tarmac riders America has ever produced.

As the 1970s wore on, Harley-Davidson's championship form gradually slid away and by the 1980s, American motorcycle fans were forced to turn to dirt track action if they wanted to see homegrown irons taking race honors.

At least they did until the advent of Battle of the Twins, the AMA's popular road-racing series for tuned production machines.

The BOT rules, which included a 1,000cc limit, gave Harley-Davidson another chance to compete against Japanese machinery from Yamaha, Suzuki and Kawasaki with a realistic chance of success.

Ducati won the first series in 1982. Then, in 1983, three-times national champion Jay Springsteen thundered to victory in the BOT

series aboard a machine christened with the unholy moniker "Lucifer's Hammer."

Basically a former ex-works road race chassis from the early 1970s with competition running gear, mated with an engine poached from the potent XR1000 street bike, the awesome "Hammer" was the warped creation of Harley racing manager Dick O'Brien.

With Springsteen at the helm, this celebrated mutant superbike stormed to victory at Daytona in 1983. Then, ridden by

Gene Church, tweaked by tuner Don Tilley and sponsored by HOG — the factory-supported Harley Owners Group — the mighty Hammer continued to thrill patriotic American crowds by grabbing three successive titles from 1984 to 1986 in the BOT Grand Prix class.

In 1988 Harley-Davidson launched a new semi-pro, one-make racing class, the 883 Sport Twins series. Featuring stripped-down Sportsters, it quickly proved a big hit with U.S. race fans. As in other one-make classes, the equally-

matched, lightly-modified machinery made for some exciting, close-fought action with riders vying for every scrap of advantage. Meanwhile, similar Sportster-based machines did battle on the ovals in the 883 Dirt Track sister series.

Surprisingly, the first ever 883 road-racing champ was not a new all-American track hero but a Brit.Thirtysomething Nigel Gale, a former North Sea trawlerman and weekend motocrosser, beat all-comers to scoop the new title.

After a brief career crewing fishing boats, Gale left England

Below Left: Harley's VR1000 racing bike was the company's first venture into beam frames and an engine not based on its road-going powerplants. Ian Kerr

Below: Modern technology abounds. Ian Kerr

Right and Overleaf, Above Left: You can have any color you like as long as it's black or orange! The VR1000 in 1995. Both: Roy Bacon

back at the age of 17 to seek his fortune overseas and wound up in sunny California. He decided to try his hand at dirt-track racing and soon earned himself a reputation for speed and a slightly wild riding style.

A successful debut season in 1986 netted Gale a "Rookie of the Year" title and brought him to the attention of Jay Springsteen's sponsor Bartel's. Impressed by his ability, the California-based race backer him offered a ride in the new Harley 883 series and the rest, as they say, is history.

After years without a competitive road-racing machine, Milwaukee embarked on an ambitious (and hugely expensive) new factory project in the late 1980s when it began developing the sophisticated VR1000 racer.

The bike was a milestone in Harley-Davidson history. Unlike every previous Harley racer, the VR was not based on a production model. Conceived as a pure track tool, it was the first purpose-built racer ever built by the company, with a fairing designed by Harley-Davidson styling chief Willie G. Davidson. Harley did, however, offer a road-legal copy of the bike in strictly limited numbers with a price tag of nearly $50,000.

A bold, hi-tech design by Milwaukee standards, the 170mph VR1000 was powered by a fuel-injected 60-degree, vee-twin dohc engine with liquid cooling and multi-valves developing 135bhp. Designed with the help of engineering gurus from NASCAR and Indy Car racing, it took five years to go from the drawing board to the circuit.

Harley-Davidson's factory race department announced its intention to campaign the bike in AMA Superbike and Grand Prix racing. But when the new Harley was first ridden in anger in 1994's Daytona 200, there were disturbing echoes of the XR750's jinxed debut season back in the 1970s. The new bike handled well but top speed was down on the pack and mechanical failure forced Miguel DuHamel to retire after 20 laps.

DuHamel put in some respectable results later in the season but never quite managed to clinch a win, thanks to a lack of power and poor reliability compared with other machines on the grid.

National dirt-track champion Chris Carr subsequently joined the VR1000 team along with former Kawasaki racer Thomas Wilson but both men found it difficult to win convincing results in the AMA Superbike series. Carr surrendered the Superbike ride to concentrate on his dirt-track career and since then Harley has hired riders including Canadian Pascale Picotte

*Below Left and Right: Same bike —
but racing as number 12 in 1996.*
Both: Ian Kerr

*Overleaf: Harley short-track and long-
track racers use the proprietary single-
cylinder road tax engine like many
other bikes that compete on the dirt.*
Ian Kerr

and Christopher Rankin to pilot
the VR.

By 1999, Harley was getting
desperate for a win, having sunk
hundreds of millions of dollars.
To improve the odds of success,
Milwaukee recruited veteran superbike rider Scott Russell to kick off
the AMA season at Daytona.
Harley had high hopes of Russell,
known as "Mr Daytona" since
winning America's most prestigious road race five times between
1992 and 1998.

Yet it wasn't to be. Scott was
attacked in a Daytona bar before
the race and a knuckleduster blow
to the face smashed his cheekbone.
As the 200-mile race got underway, Russell was on his way to
hospital. When Harley team-mate
Picotte crashed out, the team's
best shot at its first Daytona
victory since 1969 turned into a
total washout.

Milwaukee's legions of loyal
fans would like nothing more than
to see a new "Wrecking Crew"
storming to victory aboard
machines decked out in the traditional black and orange Harley-
Davidson livery. Will those bikes
be VR1000s? Time will tell . . .

VR1000

Ian Kerr

VR1000

People have short memories. It's all too easy to forget Harley has a racing and sporting heritage as good as any factory had when they were at their racing best. But how to remind people of the glorious past? On the dirt-track side of things Harley continues to win, albeit with Rotax-powered bikes, totally different to the type of engines that have made them famous.

Back in the late 1980s Harley hit on the idea of the VR racing bike. Despite the company's resources, it was not all plain sailing and it struggled to get more than 130bhp out of the new motor. Other things had been simple — the fairing design, had come from none other than Willie G. Davidson, the design guru and descendant of one the founders.

Eventually in 1994 the bike sat on the Daytona grid ready to race. The very public launch may well have been thecompany's way of telling everybody they were back. However, it was no fairytale re-launch.

Mark Tuttle, Harley's vice president of engineering, was on hand to answer questions. The broadening of the customer base — i.e. advertising — the need to become more familiar with modern technology — i.e. development —

and, last, to instil a core spirit within the company were the reasons he gave for coming back to mainstream competition.

It was certainly a brave move whichever way you look at it, a brand-new untested (in competition) bike debuting before a home crowd that wanted a win. But by the time practice was over, Miguel DuHamel's qualifying time was nearly eight seconds slower than the pole position Ducati and the cynics were starting to crow. (The other rider, a gangling Fritz Kling, was not in the batting order!)

When the bike lasted just 22 of the 57 race laps, due to the failure of a weld on the balance shaft, the critics were even more smug. Two weeks later the bike failed to finish again, at Phoenix, Arizona, when a fuel line managed to starve the engine of fuel — the "I told you so" brigade surfaced again. The season continued in a similar vein, lots of promising positions that never held to the flag thanks to mechanical failures.

But that is taking a simplistic look at the whole issue. How long did it take Cagiva to feature as a serious contender in the GPs and how many millions have been spent getting there? Harley had only started on the VR some five years before and the original intention was to modify an existing engine. It was only when the engi-

neers really started looking into it they realized that approach was not going to be enough to produce a winning bike.

The design team at that time consisted of a few well-known names: Jerry Branch, best known for his Harley cylinder-head work; Erik Buell, who now designs his own Harley-powered bikes; Dick O'Brien, the former race boss, and last but not least, Don Tilley, the tuner of the now legendary "Lucifer's Hammer" thunderbike. The man in charge was Mark

Millar who actually got the whole thing up to a prototype stage.

Rousch Racing was used to get the cylinder-head work done thanks to its Nascar expertise, as well as Harley's desire to keep the whole project as American as possible. Steve Scheibe did much of the work for them and he was eventually hired to take over the project; as a result, he virtually re-designed the motor.

The engine is a very compact unit for a 60-degree V-twin. The bore and stroke are 98mm and 66mm respectively and the cylinders are nikasil-coated aluminum. The crank has two titanium plain-bearing rods running on ball bearing big ends, while the sump is a dry. The double overhead cams operate four valves per cylinder and are chain-driven, while a counter balancer is driven off the crank to smooth things out.

Water-cooling is used to keep the 996cc's from getting too hot and this also assists the fuel injection system as well. Primary drive to the "dry" clutch is by gears, the gearbox itself being a five-speed item.

The motor first used at Daytona pumped out 140bhp at 10,400rpm with the rev limiter set at 11,000rpm. Weight-wise they were at a disadvantage weighing in at 355lb, 20lb more than the minimum allowed weight under AMA rules.

While the use of magnesium for crankcases would shave 8lb in one hit this would mean that all the road bikes produced would

also have to use this expensive commodity. Harley built seven in order to race and if the dream of challenging in world Superbike is to come to fruition, 200 will have to be available for sale to the public, and there are now quite a few to be seen around.

The original price was $49,450 and that rose thanks to the high quality components used from the home market.Rroad legal bikes went on sale with a box of racing bits for those who wish to use them on the track.

A company called Anodising Inc who specialise in aluminum extrusion made the frame after their owner contacted Harley and offered his company's services. Tuttle originally explained: "He is a motorcycle nut and found out what we were working on and offered to provide us with aluminum in any shape we wanted." The chassis is now a conventional aluminum beam item with a massive head area.

Despite using Penske suspension front and rear, Harley found that the Indy car team could not match Ohlins for handling, so the Dutch firm had its 46mm inverted items supporting the front end. The brakes were also from the car-racing world; Wilwood supplied the calipers, which feature pistons of different sizes for better load distribution across the pads.

The tail-piece had the stars and stripes on the back edge; Tuttle told the press at the time: "We wanted that to be the last thing people saw as Miguel went by!" Tuttle made a brave decision to go racing and leave the secrecy of the test rigs and tracks behind before really completing the development program.

But, as far as the chassis and handling there did not seem to be much of a problem. Du Hamel, apparently, was letting go of the bars on the banking and sliding the bike around the first time he rode it. Tuttle claimed Miguel "had signed to ride before ever having ridden the bike. He signed on our dream of what we were going to do."

The main development at the time centered on the fuel injection (another American system this time from Webber) and sorting out electrical problems stemming from EMI. It seems that all the various electrical items were confusing each other and in some cases the ECU would completely shut down.

It seems ironic that the road bikes had already been through this problem when fitting options to the touring bikes such as stereos etc. When the two parts of the factory talked to each other, the problem was quickly sorted out, but there were several teething problems during practice week,

many of them minor and avoidable like omitting gas from the tank!

By the end of the first year Du Hamel was frustrated and left leaving the hot seat to GP veteran Doug Chandler, who was joined by dirt track racer Chris Carr. Despite these experienced campaigners helping to set up the handling, victory was still a long way off, as they could do nothing about the engine's unreliability.

In fact it was not till 1998 that the bike was in real contention, but poor pit stops at Daytona stopped Pascal Picotte from recording the bike's first major win. Ironically, it was taken on a Yamaha by Georgian Scott Russell, who has been signed to ride the VR Harley in 1999.

However, despite all the development work over the last five years, the bike still lacks horsepower, still only giving 160bhp compared the 170 plus put out by rival machines. As a result some things have had to go and foreign parts have had to be used.

Magneti Marelli ignition now controls the sparks, and fuel injection. Engine work has fine tuned weight and it is now no longer as agricultural as the first 1994 spec motor. On the chassis front Showa now supplies all the suspension components.

While engineering firm Roush is still involved, so is the

Ford Car Company. A new holding company allows different working practices to those at the main Harley factory, which has allowed lots more development to take place with off-season testing. A complete race-tech race shop has also helped bring the bike to race times and given the factory more confidence.

This has translated (along with the extra cash from backers) to hiring Scott Russell to ride as number one rider alongside Pascal Picotte. Russell's immense home and world-wide racing experience, along with the up grades should see Harley achieve the success they crave. However, as Bill Davidson said after another disappointing Daytona in 1999, "We have been at this since 1916 so we appreciate it is a long haul!"

Right: Jay Springsteen on the Japanese-prepared Golden Balls machine.
Ian Kerr

Sundance Daytona Weapon

The Sundance "Daytona Weapon" is the fastest pushrod Harley to ever lap Daytona's banked circuit. In 1998 it made its sixth appearance and took a long-awaited win in the Battle of the Twins Formula 1 event, on the first of the AHMA classic race days that start the main Daytona race week.

Constructed in 1992 by Japanese Harley guru Takehiko Shibazaki, it represents a no holds barred approach to chassis and engine design. On its first appearance it attracted as much attention as the Britten from New Zealand, and had a throng of onlookers and cameras around it.

It was no fairytale debut, because 250 GP rider Katsuyoshi Kozono had to retire during the race with mechanical problems — but not before he had proved this was a bike that had potential and would be back. The all-black machine with its team of similarly clad personnel had attracted media attention in a big way. The team had become known outside Japan where they were already big news, for several reasons.

Team boss Shibazaki worked as a car mechanic establishing himself as a gifted tuner for Harleys at the same time, being a big fan of the American marque. He decided to go it alone and opened his own "Harley Only" shop in Tokyo and quickly established a reputation for high quality engineering, not only in Japan but also worldwide.

In the mid-1980s he took on the Buell distributorship and then in 1988 started racing his own version of the Buell-framed Lucifer II that had been campaigned with great success in the United States by Gene Church. In 1989 he actually won the modified class of the Japanese BOT providing Buell with its first racing success.

Other success followed, with several top class finishes against some well-prepared competition in the shape of Japanese and Italian twin-cylinder machines. Shibazaki had been supported by a major TV star, George Tokoro, who runs a comedy game show that tops the Japanese ratings. A serious motoring fan, especially of American products, he had become a customer not long after the shop had opened and had started sponsoring the Sundance effort locally.

Tokoro wanted to go to America and race, and he felt his influence would help attract sponsors to enable the trip to be made. Things are not always easy and it was not until the end of 1991 that his own TV station, Channel 10, agreed to cover the assault on Daytona; as a result they were able

Left, throughout section and Below:
Team Sundance mechanics run up the
"Weapon II." Ian Kerr

Below Left: Daytona "Weapon" with
Jay Springsteen on board. Ian Kerr

to attract some sponsors from outside.

Four months was the timescale to build and ship a bike to Florida ready for the races in early March. (This requirement later turned into two bikes, but that is another story.) Knowing what he wanted thanks to his experience with the Buell, Shibazaki approached "Over" racing boss Kensei Sato to make him a frame using a version of the uni-planer mounting system that Buell use for its engine mounting.

The finished frame was in oval-section alloy tubing (the Over trademark) with two rubber mounts for the engine. In addition three unit-planer type mounts with adjustment built in were also fitted to allow the engine to move back and forward but not to twist and crack the frame. This also helped isolate the rider from the vibes.

(Since that first machine saw the light of day, the mountings have been revised to improve the overall balance and handling. In fact, it now features eight mounting links!)

As one might expect, the front forks came from Ohlins and were of the inverted type. They also supplied the rear system, which was operated by a rising rate linkage. 320mm floating Brembos graced the front end with four-piston calipers. These

have now been uprated to Nissin six-piston calipers and discs as part of the continuing development process.

The 17-inch wheels came from PVM, the rear being massive six-inch item, both being shod with Dunlop racing slicks. Initially the steering angle was set at 25 degrees although the latest version has 22.5 degrees and 2mm less on the original trail at 98mm, with the wheelbase remaining at 1,450mm.

While all this was happening, elsewhere Shibazaki was hard at work on a late model 1200 Evo engine using all the skills and knowledge that had gained him his

reputation. The stock crank was retained, but had weight added to keep the motor spinning hard at high revs rather than have it run out of steam.

The cylinders were fitted with Nikasil-coated chrome liners and forged 120-degree pistons, heavily modified before being attached to Carillo rods. Both barrels and cylinders were coated with FA coat from the Nissin firm to draw off heat from the motor. This is a technique used very successfully in car racing and helps to keep the air-cooled 45-degree lump from self-destructing.

The cylinder heads were heavily modified by the man himself, laboriously carrying out all the work personally. Both inlet ports were welded up and reshaped by hand to give 45 degrees of downdraught.

Shibazaki then cast up new rocker boxes in the style of the famed XR motors to give more support to the rocker shaft bosses. High lift "Red Shift" cams were added to operate the 49mm inlet and 41 mm exhaust valves via adjustable steel push rods. (These are now non-adjustable carbon fiber rods and the valves are now 51mm and 44mm Del West Titans.)

• *Harley-Davidson* •

Two 41mm flat-slide Keihn carbs were added to feed go juice from the 17-litre tank and a gear-driven oil pump used to keep three quarts of oil circulating from a separate aluminum oil tank.

The standard Harley gearbox was retained but the shifter was modified to smooth out the changes, while a three-spring Bandit clutch with Kevlar plates ensured all went well with shifts. Primary drive is by belt to a 520 chain at the end of the drive train.

What this added up to initially was that the 1,199cc pumped out 99bhp, which was rapidly upped to 109 by the time

of the race. Since then further mods, including altering the gas tank to provide a chamber underneath for more cool air for the carbs, had seen this rise to 112bhp, not bad for a pushrod motor!

Lack of time meant the standard ignition set up was used and this was to cause them most of their initial problems as it kept breaking. Nowadays a Screamin' Eagle system with Nology coils has solved this problem.

Just to prove there was no limit to his talent, Shibazaki designed and built the fairing from carbon/kevlar. No wind tunnels were used, just the basic shape of a

"Kabuto" — the helmet of a Samurai warrior. It seems to work well with speeds in excess of 170mph attainable!

It was inevitable that such a rushed development would not have fairytale ending. In the race, Kozono managed five laps before some asbestos sheet on the bottom of the petrol tank dropped down and partially blocked the carbs.

It was enough, however, to alert the media and the fans. Japanese TV showed a 90-minute documentary in May 1992 and Shibazaki started to get requests from all over the world for his expertise. He soon became a media

Harley Racing

399

personality appearing regularly on the TV.

It was not until 1994 the team returned to America, winning the Formula 2 BOT at Roebling Road prior to Daytona. The "Weapon" was then battling for second place at Daytona when a broken primary belt forced rider Yoshiyuki Sugai to retire midway through the race.

It was a similar picture too in 1995 when, once again, the primary belt let go, this time on the last lap when Sugai was lying second. To add insult to injury, the winner was disqualified after the race on a technicality!

In 1997 the team turned up with a second bike called "Golden Balls," an unfaired racer with different mods to the Harley. American legend Jay Springsteen won the Battle of the Twin F2 race on the naked bike and confirmed his allegiance with the Japanese team that had started a year earlier with a ride on one of their flat-track bikes in Japan.

Although seeking a win with the "Weapon" (which failed due to a shorted battery on the first lap), Shibazaki had the satisfaction of knowing he can make what most regard as an antiquated motor, perform well against the might of the Japanese factories.

Spurred on with this success, he returned again in 1998 not only

with the original "Weapon" but "Weapon II," an incredible looking bike that utilizes a British frame from Saxon Racing.

This state-of-the-art machine uses the latest 1,200cc Super XR engine built on standard Evolution Sportster cases. The motor, while incorporating many of the design features of the first bike, is based on the motors he builds for his flat-track bikes and that I have had the pleasure of riding!

The frame comes from Nigel Hill's Saxon works and uses Saxotrack front fork system that uses a lower "A" arm in a system that combines many of the merits of both standard telescopic forks and hub centre steering. The latest machine also has eccentrically adjustable rake and trail.

The carbon and Kevlar bodywork which clothes the new bike was specially designed for it and the frontal area mirrors the leading edge of a jet fighter complete with the large air ducts used for a ram-air effect. The right side feeds the dual flat slide carbs whilst the left duct delivers cool air to the rear cylinder.

Like its predecessor, "Weapon II" failed to get success on its first outing thanks to an oil seal failure. However, Shibazaki intends to run it in the X-Formula class at the Suzuka 8-Hour endurance race. This will be the

first time a Harley has ever entered this event!

While "Weapon II" may not have won, the original did fulfill its promise and with the 31-year-old Japanese rider Yoshiyuki Sugai on board took the chequered flag ahead of Pete Johnson's Moto Guzzi 1200 and Eric Woods Bimota.

There was no disguising Shibazaki's delight at having finally been rewarded for his devotion to the classic American engine. The win was even more poignant as the bike was wearing the number 55 plate in memory of Roger Reiman who died at the Florida track in 1997. The ex-works Harley rider was one of many top names that have supported the 38-year-old Japanese tuner over the years with help and advice.

The hog-riding "wild man" from Tokyo who runs the largest Harley dealership, called the "Armoury," has promised to be back with even more developments.

Right: Harley legend Jay Springsteen on the Golden Balls machine although he was to have more success with the fully faired "Weapon." Ian Kerr

Custom Harleys

photo section

Below, Right and throughout chapter: A custom for those short on inside leg inches and a love of chrome. Ian Kerr

Why customize? And why, when they do customize, do so many people chose Harleys?

While it may seem complicated, both questions are easily answered. To begin with, it's human nature to personalize both oneself — by the clothes we wear — and our property, by choice of decor, furnishings and style. With motorcycles, the same instincts apply: the customizers have the pleasure of creating something unique and the owner (often not the same people) gets to be noticed wherever they ride.

405

Whatever paint, chrome or bodywork is used the engine still normally ends up as the focal point of a good custom.
All: Ian Kerr

Customizing really started in the aftermath of World War Two, just as large numbers of service Harleys were disposed of into the civilian marketplace. Harleys were available, people had used them and knew about them, and they were easily bobbed, chopped and dropped.

Then there was the image: helped by Hollywood's influence in the form of films such as *The Wild One* and, later, *Easy Rider*, the feelings of rebellion led naturally to an expression of a lifestyle and style that really did speak

directly to the many people who wanted "to do their own thing."

Today the customizing scene is less rebellious than big business, with a standard of design, manufacture and machining that stands comparison with the best showbikes. Quality control and the widespread use of materials such as forged billet aluminum means that the components available to the customizer do not take skilled engineers hundreds of man hours to machine — and so more people than ever do it.

So, why Harleys?

At first, after World War Two, because they were available. Then it was because of the lifestyle connotations. But always lot of it has been about the classic Harley big V-twin engine, that puts out a unique sound, plenty of power and lasts forever. And if you have to ask about that, then you certainly won't understand!

The photographs in this chapter show a small selection of the vast range of the customizers' arts — fantastic shapes, stretches, chops, bobs, drops and paint jobs. You could write a book about many of them: we've only got space to show them off.

Right: Only Arlen Ness could build a fully integrated bike and not paint it, but still end up with a head turner like this. Ian Kerr

More wonderful creations on show at Daytona. All: Ian Kerr

The custom art knows no bounds other than the builders imagination.
All: Ian Kerr

Above: Nitrous Oxide makes it go faster. Ian Kerr

Left: A "Rat" bike shows the other end of customizing! Ian Kerr

Above Right: More lights than a Christmas Tree. Ian Kerr

Right: The "Voyager." Ian Kerr

All built for show rather than real long distance go! Ian Kerr

Below: The star of Easy Rider was that Harley Chopper. Remember those fishtails? All: Ian Kerr

Left: Pinstriping is not for you if you can't paint a straight line. Garry Stuart

Right and Below: "Flame Job."
Both: Garry Stuart

A bike and riding style made popular by the 1960s cult film Easy Rider. *This is Dick Tree's Evo chop.* All: Garry Stuart

• *Custom Harleys* •

Below: Customising is open to both sexes even if it panders to a very un-PC image. This is "Rat's Hole" from Daytona. Garry Stuart

Below Right: "Hog Farm." Garry Stuart

430

• *Harley-Davidson* •

434

Motown Harley-Davidson in Taylor, Michigan, welcomed photographer Simon Clay who took the photographs shown in the rest of this chapter. Thanks to Eric Fisher for making it happen.

Previous Page and this spread: Superb attention to detail on this Softail Springer custom! All: Simon Clay

Below: Milwaulkee line-up. Simon Clay

This spread and Overleaf: High quality
paintwork on this Modern Evo custom.
All: Simon Clay

438

• Harley-Davidson •

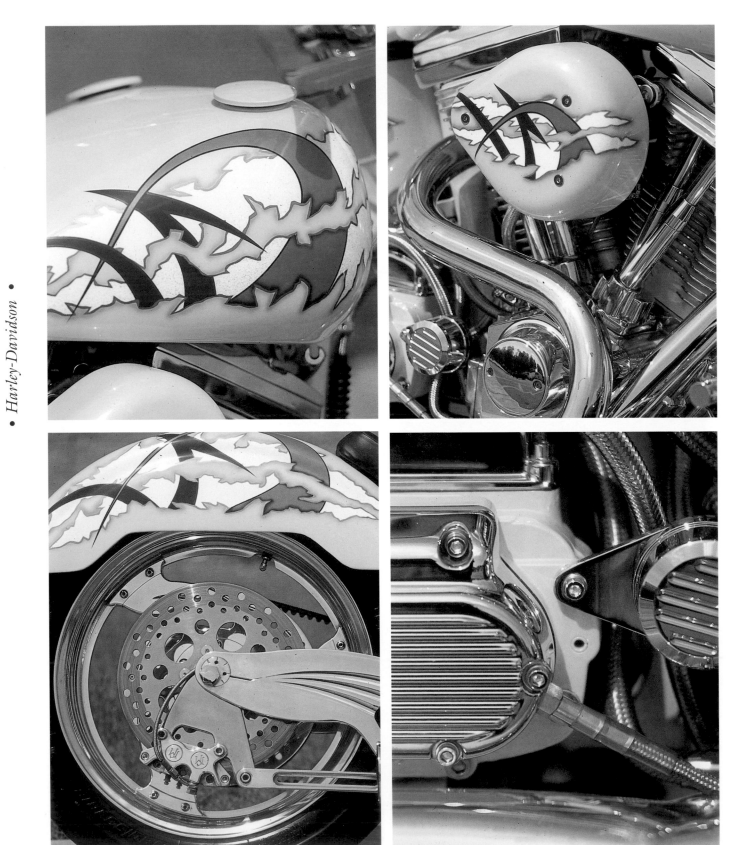

This spread: Harley's 90th birthday celebrated on this retro Shovelhead. All: Simon Clay

• *Harley-Davidson* •

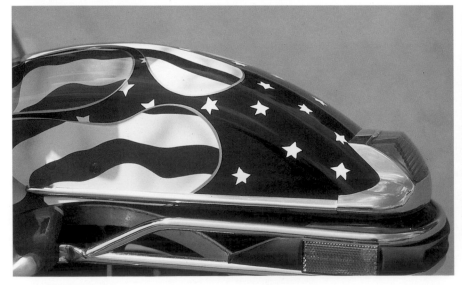

This spread: Superb paint job on this customized police special that highlights those Vietnam MIAs — missing in action — who were captured and held by the North. All: Simon Clay

Harley Lifestyle

Ian Kerr

95th Anniversary Party

It can hardly have escaped anybody's notice that in 1998 Harley celebrated 95 years of motorcycle production. Although the current big 45-degree V-twins are a far cry from the little 3bhp single-cylinder motor that powered the first bike to bear the name Harley-Davidson, they come from the same heritage and from a company that is moving forward as well as remembering the past.

Little did the company founders ever realize that not only were they creating a manufacturing company, they were creating a legend and a modern icon. Harley has always been shrewd enough to protect that, keeping a tight rein on the name by licensing it out for products as diverse as clothing and after-shave.

This chapter looks at the range of Harley products and the people who use them — and how better to do so than with the 95th anniversary party.

Harley's bikes are big and so was the birthday party: 36,000 bikes made the Milwaukee parade, with an estimated 200,000 people cramming themselves into town.

Not all were going to get there so, a European party was arranged, too, hosted by the small Austrian town of Faakar See close to the Italian Border in the picturesque Tyrol region. Willie G. Davidson and other top brass made the bash to make sure nobody felt they were going to a second class happening!

With an estimated 20,000 people visiting the area over the three days, there was plenty to do. A Harley Village provided the main focal point, but there was a Safe Riding area, a workshop to help out those in mechanical distress, Poker Runs, a three-country tour taking in Italy and Slovenia, as well as the usual bars and eating stalls.

The third day saw the big parade which took an hour to pass with 10,000 bikes taking part continually with approximately another 5,000 dipping in and out of the circular route. Local police chose to turn a blind eye to the massive disregard of the helmet law in an effort to keep the festivities going without too many regulations!

The event ended with a massive open-air concert headed by Jon Bon Jovi. It goes without saying that, apart from a few spills, the event was peaceful and full of happy people.

The hills were alive with rock'n'roll and the only thunder came from the massive numbers of bikes all stuck in jams created by bikes. Julie Andrews and the Von Trapp family would not have approved!

Plans are already underway for the 100th celebrations, so you had better book a place now because if this year is anything to go by it is going to be really massive. See you there!

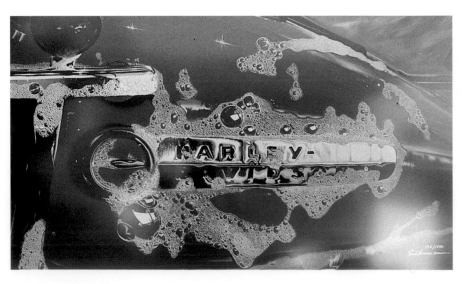

The photographs in this section speak for themselves and are, for the main part, uncaptioned except to show provence.

All photos on this spread: Ian Kerr

All photos on this spread: Ian Kerr

All photos on this spread and overleaf:
Ian Kerr

Note miniature (Below).

• *Harley-Davidson* •

All photos on this spread: Ian Kerr

• Harley-Davidson •

458

Daytona is one of the high points in the Harley calendar.

All photos on this spread and Overleaf: Ian Kerr

FRANÇOIS BRUÉRE

Above: French artist Bruere normally paints them but occasionally uses metal for his art.

All photos on this spread: Ian Kerr

466

• Harley-Davidson •

• Harley Lifestyle •

Left: More views from the Tyrol run.

Below: Willie G Davidson, styling Guru and direct descendent of co founders, at the European leg of the 95th Anniversary celewbrations.

All photos on this spread: Ian Kerr

Hog owners on the three countries' run.

All photos on this spread: Ian Kerr

All photos on this spread: Ian Kerr

Below Left and Bottom Left: Wyoming.
Garry Stuart

*Below: Sturgis — the other big event of
the Harley calendar.* Garry Stuart

• *Harley Lifestyle* •

Harley-Davidson •

This spread and Overleaf: More views of Sturgis. All: Garry Stuart

• Harley-Davidson •

• *Harley-Davidson* •

Below Left and Bottom Left: Block party at Sundance, Wyoming. Both: Garry Stuart

Below: Sturgis. Garry Stuart

Bottom: Bikini bike wash. Garry Stuart

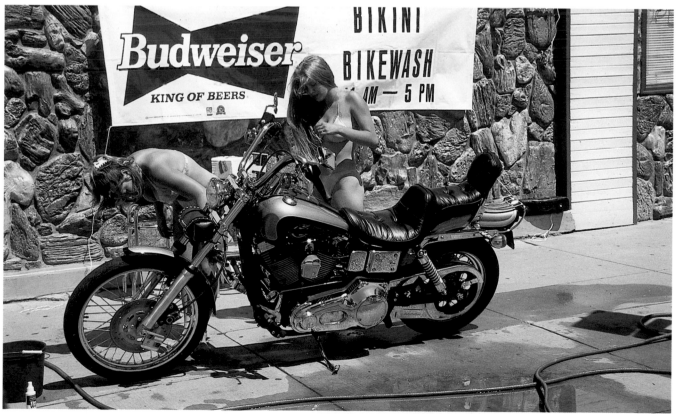

• Harley Lifestyle •

Previous Page and this spread: More great Sturgis views. All: Garry Stuart

Harley Lookalikes

Ian Kerr

The Sincerest Form of Flattery!

The Harley-Davidson has become a modern icon through clever marketing and extolling a lifestyle image. Mechanically and technically the bikes are some way behind other machines, despite the recent advances. However, Harley's PR has been so good (as well as sales) that leading manufacturers all over the world have tried to emulate its success.

The Japanese, for example, renowned for high-powered sports bikes bristling with technology, have tried to grab a slice of Harley's action. Utilizing their vast resources they have designed and built bikes that echo Harley's form and function.

While at first some of these bikes were just parodies of the American V-twin, they are now almost exact copies, even down to color schemes and sounds. So much so that Harley tried to copyright the "potato potato" exhaust note (without success) and forced at least one manufacturer to change the crankpin angle so the bike did not sound exactly like a Harley!

These machines are now so good that the average person cannot tell the difference until they are close enough to read the name on the petrol tank or engine cases.

While it must be said that many are excellent bikes in their own right, they actually fail to hit the Harley bullseye due to their sophistication. Made to exacting high standards using modern electronics, fuel injection and employing balance shafts and liquid cooling, they take away many of the "rough" elements that make Harleys so individual.

For instance the shaft-drive used on many copies may be more practical and cleaner in looks, but it is not a belt or chain and the bike drives differently. Chromed plastic or color-impregnated resin has not got the same depth or feel as chromed or painted steel, nor the durability. It is these little things that take away the soul that makes the Harley what it is.

However, while the Far East continues to make exact copies, Europe has taken the pastiche route. BMW copied the Cruiser look, if not the V-twin motor, with its distinctive James Bond 1200C. Triumph in the UK has come up with bikes like the Thunderbird, but it is Harley's own American rivals that are stealing sales.

The re-born Excelsior-Henderson now markets a V-twin based on one of its 1930s bikes. Excelsior was originally one of the American "Big Three" in the 1930s with Harley and Indian.

Indian itself is on the comeback road using thinly disguised Harley motors to power the new Cruiser.

A new player, Victory (made by the Snowmobile Company, Polaris) has now joined in with the world biggest V-twin motor, over 1,500cc. It is, despite employing modern systems and engineering practices, a direct copy of all the things that make Harley-Davidson bikes what they are.

Despite the challenge, the Milwaukee firm continues to make the type of bikes, complete with that indefinable "something" that has kept them going for over 95 years. As they approach their own "magic ton," here is a brief glimpse of some the bikes Harley-Davidson has inspired.

Right and Overleaf: The Honda opposite could easily be a Harley Sportster from the rear at a quick glance, illustrating the point only too well! Ian Kerr

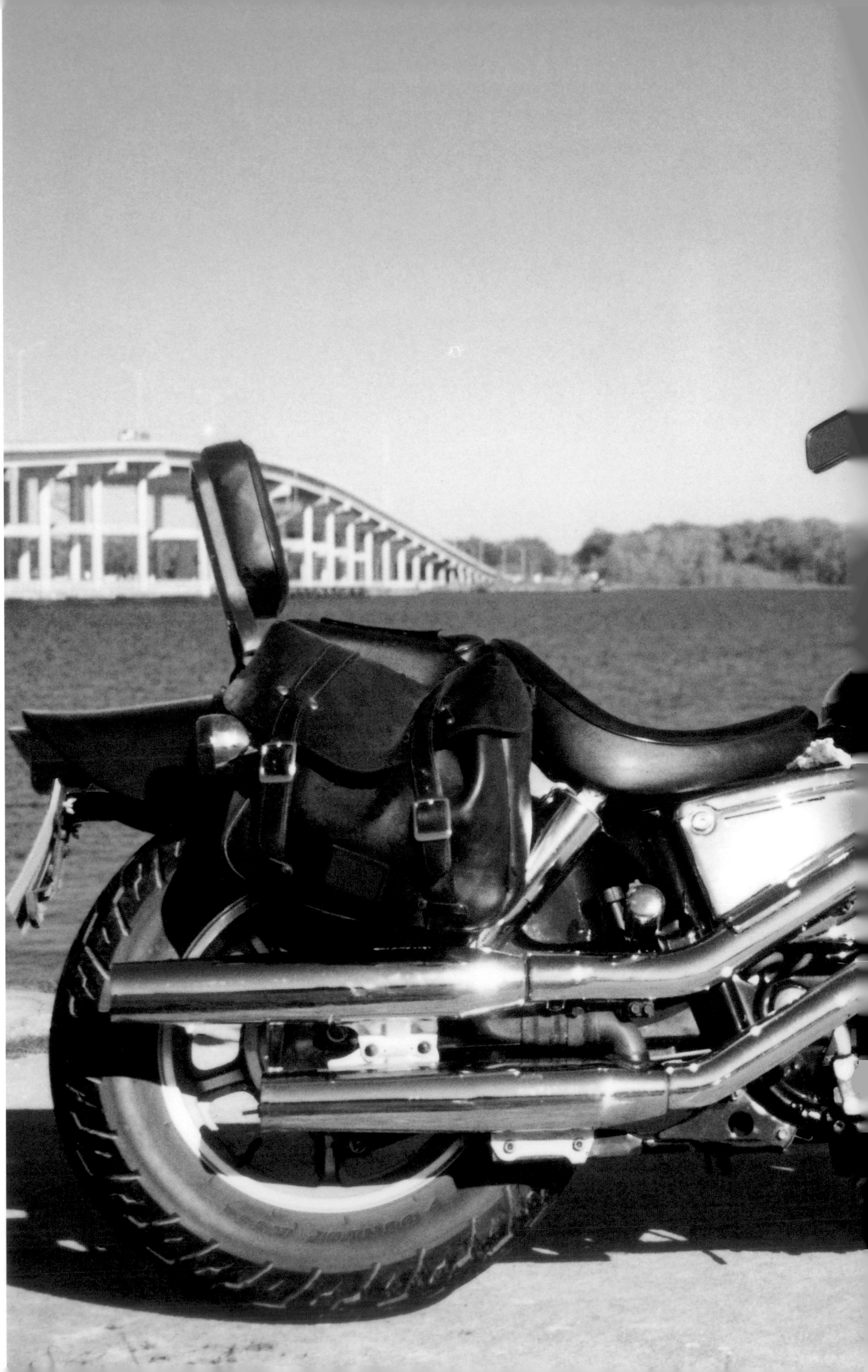

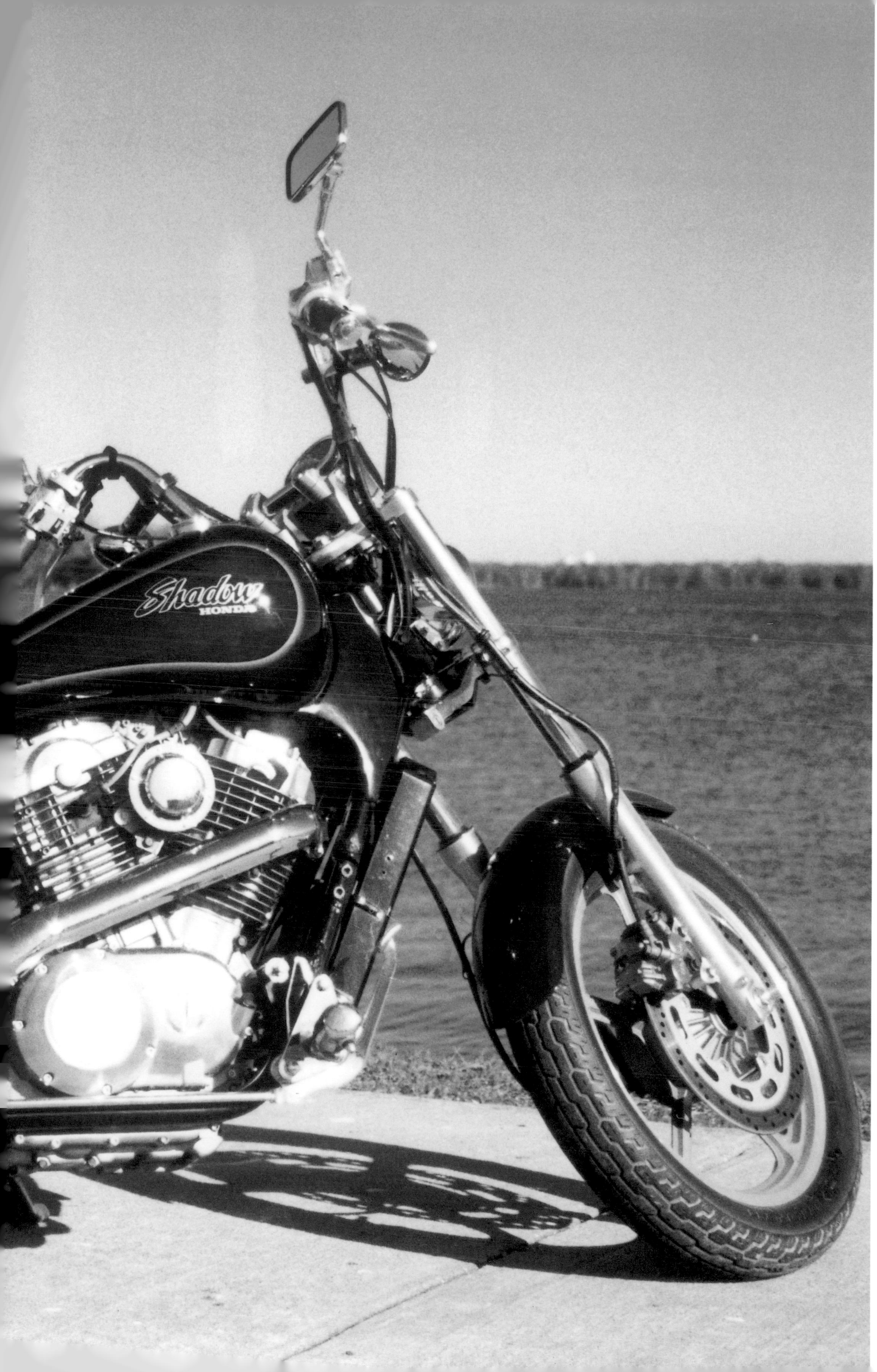
Shadow
HONDA

Left and throughout chapter: Kawasaki VN1500 Nomad. Ian Kerr

Right and throughout chapter: Kawasaki custom. Ian Kerr

Left: This early version of Kawasaki's VN1500 looks the part from a distance although the traditional Harley air cleaner is missing between the slant of the cylinders when you look closely. Ian Kerr

Left: The latest Kawasaki 1500 Vulcan now has the air cleaner to complete the looks! Ian Kerr

Below: The same Kawasaki 1500 showing it probably handles well, although like the real thing, it is limited by ground clearance. Ian Kerr

Bottom: A BMW shows the same style and theme although it is very different. Ian Kerr

495

Above and Left: The bike that Willie G. thought was good effort and kept James Bond safe! It's horizontally opposed and not a V-twin but the German machine is as well made as the American bike. Ian Kerr

Right and Overleaf: A Honda Magna, just one of the many mass-produced copies. Ian Kerr

Left: The reborn Excelsior motor with its black finish looks just like an "Evo" engine. Ian Kerr

Above and Right: The Triumph from the reborn English firm extols the "Cruiser" image even if it uses an across the frame multi-cylinder motor. Triumph, too, draws on its history using the old style tank badge. Ian Kerr

• *Harley-Davidson* •

Left: Excelsior Henderson's bike is based on a late 1920s early 1930s bike, even down to the old style forks. This is probably one of the most serious threats to Harley's domination of the American market in the past 20 years. Ian Kerr

503

• Harley-Davidson •

Below Left: A Honda Shadow, another of the mass-produced clones, but nonetheless a useable bike in the right image at a fraction of the cost. Ian Kerr

Bottom Left: A Kawasaki fitted with a host of customizing extras, enabling it to become something different to others from the same production line — just as a Harley is so often customized. Ian Kerr

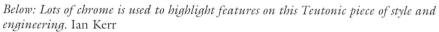

Below: Lots of chrome is used to highlight features on this Teutonic piece of style and engineering. Ian Kerr

Left: The Honda Magna suits those short in stature, thanks to its low seat height and light weight. Many of these lookalikes come in smaller engine sizes than Harley's, thus proving popular abroad as they cost less to insure as well as buy. Ian Kerr

Above and Right: The Excelsior Henderson — large, American, with a pedigree and a threat! Both: Ian Kerr

Right: The very latest Kawasaki VN1500 Nomad, complete with integrated panniers and screen. Probably the best Harley clone ever from a Japanese company, it looks so similar to a big tourer like the Road King. To the real enthusiast, however, it lacks that indefinable something
Ian Kerr